For the Sake of Sanity:

Doing things with humour in Irish performance

For the Sake of Sanity:

Doing things with humour in Irish performance

Edited by Eric Weitz

Carysfort Press

A Carysfort Press Book

For the Sake of Sanity:
Doing things with humour in Irish performance
Edited by Eric Weitz

First published in Ireland in 2014 as a paperback original by

Carysfort Press, 58 Woodfield, Scholarstown Road

Dublin 16, Ireland

ISBN 978-1-909-325-56-2
©2014 Copyright remains with the authors

Typeset by Carysfort Press

Cover design by eprint limited
Printed and bound by eprint limited
Unit 35
Coolmine Industrial Estate
Dublin 15
Ireland

This book is published with the financial assistance of
The Arts Council (An Chomhairle Ealaíon) Dublin, Ireland

TABLE OF CONTENTS

1 | Introduction

Eric Weitz

There is no getting around the fact that humour in performance is an unruly mess from an analytical perspective. Not that people from any walks of life – scholars, practitioners and civilians alike – can resist the call to ruminate upon laughter and its causes. Drama (of any medium) and humour are two areas in which diverse and strongly held opinion remain the ways of the world – and very much the point. 'Funniness' is not a property of things – it's an uncertifiable effect that writers, actors, directors and comedians venture, and so it is a seductive yet dangerous subject for any kind of earnest contemplation.

Let us start with what we know: All humans laugh, the scientists tell us, but decidedly not at the same things nor necessarily under the same conditions, due to the deep nesting of humorous laughter in cultural root systems and the precise context in which it occurs. Every joke – or, perhaps, every *good* joke – is a risk taken, a stress test for the relationship. A hearty laugh from your audience (from one close friend to a theatre full of strangers to the internet's quasi-infinite sprawl of virtual spectators) usually demands an element of surprise, and often a testing of boundaries: sufficient knowledge/awareness to 'get' the joke, an involuntary inclination to endorse its ridicule, and, ideally, some hint of 'newness' to the point, a sense of someone having momentarily stepped into your body to perceive the world *exactly* as you do.

Humour – a social transaction dedicated, among other things, to causing laughter – is a highly sophisticated interactive tool, charged with smoothing discomfort, gaining consensus, assuring lack of ill will, seduction (in various senses of the word), and other interpersonal projects. When deployed in performance, that is, in circumstances pointedly public, if not commercial, there are many additional permutations, as a joke made to an audience of more than one is made co-presently to each individual *and* to the collective body of spectators (and think of what that means for the age of stand-up gigs recorded live for later viewing by television audiences).

Under the subtitle, 'Doing things with humour in Irish performance', the guiding rationale for this collection has from the start been to ask a bunch of people to provide some personal perspective on just the kinds of issues mooted above. A main title was harder to come by, requiring, as it does, certain weight-bearing capabilities: an obligation to catch the eye and the fancy, while presenting some crystallizing image of the collection's broad embrace.

In fact, the collection started life a few years ago under the title, *Dublin City Comedy*, an allusion to a dramatic sub-genre identified on London stages in the early years of the seventeenth century. One of the defining characteristics of City Comedy was that it consciously 'did things with humour'; it is characterised generally as driven by satiric impulse and arising from the brew of socially recognisable figures mixing and conniving in localised contexts spawned by advancing economic influence. While the description evoked something of the book's guiding spirit and resonated with something in the contemporary Irish air, the phrase itself came to misrepresent the range of contributions by a good two-thirds, with restrictive notions of Dublin and city left by the wayside. The catchphrase, 'only jokin', was considered briefly, with its vernacular familiarity symbolizing with useful fuzziness the fact that we do things with humour all the time in everyday life, and that the mechanism is no different from the variously customized models deployed in theatre, film, television, stand-up and online performance.

Sean O'Casey's essay, 'The Power of Laughter', however, had supplied the title of my first collection ten years ago, and I saw no reason to resist returning to the well. O'Casey's short, unassuming essay carries no shortage of insight into the nature and purpose of laughter, and this time through, I found the following: 'We're all very low fellows, for all of us, sometime or another, are conscious humourists. And well we are, for our soul's sake, and for the sake of man's sanity. We couldn't live without comedy. ...'[1] So it is for the sake of sanity that humans come equipped with senses of humour, for the purpose of psychic survival in an uncooperative, ridiculous and infuriating world. It can be no surprise, then, that humour features in our dramatic confections and other performance structures.

Back, now, to all those perspectives you might not always get in a scholarly collection. It has long been my contention that insightful thinking need not adopt only the language of the academy, and so this book may well prove an unruly melange for some readers. But the kinds of points we make are inseparable from the language we use to make them, and so, for me, it was important to include a range of voices in terms of discursive orientation and political bearing. Make no mistake: Humour claims no ideological affiliation – its workings merit inspection in any and every individual case, in light of the who, what, where and when of a joke, including the socio-cultural context, the target of ridicule, and who knows how many other factors particular to the instance.

By inviting practitioners and journalists as well as academics to contribute to the collection, I have sought to avail of a broad range of subjective responses, and so the exceedingly multi-vocal nature of this collection includes insights into creative process, opinions on social/cultural/theatrical trends and other pronouncements one would not ordinarily expect to find in an academic collection. The contributions sometimes overlap and sometimes contest one another. The common starting point is that all the contributors have been asked primarily to put their minds to the subject of humour used or found in some Irish performance-related context over the past hundred years.

As a result, we have a scholarly and personal reflection by Christopher Murray – who in making a case about the comic heart of Hugh Leonard's dramatic works furnishes an historical overview of the past hundred years or so – alongside impassioned arguments about the state of Irish humour by Meadhbh McHugh, who highlights a robust appropriation of humorous discourse in a next wave of feminist agency; and John Waters, who, in setting out to ruminate upon the state of comedy on Irish television (or is it Irish comedy on television?) goes on to venture some wide-ranging and provocative thoughts about comedy and the current orthodoxy of public discourse.

Two stage directors reflect on the comic transaction for audiences home and elsewhere: Sarah Jane Scaife exposes a particularly Irish manifestation of humour's critical edge, thereby gaining access to broader issues of theatre and laughter across cultural divides. Jim Culleton gives a sense of comedy's capacity to temper serious subject matter at a variety of frequencies. From the perspective of playwright, Bernard Farrell offers personal observations and telling anecdotes in search of the enigmatic heart of comedy. Rhona Trench looks at Blue Raincoat's comedy-friendly physical approach in transposing to dramatic terms the comic literary masterpiece, *At-Swim-Two-Birds*; Marie Kelly assesses the surreal comic jabs delivered to real-life political targets in Tom McIntyre's dramatic fantasia, *Only an Apple*.

A few essays look to Ireland's theatrical past to focus on specific and revealing texts and character types: Christopher Collins casts a critical eye upon J.M. Synge's, *The Well of the Saints*, to illuminate a comic critique that may not be apparent to today's reader/spectator; Ian Walsh looks at the practice and resonance of what he calls the Dublin Dame, a cross-dressed comic character from popular tradition, in two prominent guises. My own offering considers some of the political inclinations of clown humour as re-spun by Barabbas Theatre Company in its ground-breaking *City of Clowns*, a few years ago.

It was intended that this collection spread its net beyond the theatre and Eamonn Jordan takes on Mark O'Rowe's *Intermission* and Conor McPherson's *I Went Down*, two films that give a Dublin-city accent to the pitch-black gangsterese comedy that emerged more broadly in the 1990s; Susanne Colleary looks at the satirical television series, *The Savage Eye*, through just the 'city comedy' lens that originally animated this project; Kunle Animashaun thinks upon the workings, coups and traps of stand-up comedy in contemporary Irish society when African-born performers hold the microphone; and we include a sampling of thought on Irish stand-up from interviews conducted on the Irish comedy circuit in the summer of 2013 by Declan Rooney, with distillation, introduction and additional material by Justin Murphy. Far more material was gathered than could possibly have fit into a single 'essay', and so I would like especially to thank contributors like Barry Murphy who gave generously of their time and thought, but whose words do not appear in this volume. It should be acknowledged readily that there are holes in the fabric of thought assembled here, some because invitees were unable to participate at this point in time and others because you don't always know what is missing until you have it all in front of you. Even now, they provide a starting point for a next collection.

I would like to make a public pronouncement of my gratitude to all who contributed to this effort. Thanks to Mairead Delaney, keeper of the Abbey archive; and also to Margaret Dunne and Danielle Byrne – I'm sorry we could not find just the right photo from *Da*. Modest collections like this do not readily claim a place in today's return-on-investment driven culture – all the more reason that Carysfort Press deserves special praise, with deepest appreciation to Lilian Chambers and Dan Farrelly; and the most strenuous of thanks to Eamonn Jordan, who has once again shepherded me through the gauntlet.

---

[1] Sean O'Casey, 'The Power of Laughter' in *The Green Crow* [1957] (London: Comet, 1987), 206-7.

2 | The Masks of Hugh Leonard: *Da* as an Irish Comedy

Christopher Murray

It might be thought superfluous to address anything written by Hugh Leonard, pseudonym for John Keyes Byrne (1926-2009), as Irish. But the initial point to be made in creating the framework for this essay is that he himself fought against the categorization as too narrow. He had a problem with the nationalistic character of Irish drama as supervised by the notorious manager of the Abbey who succeeded Yeats and remained in control until after the new Abbey opened in 1966. This was Earnán de Blaghd, a former fighter for Irish independence, subsequently Minister of Finance in the new Free State, and after he became manager of the Abbey a man who insisted on the primacy of the Irish language in all its administration. Leonard's negative view of the tradition of the Irish drama as founded by Yeats and his friends, had de Blaghd known it in 1956 when Leonard's first play was staged by the Abbey, would have caused such uproar that he would likely have been banned:

> With the coming of the Irish Free State our drama became even more parochial. We had a peasant government and a reactionary clergy, both of which were intensely anglophobic. What passed for Irish culture was imposed on artists and audiences alike: not for its intrinsic values but as a deliberate negation of all things English. Our art, music and literature became not a part of world culture but, like a limb that has been hacked from the body, a separate, atrophying entity. [...] For more than thirty years – from the 1920s until the mid-1950s – Irish theatre has concerned itself with Irishmen first and men later.[1]

Almost alone among the Irish writers of this time, Leonard looked to America and England for his standards and models. It should not be forgotten that he was a very good theatre critic for *Plays and Players* in the 1960s. His knowledge of and admiration for American film were lifelong, and, as occasional reviewer of biographies and of film history for *The Irish Times*, he displayed both attributes alongside his customary caustic wit. His late novel *Fillums* (2004), the spelling an old jibe against the pronunciation of continuity girls on RTĒ as they introduced a classic film, gives some idea of his taste in this area.

Consequently Leonard was regarded as something of a maverick among his peers of the day. Further, his political views, anti-republican and anti-Fianna Fáil, voiced fearlessly in his 'Leonard's Log' for the *Sunday Independent* all through the 1980s and 1990s marked him out in certain quarters. One sample from 1985: 'Mr Haughey's mistake [Charles J. Haughey was Taoiseach at the time] is that while our young people crave for bread, he offers them circuses in the sweet by and by – with Northern Protestants being fed to the lions.'[2] When Leonard wrote the satiric comedy *Kill* for the Dublin Theatre Festival in 1982 he made more than plain his alienation from contemporary Ireland. The play has been described as 'blatantly a political allegory' directed at 'several of his regular journalistic targets, primarily at what he considers the hypocrisy of official attitudes towards Northern Ireland.'[3]

So, when it came to the *Field Day Anthology* some years later it can be seen that Leonard might have a problem over inclusion. The editor of the section on modern Irish drama was D.E.S. Maxwell, author of a book on that subject, who already had a negative view of Leonard's achievements: 'Journalist, scriptwriter, adapter, Leonard is an enormously prolific writer, unfailingly a witty entertainer. He consequently invites the suspicion that he constructs his plays – with great skill – around good lines.'[4] As to his 'perversely disparaging' remarks about the Irish dramatic tradition, Leonard was 'clearly wrongheaded'[5] Maxwell wanted to include only excerpts from Leonard's work in the *Anthology*. When Leonard discovered that Friel and Murphy were to get a whole play each in it he demurred, and after some further, futile discussion withdrew his permission entirely. Without explaining Leonard's omission from the selection of contemporary playwrights, Maxwell felt free to underline how wrong Leonard was in his view of the tradition by contrasting his work with that of M.J. Molloy, commonly regarded as a successor to Synge: 'The country people of the West, those who filled the emigrant ships to England in the 1950s, retain an imaginative vitality that has disappeared from the suburban world of Leonard, where the present is in intermittent conference with a past that has been trivialized or erased.'[6] Leonard was not admissible as a major playwright.

It can be added here in passing that the launch of the *Field Day Anthology* was a major affair, and the man who launched the publication was Taoiseach Charles J. Haughey. Given this history, it is to rub Leonard's work against the grain, perhaps, to argue that in *Da* – his best play – the comedy is Irish before it is international. But such is the intention here.

As the Irish actor-playwright Charles Macklin had ruefully to concede when his comedy *The True-born Irishman* (1762) flopped under a new title in London following its Dublin success, there is such a thing as 'a geography in humour as well as in morals'.[7] Different century, same problem. Ethnicity rules where humour is concerned. Some jokes simply do not travel; stereotypes tend to get in the way. Situations found hilarious in one country remain puzzling to audiences in another. But if there is a geography at play there is also a history. British comedy from the Restoration period, when it reinvented itself through French influence, is based on the love chase, polished wit, and the class system. As comedy of manners it thrived with remarkable consistency from John Dryden to Noël Coward; in more recent times a lower-middle class style has grown through Alan Ayckbourn's abandonment of wit in favour of stupidity and of the conventional love chase in favour of 'sheer invention'.[8]

American comedy grew out of English comedy of manners and in due course evolved in rather different ways to become democratically based versions of the American Dream: the pursuit of happiness, featuring ordinary hard-working couples, struggling in the land of opportunity and succeeding. I should say Neil Simon represents the pinnacle of contemporary American writers of comedy, and *The Odd Couple* (1965), an early success, the quintessence of the well-made Broadway hit. It is important to note that the situation in that play is not 'sheer invention' but based on the break-up of the marriages of Simon's brother Danny and Danny's friend Roy Gerber, who to save money lived together, with Danny doing the cooking. 'This union didn't prosper any better than either of their first marriages', Simon comments in his memoir.[9] However, he himself did and that's life. It's also, in the hands of a master, comedy.

It can easily be said that Hugh Leonard is a lot closer to Simon as a playwright than he is to Ayckbourn. The proof is in the one-liners. Here are just a few from *Da* alone: 'Blessed are the meek: they shall inherit the dirt'; of marriage: 'the maximum of loneliness and the minimum of privacy'; 'if you ran into him with a motor car he'd thank you for the lift'; 'There are no shallows to which you won't sink, are there?'; and (most significantly), 'the dangerous ones are those who amuse us.' Similar *bon mots* have crept into many recent books on humour and wit.[10] They are no more proof of the vacuity D.E.S. Maxwell implied than the epigrams of Oscar Wilde of that author. And it may be no harm to note that the lead character in *The Odd Couple* is called Oscar, while the two girls are Cecily and Gwen. Boom-boom. This may show the affinity that exists between Irish and Jewish humour, which tends to bypass the English version.[11]

In spite of this kinship between ethnic senses of humour, the geography persists as a distinguishing mark. Leonard's work is based on what he experienced growing up in Dalkey, Co. Dublin, in the 1930s and after. The details are in his memoir, *Home Before Night* (1979) – six years after the premiere of *Da*, which anticipates some of it. Like Flann O'Brien before him, Leonard worked for years in the Irish civil service before he made a name for himself, and was to adapt O'Brien's *The Dalkey Archive* for the stage in 1965; following his successful adaptation of Joyce's *Stephen Hero* and *A Portrait of the Artist* in 1962 under the title *Stephen D*, his psychic geography was well established. His material was Dublin city. What drew him to the theatre for the first time was a production of O'Casey's *The Plough and the Stars*, and it was the realism that astonished him: 'The life that roared through the play itself [apart from the acting] had spilled over from the stage, sweeping him with it so that he knew he would never again be content just to sit and watch and applaud with the rest of them.'[12]

Soon Leonard was submitting plays to the Abbey himself, *Madigan's Lock* (1957) the only one to be published. It is thoroughly Irish in setting, characterization and vocabulary, even though the redoubtable Earnán de Blaghd rejected it: 'I don't like plays with a ghost in 'em', he said, 'and there, I thought, go *Hamlet* and *Macbeth*'.[13] Leonard took the play to the new Globe company then playing at the Gate. It was to be nineteen years before he had another play at the Abbey, this time the new Abbey under the direction of Joe Dowling, who was an enthusiast. As a fellow Dubliner he understood the Irishness and wit of Leonard's plays and directed the sequel of *Da*, namely, *A Life* (1979), as well as revivals of *Da* and *Stephen D* at the national theatre. In later years, artistic director Patrick Mason directed other new work, such as *Love in the Title* (1999). Leonard's credentials, then, seem impeccable.

Da marks a special turning point in Leonard's career. This is the play that was to bring him a Tony award on Broadway for best play. This is the play that was to expose him publicly on the Dublin stage when it had its Irish premiere in 1973 at the Dublin Theatre Festival. But it is so artful that it manages to mask reality once again, or rather perhaps transform it in order to dramatize the doubleness (it cannot be called duplicity) in Leonard's very being. He was illegitimate. His Da was not his father; Mother was not his natural mother. Therefore the story he had to tell, the comedy he had to contrive, was a form of confessional catharsis – for even comedy can create purgation.

This double identity, which is such a major element in Leonard's creative life, was rooted in traditional Anglo-Irish comedy. While not arguing that Leonard was influenced by Goldsmith's *She Stoops to Conquer*, Sheridan's *The Rivals*, Wilde's *The Importance of being Earnest*, and Shaw's *John Bull's Other Island*, all plays recording the colonialist stratagem of two conflicting selves as a way of expressing the Irish need for a mask in English society, I would see a continuity here. To be sure, with the foundation of the Irish dramatic movement in 1897, the emphasis was on authenticity without duplicity. Yet if Synge's *Playboy of the Western World* (1907) is looked at in this context, it is an examination of how *becoming* the mask (in the Yeatsian sense) is the colonialist's route to freedom. I am inclined to see Synge's *Playboy* as the paradigmatic comedy in the modern Irish theatre; I don't see it divorced from what went before.

The relationship between the Irish drama staged at the Abbey theatre and the evolution of the liberation of the country is a complex one, but it is there and it is compelling. One of the things it brings out is how deep 'performance' has always been in the history of Irish colonialism. The Anglo-Irish tradition gave us the language and the technique, the idea of a theatre, through which we could transcend our disadvantages and achieve mastery over our lives. Because many of the playwrights around the turn of the twentieth century were, like Synge, renegades from Anglo-Irish stock, they provided a bridge between the old and the new styles and intentions. That is the nub of the development of a native Irish drama.

In postcolonial Ireland, where the country itself was divided in two, this sense of double identity intensified rather than dissolved. In drama, O'Casey was the first to represent this troublesome phenomenon as comedy verging on tragedy. In his *Shadow of a Gunman* (1923), Donal Davoren begins as a poet and ends a poltroon. Shunning the world in order to concentrate on his writing he accepts the role of hero when it is thrust upon him through the misunderstanding of those around him in the tenements. The double life Davoren leads is bogus on both sides. This is the revelation he is forced to recognize in the end. He is more shadow than substance of any denomination.

Everywhere one looks in O'Casey's work there is this duality: the real Jack Boyle the waster in *Juno and the Paycock* (1924), as against the self-styled captain with a history of world travel, living in a dream world; Joxer Daly, Boyle's other self, his feed, his parasite, sometimes his mask and at other times his leering anti-mask, serves well the world of Boyle's illusions and dishonesty. Meanwhile, young Johnny Boyle, that frightened image of post-traumatic stress, pins his hope of survival on the flickering of a candle before a little shrine. In the greatest of O'Casey's plays, disillusion plays its greatest role. One can see how it would fire a disadvantaged youth like Hugh Leonard circa 1955. 'Is there anyone goin', Mrs Clitheroe', asks the consumptive child Mollser Gogan 'with a titther o' sense?'[14]

Hugh Leonard was born in the year *The Plough and the Stars* was first staged; its truths caused riots in the theatre. The pathology of the divided self was to endure into de Valera's Ireland as Leonard's inheritance. A post-O'Casey further example of this Irish characteristic is Friel's *Philadelphia, Here I Come!* (1964), where two actors are needed to play Private Gar and Public Gar. Leonard does something similar. In *Da*, Charlie the forty-two-year-old writer who returns from London to Dalkey for the funeral of his adoptive father is clearly a representation of Leonard himself. He had already written a television play by then on the theme of the encounter between the young self and his middle-aged counterpart. It would later be redrafted to fill a Theatre Festival bill as a one-act, under the title *A View from the Obelisk* (1983). The idea of time as allowing such coincidences fascinated Leonard as it fascinated the playwright he sometimes thought his natural father, Denis Johnston (1902-1984). Johnston saw time as capable of replaying itself. He developed the philosophy and physics of this idea in his strange book *The Brazen Horn* (1976), but it was in his plays that, rather in the style of Priestley's *I Have Been Here Before* (1937) and *An Inspector Calls* (1946), Johnston revealed its possibilities. There was in 1957 a significant revival of Johnston's first and most exciting play, *The Old Lady Says 'No!'* (1929), in which Micheál MacLiammóir reprised the role of Robert Emmet he had played when the play first opened at the Gate. This time it opened the first Dublin International Theatre Festival. It is very likely Leonard saw it. It is a play in which the actor playing the Irish hero, Emmet, is injured onstage and thereafter, while out cold, seems to wander around 1920s Dublin only to find it shrunk morally and politically from what it was in Emmet's day of glory (in 1803). Then he wakes up to find only moments have passed in real time. Johnston has superimposed one time frame on top of another as a kind of theatrical palimpsest. Leonard does something similar in *Da*, though in a different style. The use of flashbacks, the defiance of the fourth wall by both Da (who is dead) and Young Charlie (who exists only in Charlie's memory), the scenes shuffled in discontinuous yet continuing time are all modernist techniques of the early twentieth-century theatre, but made Irish by Denis Johnston in 1929. In taking them over here in *Da*, as well as in many other of his plays (*Time Was, A Life, Love in the Title* among others), Leonard was at the same time appropriating for his own use those much earlier dramatic ideas on duality, masking and identity found in Goldsmith, Sheridan, Wilde, Shaw, and so on, up to Brendan Behan – Irish writers who had to struggle with pleasing an English audience. Like Goldsmith and these others the writer Charlie *qua* Leonard can put the question in *Da*: 'how could I belong there [in London] if I belonged here [in Dublin]?'[15]

In *The Irish Comic Tradition* Vivian Mercier discussed Irish humour, understood as fantasy, under the headings 'macabre' and 'grotesque'. I have written elsewhere on 'Irish Drama and the Fantastic'.[16] About Leonard's use of fantasy there is no question whatsoever. From *Madigan's Lock* on, he invariably had a paradise to search for. *Lost Horizon* (1937) was a favourite film, Alain Fournier's *Le Grand Meaulnes* (1913) a favourite novel. Leonard's use of time, already noted, is also a means of basing many of his plays in fantasy. By the macabre Mercier means a peculiar sense of and attitude towards death. It is true we as a people are inordinately preoccupied with death. Didn't Yeats say there were only two major themes, sex and death? At any rate, much Irish humour is about death; much of Irish drama is bound up with gallows humour.

Synge provides the best example. His poor health may have something to do with it, but all he wrote was either morbid or gloriously defiant of the inevitability of death. *Riders to the Sea* (1903) is one thing: we can accept a piling on of agony in a tragedy, even a dwarf one as Joyce regarded it. But in comedy? *The Shadow in the Glen* (1903) opens with an old dead man laid out by his young wife and a passing Tramp asking for shelter in the night. Then she goes outside and whistles piercingly for her lover. Later the dead man sneezes when the

Tramp is alone with him and the play takes a fresh, comical turn. Dan Burke has merely pretended to be dead in order to catch his wife, Nora, with her lover and exact revenge. In the end the unexpected takes place, the wife stands up to her husband, the Tramp stands up for her, and in a burst of lyrical victory the pair of them leave for a life on the roads. The traditional death-and-resurrection theme makes Synge's play comic, as in Boucicault's *The Shaughraun* (1874) before that, and after that in the ballad, 'Finnegan's Wake,' on which Joyce was to base his comic novel. The funny and the macabre sit easily together in Irish literature. Synge first heard the story for his little play on the Aran Islands, though he gave it a new, subversive, ending. His style helped to establish the modern Irish dramatic tradition.

The death-and-resurrection motif, then, as derived from folklore, was available to modern Irish writers of comedy. Synge would have known that as a scholar. Behan would have known it as a Gaeilgeoir and an Irish Catholic who described himself as 'a daylight atheist'; when the dark came 'he said his prayers.'[17] He dealt with this dread of death through comedy. *The Quare Fellow* (1954) is written like an Irish wake, with comic scenes all through, a traditional mark of respect for the man due to hang. *The Hostage* (1958), if one can set aside the fact that Behan's text was altered by Joan Littlewood and her Workshop Theatre, ends with the resurrection of the eponymous hostage, the British soldier captured by the IRA and shot while trying to escape. It is an extraordinary moment when he rises again to sing his parody of Saint Paul:

> The bells of hell
> Go ting-a-ling-a-ling
> For you but not for me.
> Oh death where is thy
> Sting-a-ling-a-ling
> Or grave thy victory?[18]

A later, more thorough application of the theme in Thomas Kilroy's, *The Death and Resurrection of Mr Roche* (1968), gave it a new and profound twist. As Kilroy has said: 'When I was writing it I did have a certain private academic fun in trying to write an ironic version of the old resurrection-fertility comedy.'[19]

This is where Hugh Leonard comes in. *Da* is a wake disguised as a comedy. The macabre note is muted, to be sure, and yet the scorn son piles on father and the constant jokes for which Da is responsible nevertheless lend what David Krause calls the 'profanity' necessary to comedy.[20] It may be that Da's line, 'There's some queer people walking the ways of the world' (44) is a parody of Synge, raising the prospect of seeing *Da* as a version of Old Mahon in *The Playboy of the Western World*. Whatever about that, the Oedipal theme is present in the play in spades, even though Da is not Charlie's natural father. Leonard's variation is that Da is already dead at the opening of the play, which makes the parricide redundant and at the same time ironic. The gruffer and more insolent Charlie becomes in discouraging Da from displaying his lovable qualities, the more the audience feels drawn to Da in his warm-heartedness and incorrigibility. However often Charlie insists that Da is dead and exists only in his memory, no character could be less ghostlike; no Blithe Spirit he, for Da is there corporeally before our eyes. The role was recently played (at the Gate in 2012) with great effect by Owen Roe, Ireland's answer to Simon Russell Beale, whose stage presence communicates vitality with every sound and movement. Roe played Da resurrected as the most alive figure on the stage.

Yeats drew a distinction between comedy and tragedy on the basis that character 'is continuously present in comedy alone', whereas it is passion that gives to the figures in tragedy their sense of life. To be alive, to be 'real' to us, Da has to be comic, like Falstaff, who, Yeats says, 'has no passionate purpose to fulfil'.[21] Yet Da has his great passionate explosion of jealousy in Act II when he forbids his wife ever again to venture where she might see 'curse-o'-God-Ernie', the man she loved and did not marry. The stage direction is explicit: '*Even* MOTHER, *who knows him, is alarmed by the violence of his rage*' (64). Leonard presents the scene as a flashback, conjured by Charlie, who is helpless to intervene. He can only convey his horror: '(*remembering*) And the floorboards barked like dogs, and the cups went mad on their hooks' (64). This magnificent scene, so well played by Roe and Ingrid Craigie in the Gate production, lifts Da well beyond the category of fool Charlie has foisted on him up to this point. Mother's throwaway line after he has made his raging exit restores the play to comic mode: 'The jealous old bags' (65). *Da* exists to prove Yeats wrong.

Mercier is inclined to associate the macabre with the grotesque, citing the stone Sheela-na-gigs as evidence, with their blatant sexuality distorted by haggish facial features. Fear of sex within Irish culture can be associated with such distortion in female representation. Leonard exploits this feature also, but as a modernist transforms the grotesque into harmless mockery. A key scene in this regard occurs in Act I, in which Young Charlie lusts after the Yellow Peril. In a sense she is a Sheela-na-gig figure, except that she is young and beautiful, being a sex symbol, a goddess who could 'both destroy and create'.[22] Charlie

describes her for Da in 'real' time just before the re-enactment of his
encounter with her:

> We all dreamed, privately and sweatily, about committing dark
> deeds with the Yellow Peril. Dark was the word, for if you were
> seen with her, nice girls would shun you and tell their mothers
> [...] The Yellow Peril was the enemy of mothers. And the
> fellows [pals] would jeer at you for your beggarman's lust – you
> with your fine words of settling for nothing less than Veronica
> Lake. [...] The Yellow Peril never winked, smiled or flirted: the
> sure sign of an activist. (38)

As Young Charlie and Oliver stroll past her sitting on a bench and
flicking through *Modern Screen,* the male gaze is openly enacted. 'They
say she'd let you. All you have to do is ask', Oliver says. But she would
'make a holy show of you', perhaps, Young Charlie muses (39). The
grotesquerie is all in the mind. When the young woman raises her head
she has *'a calm direct look, neither friendly nor hostile'*, though Charlie
is inflamed by 'lust' (38). Oliver, alarmed, beats a retreat. Urged on by
his older self (the scene is, like many in the play, in double focus),
Charlie sits beside her and, *'What follows is ritual, laconic and fast'*
(40). As he is making progress, pawing the girl's knee and attempting to
touch her breast from across the back of the bench, but actually
'kneading and pinching her handbag, which is tucked under her arm',
the older Charlie remarks, 'I think you're getting her money all excited'
(42). 'If you won't stop', she tells Young Charlie, 'I'll have to go down
the back [...] If you won't stop.' (42) He hoarsely accepts the invitation
when suddenly there is a blast of an Irish song, as Da enters on his way
home and in shock addresses his son. 'Bruce' from Trinity College, as he
has just called himself, cringes while Da addresses Mary Tate (as she
now identifies herself) cheerfully. 'If my hand was free', says older
Charlie, 'I'd have slashed my wrists' (43).   Da sits on the bench
and settles in for a chat with Mary: 'Your mother was one of the
Hannigans of Sallynoggin. Did you know that?' He pursues her
genealogy until he can avow: 'Don't I know the whole seed and breed of
yous!' As Charlie notes, Da has turned the Yellow Peril into 'a person'
before his very eyes: 'Sure this is a grand girl' (44). A potential sex scene
is transformed into the unmasking of Charlie's immaturity. After Da
has gone off happily into the night, Mary repeats her invitation more
personally to Young Charlie: 'Well, will *we* go down the back? (44,
emphasis added) but the unmasked youth makes his excuses and the
scene ends. In a subversive way the scene can be read as Da making a
man of Charlie.

Irish comedies do not usually end in a marriage. Synge's *Playboy* is the standard here, because Pegeen Mike's loss of Christy Mahon underlines the element of bittersweetness in the Irish representation. To be sure, Northrop Frye has outlined the myth of spring, whereby the victory of youth over age and new life over old is symbolized in the end by marriage as historically the pattern of romantic comedy. The final 'festive ritual' acts as symbol of 'crystallization around the hero' as a new society is germinated.[23] Synge showed the opposite. He showed comedy enacting the break-up or denial of a marriage, overturning audience expectation in order to expose hypocrisy. By the time Hugh Leonard was writing, Synge's model, in which 'I've lost him surely' is the endnote, had become too romantic (in Siobhán McKenna's interpretation[24]) to satisfy. Leonard does include a marriage towards the end of *Da* but it is essentially a ritual of leaving. Young Charlie is being bustled out the door to catch his plane to Belgium to marry out of the tribe. Oliver goes with him as best man, but not his adoptive parents. The liminal moment is understated in order to keep the focus on them. There is to be no 'crystallization' around this hero, no new society in the formation. 'You may as well be off, so. There's nothing to keep you', is about all Mother can say. So, even though Leonard avoids romance in his comedy, he nevertheless retains Synge's paradigm in which the ending marks a leaving which is a critique of society. The older Charlie, reliving the painful parting, urges his younger self to go quickly: 'Now. Goodbye, and out' (75). After the wedding Charlie's new life will grow in London, where he will pursue his career writing for television. He remains, while his young self departs. But what Young Charlie sees as 'a beginning' Mother sees as 'the end'; he is outside the house, she inside; neither hears the other's line but the audience hearing both sees the moment as powerfully ambivalent.

The final scene is in the present tense only. Drumm, who is in a sense Charlie's alternative father, arrives before Charlie locks up and leaves forever. There is a kind of reckoning between them. Though Drumm believes Da was 'an ignorant man', at least he never knew disillusion (82). Drumm tells Charlie about the money, how Da had never used what Charlie sent over the years but set it aside as a lump sum to leave him. The shock leads to a recognition scene when Charlie confronts Da on the matter. What Charlie recognizes is that one cannot pay back love given freely; though he is more than ever in debt to Da there is no way to abolish it. He thinks that by tidying up the house and destroying almost all records he will be free. Even when he locks up and throws away the key to the little house he finds Da happily by his side, having ignored the stage's fourth wall.

This Old Mahon and Christy leave for London together, even though one of them is dead. All tenses are now combined. Da was the patriarchal Ireland Leonard could no longer abide circa 1960; Da is the ghost who will be Charlie/Hugh Leonard's muse; Da will prompt his writer-son to avenge himself as satirist and commentator on Haughey's Ireland. The manager of the old Abbey told the young Leonard he didn't like plays with ghosts in them. Twenty-five years later Leonard proved him wrong. By laying his private ghosts to rest he helped to liberate the ghosts of a nation, poverty, humiliation, fear of sex and death, and to renew Irish comedy in many of its ritualistic preoccupations.

---

[1] Hugh Leonard, 'Drama: The Turning Point', in *Ireland at the Crossroads*, ed. Patrick Rafroidi and Pierre Joannon (Lille: Université de Lille III, 1979): 78.

[2] Hugh Leonard, *Leonard's Year* (Dublin: Canavaun Books/Brophy Educational, 1985), pp.104-105. These collections began with *Leonard's Last Book,* ed. John Feeney (Enniskerry: Egotist Press, 1978), from pieces in *Hibernia* 1973-76 and the *Sunday Independent* 1976-78; and *A Peculiar People and other Foibles*, also ed. John Feeney (Enniskerry: Tansy Books, 1979). Kevin Brophy, who published Leonard's Year, following the sudden death of journalist John Feeney, took up the task and followed *Leonard's Year* with *Leonard's Log* (1987) and *Leonard's Log – Again* (1988), edited from the *Sunday Independent* column.

[3] S.F. Gallagher, ed., Introduction to *Selected Plays of Hugh Leonard* (Gerrards Cross: Colin Smythe, 1992): 11-12.

[4] D.E.S. Maxwell, *A Critical History of Modern Irish Drama 1891-1980* (Cambridge: Cambridge UP, 1984): 175.

[5] Maxwell, 177.

[6] D.E.S.Maxwell, ed., 'Contemporary Drama 1953-1986' in *The Field Day Anthology of Irish Writing* (3 vols., Derry: Field Day Publications, 1991):3, 1138.

[7] William W. Appleton, *Charles Macklin: An Actor's Life* (Cambridge: Oxford, 1961): 141.

[8] Alan Ayckbourn, *The Crafty Art of Playmaking* (London: Faber, 2002): x.

[9] Neil Simon, *Rewrites: A Memoir* (New York: Simon and Schuster, 1996): 143.

[10] For example, Rosemarie Jarski, *The Funniest Thing You Never Said: The Ultimate Collection of Humorous Quotations* (London: Ebury Press, 2004); Rosemarie Jarski, *The Funniest Thing You Never Said*

2 (London: Ebury Press, 2010); Des Mac Hale, *Wittypedia: Over 4,000 of the Funniest Quotations* (London: Prion/Carlton, 2011).

11 Leonard was inordinately proud to have a fan letter from a man named Silverman after the premiere of *Da* in Olney, Maryland, thanking him for writing 'a lovely Jewish play.' Leonard,'Drama : The Turning Point', 85.

12 Hugh Leonard, *Home Before Night* (London: Andre Deutch, 1979): 187.

13 Hugh Leonard, Introduction, *Madigan's Lock and Pizzazz: Two Plays* (Dublin: Brophy Books, 1987): 4.

14 Sean O'Casey, *The Plough and the Stars*, in *Collected Plays 1* (London: Macmillan, 1949): 191.

15 Hugh Leonard, *Da, A Life and Time Was* (Harmondsworth: Penguin, 1981): 37. All subsequent quotations from *Da* are from this edition, to which page numbers refer.

16 Christopher Murray, 'Irish Drama and the Fantastic', in *More Real than Reality: The Fantastic in Irish Literature and the Arts,* ed. Donald E. Morse and Csilla Bertha (Westport, CT: Greenwood Press, 1991): 85-96.

17 Seamus de Burca, *Brendan Behan: A Memoir* (Newark, DE: Proscenium Press, 1971): 28.

18 Brendan Behan, *The Hostage* (London: Methuen, 1958): 92.

19 Thomas Kilroy to Christopher Murray, 9 July 1973. At the time I had put *The Death and Resurrection of Mr Roche* on a First Year course on comedy at UCD. The text was first published by Faber and Faber, 1969.

20 David Krause, *The Profane Book of Irish Comedy* (London: Cornell, 1982): 32-47.

21 W.B. Yeats, 'The Tragic Theatre', in *Essays and Introductions* (London and New York: Macmillan, 1961): 240.

22 Mercier, *The Irish Comic Tradition* (London: Souvenir, 1991): 55.

23 Northrop Frye, *Anatomy of Criticism: Four Essays* [1957] (New York: Atheneum, 1966): 163.

24 See Adrian Frazier, '"Quaint Pastoral Numbskulls": Siobhán McKenna's *Playboy* Film', in Adrian Frazier, ed., *Playboys of the Western World: Production Histories* (Dublin: Carysfort, 2004): 59-74.

3 | Dead Funny: Mortality and comic comeuppance in Tom Mac Intyre's *Only an Apple*

Marie Kelly

As Walter Nash states in *The Language of Humour,* 'humour is a serious business [...] more than an amiable decoration on life; it is a complex piece of equipment for living.'[1] Theories of humour from cultural studies, psychology, and philosophy corroborate this view asserting that laughter is fundamentally conditioned by our environment and comedy brings us closer to covert, taken-for-granted, and unspoken values entrenched in the culture at large. Some of these theories link humour to aggression, hatred, sex, and death. In this essay I explore the latter contention in Tom Mac Intyre's play, *Only an Apple,* which premiered at the Peacock Theatre, Dublin, in 2009.[2]

When *Only an Apple* was publicised in the lead-up to its opening night there was more than a hint of comedic promise in the air. Marketing material described a play of 'somber colours and comedic *rí-rá*' [Irish for rough and tumble] about an 'ailing playboy Taoiseach' on 'the brink of being overthrown.'[3] Pre-performance publicity issued a photograph of the said 'playboy Taoiseach' sitting with his lovers and cohorts behind a table piled with apples and guarded by a peacock and two Irish wolfhounds (see Fig. 1). At a time when corruption in the Irish State's leadership was making headlines across the world, the play's content, and the image of this fictional Taoiseach juxtaposed with the biblical scenes of Leonardo da Vinci's *The Last Supper* and Wenzel Peter's *Adam and Eve in the Garden of Eden,* playfully pointed towards sexual temptation and the ousting of the Irish political leader, Charles J. Haughey.

Charles Haughey (1925-2006) was leader of Fianna Fáil (Ireland's Republican Party) and Taoiseach (Prime Minister of Ireland) at various stages between 1979 and 1992. He was an adept but controversially corrupt politician with a hugely lavish lifestyle. At the same time that Haughey advised the Irish public to 'tighten their belts' in the 1980s he was living in Abbeville, the eighteenth-century mansion in Dublin designed by James Gandon. He was in possession of a sizeable art collection and an island off the West coast of Ireland (Inishvickilane). He enjoyed splashing out on exotic foreign holidays, fine dining, French tailoring, and the company of his long-term mistress, the gossip columnist Terry Keane. Haughey and his political allies were unmasked publicly on more than one occasion in the decades between 1970 and 2009: Haughey was sacked as a young government minister in 1970 on suspicion of importing arms and ammunition into the Irish State. When presiding as Taoiseach, Haughey's Attorney General (Patrick Connolly) was found to be harbouring a fugitive murderer (Malcolm McArthur) at his home in North Dublin in 1982. In the same year, Minister for Justice Sean Doherty intervened in the prosecution of his own brother-in-law who was due in court on an assault charge. In 1992 Haughey resigned from political life when the phone-tapping of two prominent journalists, authorised by Doherty, was exposed. Haughey's house of cards completely collapsed in his retirement, however, when the Moriarty Tribunal began to discover the personal profits garnered by Haughey and several other Fianna Fáil politicians through back-handers from various businesses and individuals in the corporate world. The media had a field day as one headline exemplifies: 'Disgraced former Taoiseach stole £45m in today's money from taxpayers.'[4]

By the time of *Only an Apple*'s premiere both the stronghold of the Fianna Fáil leadership and Ireland's Celtic Tiger economy had disintegrated. Haughey's previous right-hand man, Bertie Ahern, was now leader of the party and Taoiseach. Following in his predecessor's footsteps, however, Ahern was also leaving in disgrace and under investigation at the Mahon Tribunal for accepting payments from property developers and others seeking leniency in planning permission and land rezoning. Meanwhile the 'Tiger' economy, precipitated by Fianna Fáil policies and once the envy of international markets, was in collapse and exposed as a pseudo-boom built on multinational investment, inflated property prices and a culture of massive over-borrowing and over-spending.

From the outset of his writing career Tom Mac Intyre has had an interest in powerful male figures – mythical, political, or literary – as subject matter. One of his first prose works, *Through the Bridewell Gate* (1971), was a journalistic account of the arms trial that led to Haughey's sacking from government in 1970. In the course of this account Mac Intyre describes the young Haughey:

> [H]e is a man who wants power, they say, he has everything else, deprived of the chance of power now – for how long?, monied still though – rich beyond the calculations of rumour, a tongue in his head too – that was evident straight off this morning – years of experience in the House behind his finesse in handling answer, qualification, elaboration; and this gruesome control, and, of course the vanity – dear Jesus, what strange nectars and stranger vinegars this man must have sipped these past years besides coffee that makes the politician wise, and see through all things with his half-shut eyes.[5]

Hints of Mac Intyre's interest in the exploration of interior landscapes are present in this early prose, an interest which dominates the main thrust of his dramatic work: *The Great Hunger* (1983) enters into the repressed psychology of Patrick Maguire, the character of Patrick Kavanagh's poem of the same name; *The Bearded Lady* (1984) joins Jonathan Swift as he lapses into a dream in which his Freudian fantasies are played out through the fictional character of Lemuel Gulliver; *Rise Up Lovely Sweeney* (1985) recreates the hallucinogenic world of an ex-IRA man who is exiled and unable to reach out to wife or lover; *Good Evening, Mr Collins* (1995) stages the libidinous dream world of Michael Collins (Irish revolutionary leader, killed in 1922 during the Irish Civil War). Across all of this work Mac Intyre has cultivated a distinct style and theme, a dramaturgy that is non-linear, imagistic, and framed by dream, the unconscious, the unreal, and the surreal. These plays are densely poetic and as funny as they are sad, as invested thematically in sex as they are in death. Thus *Only an Apple* is a play of two halves; the first act playful, sexually frivolous, and caught up with clownish behaviour and Freudian slip, the second plunging into Jungian shadows of the trickster archetype and focusing on the contemplation of death.

SEX AND DEATH

For George Bataille, 'sex and death' represents *the* most erotic of all metaphors, which encapsulates the 'exuberance of life' and our 'assenting to life even in death.'[6] In Bataille's view:

> The desire to go keeling helplessly over, that assails the
> innermost depths of every human being is nevertheless
> different from the desire to die in that it is ambiguous. It may
> well be a desire to die, but it is at the same time a desire to live
> to the limits of the possible and the impossible with ever-
> increasing intensity. It is the desire to live while ceasing to live,
> or to die without ceasing to live, the desire of an extreme state.[7]

According to Mac Intyre the metaphor of sex and death represents,
'the hunger many of us have for intense living – and the reluctance
many of us have to pay the price for that elusive goal.'[8] His writing for
theatre mirrors this condition, taking audiences on a roller-coaster ride
that dips and swerves between bewilderment, amusement, and despair.
His texts are steeped in symbolism and metaphor, full of riddles, puns,
one-liners, sophisticated word play, and bawdy rudeness. In *Only an
Apple*, for instance, a description of Limerick as a 'posterior opening
through which Ireland relieves herself,'[9] and lines such as, 'You couldn't
be a poet, your mouth too closely resembles your anus,' (32) sit
alongside more densely poetic expressions that carry both serious and
comic undertones. The Taoiseach asks, 'why is there such pleasure,
limitless pleasure, in the full knowledge of, full consent to, disaster?'
(55). He is excited by '[t]he turbulent landscape of the new' (20) and
repulsed by the work-a-day world of clock-watching, a state he
describes as, 'Vasectomy of the soul!' (17). As he tells the audience in
the first scene of the play:

> Someone said to me once – young Deputy up from the bogs –
> first term in the house – 'You never wear a watch, Taoiseach?'
> 'No,' I told him, 'I never was. But I've known lots who *were* and
> battalions who *are*. All they do is *tick*, and when they're not
> ticking they're alarming, when they're not alarming they're
> bloodless gadgets falling to bits at forty – and then *insisting* on
> a State Funeral!' Young Deputy's eyes now one-arm-banditing
> in their sockets – he was mine for life. Kill for me. Detail.
> Everything's in the detail (5).

This abundant use of metaphor and symbolism, shot through with
equal measures of witticism and solemnity, are typical features of Mac
Intyre's writing, a textual marker of the search for 'intense living,'
heightened experience, excitement, the sensual, and the erotic.

The entire dramaturgy of *Only an Apple* is built, however, on male
fantasy, sexual desire, the drive towards death, and the necromantic.
We are seeing the world through the eyes and imagination of the
Taoiseach, witnessing his attitudes to male/female interaction, and we

are in the zone of spirits, ghosts, and the supernatural. In this respect the play exposes gender-dominated power relations surrounding sexuality, desire and the erotic, and displays features of the Funerary School in Irish drama. Nina Witoszek and Patrick Sheeran describe the *funerary tradition* in Irish culture as propagating a philosophy of life as dying and a 'necrogenic drama' or a *Theatrum Mortis* (theatre of the dead), which elevates the status of death through the centre staging of funerary rites of passage, reviving corpses, wakes, burials, revenants, and other signifiers of dying. Included in this are dramaturgies of the non-real, the spiritual, and the transcendental. The *Theatrum Mortis* is turned towards the past and suspended in time, caught in the liminal and the non-linear; it has been 'distilled by the conjunction of two imperatives: the contemplation of death and the prohibition on sex.'[10] In this drama, 'the basic condition is that of grieving, fantasising, being haunted and preparing for one's own funeral.'[11]

EVENTS *EN TRAIN*

According to Jacques Lacan's psychoanalytic theory, fantasy (phantasy) 'provides the co-ordinates of our desire [and] it is through phantasy that we learn to desire.'[12] Everything that occurs in *Only an Apple* – every man, woman, and object – has been conjured up at the Taoiseach's behest and exists only within his fantasy. Thus, the events that take place in the play are as real to him as the intensity of pure pleasure and as his desire dictates. This central male character has left behind the mundane everyday world and embarked on a chimerical journey. On this journey he is accompanied by the ghosts of two of European history's most powerful women, the Tudor Queen, Elizabeth (I) and legendary Irish pyratess, Grace O'Malley. These two women are succubi, female demons, the spirits of sex, or: 'Strays, charged particles, succubi' and 'a summons to [...] the Beyond!' (23). Central to the action, and indeed the comedy, is the seduction of the Taoiseach and his cohorts by O'Malley and Elizabeth. These fantastical seductions, or the 'events *en train*,' take precedence over the intrigues of political life and the impending 'heave' or political ousting of his main political opponent. As he tells his starchy press secretary, Hislop, in Act I: 'The heave is on the margin. There are, I repeat events *en train*, before which you, the media, the world at large, will stand amazed! (19)'.

As well as Hislop in supporting roles are: McPhrunty, the bumbling middle-aged rural politician/Taoiseach-in-waiting; Arkins, a Yeatsian figure in the form of a gay cultural attaché-cum-poet; the Taoiseach's mistress, Cherie, who looms offstage; and, lastly, the Taoiseach's unnamed 'Wife' who is engaged in a longterm affair with the butler of the house, the ever subservient Sheridan.

The opening scenes acquaint the audience with the contours of the egotistical political leader's fantasy world. The bulk of the humour in this early part of the play is derived from absurdity, incongruity, and the stripping away of the Taoiseach's pretentious behaviour. We are in the playground of the illogical, the ludicrous, and the grotesque, and it is in this playground that the audience gets to witness and laugh at the great man as his imperious demeanour is compromised by the two spirits of sex. Dick Bird's setting for the Peacock production is the aptly lavish and ornate drawing room of the Taoiseach's mansion, Taraford (aka, Abbeville). There is a great bay window to the rear, an antique table centre stage, and a host of bizarre items hidden in the surrounding paneled walls: a paper shredder, a store of raw meat and bones. The Taoiseach (played by Don Wycherley) is in leadership mode, dishing out orders to Sheridan for coffee and to Hislop about the 'banal business of the heave' and McPhrunty 'who has to be shafted. With no delay' (2). A stage direction describes the accompanying action:

> *Taoiseach strolls upstage, flings open the window. Wolfhounds begin to howl melodiously. Taoiseach dons white gloves, removes lid from a convenient bin, flings a succession of bloodied bones to the hounds. Tumult subsides, gloves discarded* (2).

Sheridan (Malcolm Adams) is given instructions on what to do with the morning newspapers:

> **Taoiseach.** [...] Morning papers singing the same old song?
> **Sheridan.** Right, Taoiseach. Claimin' he has the numbers.
> **Taoiseach.** Shredder.
> **Sheridan.** No bother, Taoiseach.
> **Sheridan** *to the shredder with the dailies, feeds the dailies to it. Vengeful hum of the shredder rouses the wolfhounds. They want more, more, more [...]* **Sheridan** *moves to placate them, goes to the bin (no need of gloves), gets the goodies, hurls them to the hounds. Happy sounds of the pack gobbling* (2-3).

Humour is extracted from the shredding of the newspapers without being read, the unhygienic handling of the raw meat being chucked out the window, the bizarre and over-the-top sounds of the '*pack gobbling*'. These elements of the action are entirely out of place in the elegant and somewhat clinical interior of the drawing room. The Incongruity Theory of humour states that the 'cause of laughter in every case is simply the sudden perception of the incongruity between a concept and the real objects which have been thought through it in some relation, and laughter itself is just the expression of this incongruity'.[13]

When confronted with an absurd or illogical action, then, it is the perception of incongruity with regard to what we know that prompts laughter. Drawing upon another strain of humour theory, such incongruity also provides an opportunity to feel superior to those at the centre of the action. Under the direction of Selina Cartmell, for instance, the Taoiseach's imperiousness is accentuated by Sheridan's formal subservience and businesslike courteousness, which both complement and emphasize the former's higher status. The Taoiseach's centrality and authority is threatened, however, when Hislop (Michael McElhatton) enters and asks, 'have you studied the morning rags?' (18). The stage direction describes the Taoiseach's reaction:

> *For answer,* **Taoiseach** *dances, giddy, to the shredder. Showers himself with ribbons of paper, romps about the space festooned with the offending newsprint* (18).

In performance this action is exaggerated by the actor's comic bravura as he showers himself in the shredded newsprint not once but twice, and by punctuating each shower with a *Tada!* gesture. On receipt of the required response of laughter from the audience he moves adeptly on to the punchline: I'm *in* the news! And I adore being *in* the news! (18), the word 'in' emphasised by Wycherley in performance.

Wycherley's Taoiseach looks ridiculous with the shredded newsprint sitting like a mad wig on top of his head. The degree to which his dance breaks or contradicts the mask of his earlier imperiousness corresponds with the degree of hilarity evoked through the combination of text and action, thus demonstrating the significant importance of the performer's skill in the delivery of the comic moment. Our laughter devalues the character of the Taoiseach in response to these actions, lessening the degree to which we take him seriously. Obviously this humour is at its most effective within specific social/political conditions and when the audience understands the joke. Since talk of the 'heave' situates the characters within the cultural sphere of Fianna Fáil politics, the humour mocks a particular individual/situation and creates a bond between those who share this understanding – presumably anyone who is reading the real news of the day and who has followed Irish politics over the past half century.

PUSSY DRIVES THE TRAIN

The main thrust of *Only an Apple's* comedic *rí rá* arises, however, in the incongruity between characters of heightened sexuality and those who appear to be sexually inept or lost. In this regard it is the main (male) characters' sexual fear, their confrontation with the opposite sex, that is showcased and most often at the butt of the joke. The Taoiseach, Hislop, McPhrunty, and Sheridan are straight-laced, formal, and utterly inept around women. On the other side of the fence all three of the female characters are represented as sexually voracious to the point of being life-threatening. Speaking of the succubi, the Taoiseach says:

> My *guests*, man, this pair of black-widow spiders I'm landed with. My perfumed banshees! Everyone they've bedded is a corpse! All right, sex and death are the only topics – *are they?* – but this is necro – necro – what is it? Necro*SARCOPHAGI!* (73).

Bawdy comic moments show: the Taoiseach terrified when he is mounted by not one but both of the spirit women on top of his beautiful antique drawing-room table (see Fig. 2); Sheridan's repressed sexuality when he gestures masturbation in polishing the doorknobs whenever a woman is in sight; McPhrunty's lecherousness when he secretly takes out a comb from his breast pocket and sweeps his one lock of hair across his bald patch as Grace bends over the drinks cabinet; and finally, Hislop's total breakdown when he staggers on stripped and dazed after his presumed dalliance with the two spirit women. Arkins stands, however, as a specialist of sensualism, describing himself as 'entirely open to temptation' (27). The all-singing all-dancing finale to Act I gives an example of the tone of the action. In the words of the stage direction:

> *The entire ensemble appear [...] and we soar into a showpiece chorale – with dance element. This (a reprise with wild variations of 'Pussy Drives the Train') is the musical director's chance of immortality and should not be missed. Note: the animals and the birds should not be left out of the vocals. They should, even, be given a gallop entirely to themselves. In short, it's a blast. This set-piece concludes Act I. Nota Bene: An essential ingredient in the above is (vid. Infra) a particular shift. As soon as the celebratory thrust has been established, the colour of the proceedings should take a turn towards the troubling, the menacing, the chasm, i.e. sure, pussy drives the train, but pussy, by the same token, is high octane, and the mere lighting of a match has blown many away (47).*

The sexual innuendo of this *'showpiece chorale'* is distinctly out of step with attitudes to sex and sexuality in the twenty-first century, the play's carnal exuberance and frivolity at odds with prevailing realties in Ireland and abroad. At a time of rapid economic decline, escalating joblessness, homelessness, bankruptcy, poverty, and at a time of wider world concerns post 9/11, the action of the play sidesteps these immediate concerns in order to make way for another kind of reality. Through the lens of the fictional character's fantasy, *Only an Apple* brings lewd and politically incorrect moments to the surface, removing such moments to a realm beyond reason and the real.

As I have discussed elsewhere with Dr. Bernadette Sweeney, the female figures are represented as formidable forces within the stage world, but they are imprisoned and debased within the vicious alterity and misogyny of the Taoiseach's fantasy.[14] The language of the male characters in referring to Elizabeth and Grace is savagely crude: 'Pixillated cunts,' (15) 'scented cobwebs,' (15) 'minges *growling* for it,' (17) 'brazen free-loaders,' (21) 'piss-flaps on the make,' (28) 'spaced-out snatches' (28). By contrast, the male characters are demeaned rather than debased through the language of the women. Grace (Cathy Belton) demotes the Taoiseach as she gives him a physical once-over: 'Show me your teeth,' she says, 'I love cold teeth in a man!' (7). Meanwhile, Elizabeth I (Fiona Bell) mispronounces the Taoiseach's name at every opportunity, addressing him variously as Teeshuck, Twosocks, Twosack, Toolsack, Rucksack, Threesock, Tassock, Trussock, Trulock, Trillock, and Tayshine.

In its alterity this form of humour exposes a misogynistic world of patriarchal power and control, and holds the potential either to breach or repeat a whole range of socially accepted yet hidden values, protocols and codes of behaviour. This begs the question as to whether the humour of *Only an Apple* provides a safe space for dealing with what is usually *suppressed*, or whether in fact this humour *expresses* what would otherwise be regarded as taboo. As Patrick Lonergan remarks in his review of the play, *Only an Apple* is

> vacuous, crude, and infantile. It is consistently sexist and occasionally homophobic. It is incoherent and self-regarding. And because it is all of those things, it is a stunningly appropriate and stimulating portrait of our political system – one that allows us to imagine what the world looks like from the perspective of a mediocre man with serious responsibilities.[15]

Sigmund Freud's approach to laughter sees it as satisfying 'an instinct (whether lustful or hostile) in the face of an obstacle that stands in its way.'[16] According to this approach – usually aligned with humour's Relief Theory – laughter releases a pressure valve for suppressed thoughts, desires, or hostilities. John Morreall has countered this explanation, however, by asserting that if the energy released in laughter is

> the energy normally used to repress hostile and sexual feelings, then it seems that those who laugh hardest at aggressive and sexual jokes should be people who usually repress such feelings. But studies about joke preferences by Hans Jurgen Eysenck (1972) have shown that the people who enjoy aggressive and sexual humour the most are *not* those who actually repress hostile and sexual feelings, but those who express them (my italics).[17]

To this extent the humour of *Only an Apple* is indicative of the funerary tradition's vernacular hatred which in the words of Witoszek and Sheeran, 'energizes the famous Irish wit; all those verbal assassinations, sneers, jests, lampoons and venomous satires'. In this regard, 'no other culture has been so negatively defined, so lacerated by its own culture'. By definition:

> Vernacular hatred and its various verbal and behavioural manifestations (calumny, distraction etc) is a diffuse, low-voltage, insidious process of dealing out death. (Just as we might say, alcoholism is slow suicide). At its most virulent – and Ireland is a pathological zone in this regard – it destroys personal identity and maims for life. It is in this sense that the manifold manifestations of vernacular hatred may be treated as tropes of funerary culture, ways of willing and wishing death.[18]

In the same vein, then, the Taoiseach asks his audience in Act II: 'Have you ever had the experience of opening your passport, glancing at your photo, and discovering that the name under it is Paddy Shite?' (96). As the play moves into its second half, such 'ways of willing and wishing death' begin to emerge more clearly from the shadowy edges of the play. To repeat the stage direction at the end of Act I, there is '*a particular shift [...] a turn towards the troubling, the menacing, the chasm*' (47).

DEAD FUNNY

In this shift '*towards the troubling*' the earlier playfulness of the dramaturgy subsides and makes way for more sombre colours of the central character's fantasy (Fig. 4). The Taoiseach plans to do away with McPhrunty (Steve Blount), his chief political opponent, by feeding him to the two spirits of sex. The presence and seductiveness of the succubi sets off a dark cosmic storm and finally McPhrunty's spontaneous combustion. In the aftermath of the crisis the Taoiseach talks of fate, sexual temptation, and death in the same breath:

> I can go *this* far with Arkins. If Fate – FATE – is being pulled irresistibly towards a line of action, then this is – they are – my fate. And if you say to me, have you been walking towards them from the cradle, I'd have to say yes. YES. *YES.* Why, Because of what they do to me. What's that? It's where I've never been before. In bed. Or outa bed. It's – it's – don't ask me what it is. *(Pause)* There's only one catch. Death. Rot. Quite. Possibly. The box. The graveyard speeches. I want *that*? (97).

To a large extent these echoes of death have been lingering throughout the stage action of the first half of *Only an Apple*, keeping vigil as if waking a living corpse. Witoszek and Sheeran explain how the Funerary School in Irish drama has appropriated the ritual of the wake which

> divides the dramatic space horizontally in terms of the opposition inside/outside. It constructs symbolic boundaries which separate the mourners – members of the magic circle of cultural community – from the outside world. The liminal space of the wake is the space of ludic initiation into the knowledge of death or death-in-life. It is the locus of memory and illusion – and of escape from the structures of power.[19]

The interior of the wake-house accommodates repression, suffering, and death, while the outside becomes the place of chaos and rebellion. In *Only an Apple* this boundary is registered both in the contrasting tones of the first and second halves of the play as well as in the contrast between the indoor luxury of the drawing room and the strange menagerie of animals existing outdoors. The presence of the menagerie becomes more pronounced as the play proceeds and comprises wolfhounds (referred to earlier in this analysis), peacocks, horses, and crows. These animals have a symbolic/mythical quality, relating both to the unconscious and to the otherworldliness of the play.[20] These animals are in communication with and take orders from the succubi. They represent the psychopomp whose responsibility it is to escort the Taoiseach to the unconscious.[21] As Sheridan says, 'Th' animals – the birds – knows the know, I always heard' (58). In Act I, Scene 2, on the arrival of Grace and Elizabeth, '*the wolfhounds go into a (well-nigh)*

worshipful chorale. The two wave, take a bow. Chorale continues (13).
The menagerie also erupts into a concert in the third scene of the
second act when matters have reached a crisis point in the play:

> *Now a sound, a medley of sounds, intrudes from the lawn. At
> first it scarcely impinges, but taking its own time, it gathers
> force and cohesion. The animals – all the animals – and the
> fowl – all the fowl – peacocks and crows in the van, are giving
> voice. There's a concert en train. The mélange is not
> discordant. On the contrary, it has a haunting valedictory
> note at its heart. [...] The magic chorale – it has a magic – lifts
> to another level of the elegiac valedictory'* (57).

From a purely political point of view the aural commotion of the
animals points to societal upheaval and the rebellious voice. The play
replicates the setting and sentiments of Adrienne Rich's well-known
poem, *The Uncle Speaks in the Drawing Room* (1951) in which an
aristocratic man observes and fears an angry mob from the safe
position of affluence and privilege. Rich's poem obliquely refers to the
advent and reverberations of change on the stronghold of a class-ridden
patriarchal society. *Only an Apple* intertextually parallels these
sentiments of impending change. The Taoiseach has been feeding the
outside menagerie as if feeding his own unconscious mind, physically
willing the women to appear through his own desire and in the process
subverting order in the household. The animals' appetite for the raw
flesh represents the magnitude of this unconscious desire. Thus the
outdoor menagerie not only contributes to the absurdity of the action,
but is crucial to the political and symbolic order of the play.

The appearance of the animals in the concluding finale/chorale of
Act I beckons the Jungian archetype and the entrance of the trickster.
According to Jung the

> trickster motif does not crop up only in its mythical form but
> appears just as naively and authentically in the unsuspecting
> modern man – whenever, in fact, he feels himself at the mercy
> of annoying accidents which thwart his will and his actions
> with apparently malicious intent. He then speaks of *hoodoos*
> and *jinxes* or of the *mischievousness of the object*.[22]

The trickster is an archetype of tragic fun. He is as unpredictable as
he is foolish and as dangerous as he is comic. He is also, however, a
shape-changing shamanistic figure,

> a primitive 'cosmic' being of divine-animal nature, on the one
> hand superior to man because of his superhuman qualities, and
> on the other hand inferior to him because of his unreason and

unconsciousness.[23]

The trickster is the shadow of the self and the spirit guide. Bubbling beneath the surface of the first half of *Only an Apple* has been the Taoiseach's conflict between reason and instinct, between the secular and the sensual. As a representation of the trickster archetype, Arkins conducts himself as special adviser and guide to the Taoiseach in all matters relating to this conflict. In the Peacock production – through choice of accent and costume – Arkins (Marty Rea) is modeled on the persona of the Anglo-Irish literary figure, William Butler Yeats. Arkins has an affinity with the succubi and is on a mission to acquaint the Taoiseach with their world. As Arkins says in Act I: 'The sensualist within – *must* be released – however we manage it' (23). In turn the Taoiseach alludes to the mitigating role of culture when he warns the audience always to '[h]ave a poet on the premises' (23). Jung explains that when an individual confronts the shadow or interacts with the trickster calamity and disaster will ensue:

> The recognition and unavoidable integration of the shadow create[s] such a harrowing situation that nobody but a savior can undo the tangled web of fate.[24]

Arkins and the Taoiseach discuss this issue in the penultimate scene of *Only an Apple* as the two come head to head, Arkins shape-changing through his wearing of the mask of a bird (see Fig 3). The Taoiseach considers the integration of his shadow and Arkins advises:

> **Taoiseach.** Am I stuck with my fate?
> **Arkins.** Madness to contest it, it's said.
> **Taoiseach.** So it's possible Grace is right – I *may* have been howling for them for at least a decade?
> [...]
> **Taoiseach.** All right. Your advice?
> **Arkins.** Follow your instincts.
> **Taoiseach.** They'll be the death of me, Arkins.
> **Arkins.** No telling. The obligation is to explore (92-93).

As the play comes to an end the Taoiseach sets out on this exploration in a staggered interior monologue. Alone under a spotlight on stage he spills out thoughts which echo the words of George Bataille cited earlier in this paper:

> **Taoiseach.** Tell you something, and for free: I'm minded to gamble – just go for it – y'know, like closin' your eyes and walking over a cliff. Donegal. Or Clare. Aran Islands. Am I going mad? I feel in balance. I think [...] I want the trip. Am I

ready to pay the price? Will there be a price? Always a price. For coming. Going. Pray for me (98).

Laughter dwindles to nothing as this final piece of the action unfolds. We are no longer in the midst of the Taoiseach's sexual fantasy, we are in the midst of his wake; no longer laughing at his comic sexual buffoonery, but contemplating culture and change, fate and instinct, sex, and death.

---

[1] Walter Nash, *The Language of Humour: Style and technique in comic discourse* (London: Longman, 1985): 1.

[2] My analysis draws on the published text of *Only an Apple* (Dublin: New Island Press, 2009) and observation of performances during the run of play at the Peacock Theatre (April/May 2009). The cast included: Malcolm Adams, Fiona Bell, Cathy Belton, Steve Blount, Marty Rea, Michael McElhatton, Don Wycherley. Directed by Selina Cartmell, Set design by Dick Bird, costumes by Niamh Lunny, lighting by Matthew Richardson, casting by Holly Ní Chiardha.

[3] http://www.abbeytheatre.ie/whats_on/event/only_an_apple/

[4] Fionnan Sheahan, Brian Dowling and Gene McKenna, 'Moriarty Tribunal: Haughey Stole 45m' in *Irish Independent*, 20 December 2006. http://www.independent.ie/irish-news/moriarty-tribunal-haughey-stole-45m-26352058.html

[5] Tom Mac Intyre, *Through the Bridewell Gate: A Diary of the Dublin Arms Trial* (London: Faber, 1971): 158.

[6] George Bataille, *Eroticism Death and Sensuality*, (trans.) Mary Dalwood (San Francisco: City Lights Books, 1986): 1.

[7] Bataille, 239-40.

[8] Tom Mac Intyre in Ron Weiskind, '"Deer Crossing": Abstract, Stylised', *The Journal, Lorain Ohio,* 5 May 1978: 10.

[9] Tom Mac Intyre, *Only an Apple* (Dublin: New Island, 2009), p.32. All future references to the text of *Only an Apple* will be noted by page number(s) from this edition in parenthesis.

[10] Nina Witoszek and Patrick F. Sheeran, *Talking to the Dead: A Study of Irish Funerary Traditions* (Amsterdam-Atlanta: Rodopi, 1998): 150.

[11] Witoszek and Sheeran, 91.

[12] Madan Sarup, *Jacques Lacan* (London: Harvester Wheatsheaf, 1992): 128.

[13] A. Schopenhauer in John Morreall, 'Philosophy of Humour', *Stanford Encyclopedia of Philosophy*, http://plato.stanford.edu/entries/humor/

[14] For further discussion on the treatment of gender in this play see Bernadette Sweeney and Marie Kelly, 'Anarchic and Strange: *Only an Apple*', in Bernadette Sweeney and Marie Kelly (eds.) *The Theatre of*

Tom Mac Intyre: Strays from the ether (Dublin: Carysfort Press, 2010): 302-14.

[15] Patrick Lonergan, Theatre Review: 'Only an Apple', *Irish Theatre Magazine,* 6 May 2009.

[16] Sigmund Freud, *Jokes and their Relation to the Unconscious* in *The Complete Psychological Works of Sigmund Freud: Vol. VIII* (London: The Hogarth Press, 1905 (1960): 101.

[17] John Morreall, 'Philosophy of Humour', *Stanford Encyclopedia of Philosophy,* http://plato.stanford.edu/entries/humor/

[18] Witoszek and Sheeran, 146.

[19] Witoszek and Sheeran, 95.

[20] The wolfhound symbolises Irish identity. Peacocks signify eternity, spirituality, personal pride, the ego, and vanity. In folklore, two peacocks are said to have guarded the Gates of Paradise and to have carried Satan into the Garden of Eden. The horse is a creature of nobility, known for its power, strength, and grace. Crows, on the other hand, carry dark connotations as messengers of death or guides for the journey to the soul. Sabine Heinz, *Celtic Symbols* (New York: Sterling Publishing Company Inc, 2008).

[21] The psychopomp is a manifestation of the anima, a mediator between conscious and unconscious mind, an escort to the soul. In Jungian psychology the psychopomp often appears in dreams as the wise old man or woman, or a helpful animal, or sometimes the shaman. Marie-Luise von Franz, *The Interpretation of Fairytales* rev. edn (Boston: Shambhala Publications Inc, 1996): p. 119.

[22] Carl Jung, *The Archetypes and the Collective Unconscious*, (trans. R. F. C. Hall), Second Edition (London: Routledge & Kegan Paul, 1959): 262.

[23] Jung, 264.

[24] Jung, 271.

4 | 'Flann O'Brien's Dublin drift': The comedy of literary disorientation in Blue Raincoat Theatre Company's, *At Swim Two Birds*

Rhona Trench

When it comes to Blue Raincoat's stage adaptations of Flann O'Brien's novels by Jocelyn Clarke, lengthy narratives, intense debating, innovative stage designs and actors playing numerous characters are customary features. In *The Third Policeman*, first produced in 2009, a man and his bicycle appear high up on the back wall of the stage, surrounded at times by a constellation of lights. Caged doors open to a darkened hallway and an eerie soundscape of bicycle chains and wind denotes some of the peculiar instances of the play. In the 2010 production of *At-Swim-Two-Birds*, groupings of two, three, four and five actors using an array of moustaches, glasses and hats, accentuate the interplay between the range of characters and narratives that tell the story of the life of a student of literature. In *The Poor Mouth* (2012), the sound of torturous bad weather opens the play, foreshadowing the misery and misfortune inflicted upon the world presented, with thunder and persistent rain accompanied by cascading terror-scapes of clanging noises which frequently fall on the map of Ireland, the floor design of the play. Such blatant displays are crucial to Blue Raincoat Theatre Company's productions, which use a diverse array of strategic visual composition that directs the audience's attention to stage images. Amidst the disorienting world of the plays, the actor's body is revealed moving in unfamiliar ways, subverting the body's habit of walking, running and orienting itself. The performance then takes the audience on a romp through comic subversion and satire.

Blue Raincoat's *oeuvre* has helped the company achieve the label 'physical theatre company'; as a company they tend to showcase works which complement their interest in corporeal mime, influenced centrally by the work of Étienne Decroux. Decroux's actor training emphasised firstly the torso as the body's core focus for movement rather than its extremities such as the face, hands or feet. His training also demanded the actor's commitment to strict physical discipline and rigour, precise gesture, mime and mask work.

Blue Raincoat's past productions range from *Alice Through the Looking Glass* (2000), adapted by Clarke from Lewis Carroll, to Malcolm Hamilton's *Time Before Sleep* (1999) and *The Strange Voyage of Donald Crowhurst* (2003 and 2009), from Eugéne Ionesco's *The Bald Suprano* (2005) and *The Chairs* (2006), to W.B. Yeats's *The Cat and the Moon* (2009/2010) and *At the Hawk's Well* (2010), and on to the trilogy by O'Brien (one of Brian O'Nolan's pen names), all demanding physical agility and high energy.

This essay will examine the ways of 'seeing' in *At Swim Two Birds*, in terms of a certain range of recurring visual comic experiences represented by means of a distinct Blue Raincoat style. The company's attention to the *visual*, a matter of seeing as a physical act, gives *At Swim Two Birds* its idiosyncratic theatrical palette. The subjective sense of disorientation suggested by O'Brien's literary original is a pretext for Blue Raincoat's visual gags and their manner of physical representation. It is the sight gags as configured by Blue Raincoat's physical techniques that comprise the audience's fundamental experience of the stage picture, since that is what s/he is guided to attend to in the company's embodiment of O'Brien's modernist text.

Bodily actions cultivated by habit are brought into comical relief as spatial qualities like distance and orientation in terms of the body's capacities to act, its dispositions, its purposes and projects are heightened, disrupted and/or exaggerated. The unusual conditions of O'Brien's world in *At Swim* then place the body in modes of comic subversion and defamiliarisation, foregrounding for reflection the body's knowledge of how to walk, its ability to personify animals, express fairies and ghosts and generally (dis)orient itself.

This essay will consider the physical world of the stage, the actors' uses of the body, the role of gender, the costumes, props, lighting, alongside the iconography of the play's postmodern tropes – disconnecting action to its reaction, the endless fascination with play and parody, and the celebration of intertextuality. This examination will focus on Blue Raincoat's production of *At Swim Two Birds* in

November 2010, directed by Niall Henry and performed in the company's home space, The Factory, in Sligo. (The play was first performed by the company in November 2009 in Sligo and played in Galway, Dublin, Glasgow and Edinburgh over the next few years.)

The exploration of ways of seeing the performance is enhanced by the play's movement around Dublin city, a journey in the story which Blue Raincoat perform as multidimensional narratives, two stories organised from a range of elements that emerge from a shared spatial context. The result produces a hyperreal map of Dublin, which takes the audience on an expedition through the city, and the mundane, surreal and metaphysical narratives encountered en route.

The term 'drift' in the context of an urban setting will frame the essay, an expression borrowed from Guy Debord, whose practice of psychogeography came from a small but significant movement begun in the 1960s and which was interested in '[t]he study of the specific effects of the geographical environment (whether consciously organized or not) on the emotions and behaviour of individuals.'[1] The concept, 'dérive', literally means drift and was 'a mode of experimental behaviour linked to the condition of urban society: a technique of transient passage through varied ambiances.'[2] The ambiences can also be abrupt and fleeting, described as:

> the sudden change of ambience in a street within the space of a few meters; the evident division of a city into zones of distinct psychic atmospheres; the path of least resistance which is automatically followed in aimless strolls (and which has no relation to the physical contour of the ground); and the appealing or repelling character of certain places ...[3]

The drifting in the play, applied through theatrical embodiment, I believe, offers the actors frames of movement in the performance space, performing psychographical contours, represented by numerous shifting between different senses of spaces. Indeed, the winking plot has a charge of humour in its own right, which in performance results in a flash-by episodic comedy. Correlating with the postmodern sensibility, scenes in the play do not evolve, but seem to just happen in a series of unhinged sight gags. The narrative functions to showcase Blue Raincoat's comic routines, including a rich array of physical acts, a variety of well-timed vocal deliveries and the strategy of visual composition, all frustrating conventional sense-making, providing potential amusement for the audience. Like the narrative, the production style is not so much interested in showing how events develop, (paradoxically they do develop logically despite the illogical content) than in presenting the actor's drifting through physical environments together with the encounters they find there, which more often than not are locations for comic moments of disorientation.

Blue Raincoat's visual compositions, then, at the level of stylistic presentation, are predicated on making the fast and furious events of the play, the concern of bodily disorganisation, which dominates the comedy. Physical elements of the action in scenes are shown as primary features for the audience to attend, but not necessarily with the physical or narrative process as intrinsic to the situation. The aim appears to be to use compositions of scenes in such a way as to put the audience in a 'seeing-that' rather than a 'seeing-how' frame of mind. Blue Raincoat's visual style then incarnates a way of seeing that is preoccupied with the physical dimensions of the world and with the motion and interaction of material things, including human bodies, as they enter networks of causal relations. Since the ensemble's attention to physical detail happens in contexts that are comic in themselves, the performance on the whole speaks to comic functionality.

A degree of playful contrast between disparate elements commonly arises in the production, proposing unexpected connections between seemingly incompatible things. A range of such connections arise in the play via the drifting expeditions that take place through the city. Characters regularly get sidetracked by unexpected encounters, the mood rapidly shifts to different registers, and the narrative is framed by dissimilar genres, which do not reconcile with the ways in which the world works. The audience are thus compelled to take leaps of logic in making these connections between mismatched signifiers, which Blue Raincoat invokes largely through physical proficiency.

The stage adaptation retains many of the core components of the novel. In the novel, *At Swim* constructs a multiplicity of dramatic spaces centred on Dublin city in which characters from Celtic mythology, American westerns and crime novels interconnect with the streetscape and social geographies of the *petit-bourgeois* and working-class Dublin to create an ever-changing *breccia* of place. The leap from one space to another within the novel's intricate and connected array of stories offers a shifting plot direction. *At Swim* contains stories within stories within stories, based in and around the life of an unnamed narrator living with his uncle, and including among his creations a writer of Western fictions, named Dermot Trellis.

Keeping the novel's elements, the play's two main narratives tell the adventures of the unnamed narrator, a lazy student who fancies himself a writer, who writes about a writer, Dermot Trellis, who has decided that composing characters is not necessary when he can borrow characters used in other books. Trellis compels his characters to live with him at the fictional Red Swan Hotel, half a block from Grogan's bar. He tells the audience, 'there's a cowboy who's in room thirteen and Mr McCool, a hero of old Ireland on the floor above.'[4] The unnamed narrator continues, cynically:

> Trellis wants this salutary book to be read by all. Therefore he has put plenty of smut in it. There will be no less than seven indecent assaults on young girls and any amount of bad language. There will be whiskey and porter for further orders. (9)

Confounding the relationship between real life and literary logic, the inner worlds of the characters come to life when they realize that while fictional author Trellis sleeps, they are free from the control of his shocking plots and can lead the lives they want. During their freedom they plan revenge on Trellis, drug him and seek to eradicate him altogether.

Already alluded to in the brief description of the student narrator's story, the multi-narrative text gives opportunity to play with various levels of imagined reality. Clarke's adaptation, keeping O'Brien's tropes and drawing upon his remarkable twists set up for comedic value, seems quite fitting to the fictional author, Trellis, who comments: 'While the novel and the play were both pleasing intellectual exercises, the novel was inferior to the play inasmuch as it lacked the outward accidents of illusion. (7)' It is therefore also quite fitting that Blue Raincoat's production of *At Swim* envisages its staging as a self-aware and self-reflexive construction within the theatre itself. Thus, Jamie Varten's design offers a stage on the stage: the actors enter the playing space upstage through a proscenium arch draped in red velvet curtains. The design therefore is a double reminder to the audience that what they are about to see is an illusion, strengthening the opening lines of the play which announce: 'All the characters represented, including the first person singular, are entirely fictitious and bear no relation to any person living or dead (2)', poking fun at the validity of the entire performance before it begins. The disclaimer is a tongue-in-cheek reminder of the legal formalities that are often a feature of films and seems all the more humorous when said in an environment which clearly performs its story in front of a live audience. From the outset, then, the audience are given an introduction into the kind of comic world to expect, something that humour scholar Eric Weitz has observed when entering the world of comedy: The 'disjunction between the content of an utterance and the register of its conveyance forms a basic mechanism for comic writing as well as comic performing.'[5]

Indeed, the disjunction continues in the representation of gender in the production, with the three female cast members (Sandra O'Malley, Fiona McGeown and Kellie Hughes) playing male roles. Clarke's adaptation keeps close to the novel which contains only male characters (the novel has only fleeting glimpses of female characters). Keeping with the social habits at the time the book was written (1939), O'Malley's, McGeown's and Hughes's costumes and physical behaviours can be attributed to men. Wearing shabby suits and crumpled shirts, they walk with their pelvises forward and hands in pockets; they spit and drink pints, made all the more humorous by removing any efforts to disguise the female voice. The effect sends up the male bravado in the play which contrasts with their rough demeanour and emphasised in the body of the female.

The characters' movements from space to space around the suburbs of Dublin together with its suddenness, encounters, strolls and acts treats the urban drifting in the play as playful literary enactments. The commitment to the relationship between the urban environment and the psychic life of the play's characters foregrounds travelling on foot as a method of theatrical exploration and representation for Blue Raincoat, constructing the drifting as a series of comic journeys.

The buildings and atmosphere encountered by drifting are immensely significant in terms of the humour in *At Swim*. The detailed portrayals of buildings and environments together with their dimensions, properties, and cultural significance offer the audience a way of seeing the actors utilize space. The importance of geometry and symmetry is constantly referenced by Blue Raincoat through acting, lights or props highlighting the complex kaleidoscopic narrative designs. The actors' skill in precise movement goes hand in hand with the plot design, allowing the actor's body to form a unique relationship to the external world. The isolation and elucidation of a selection of scenes in the performance of *At Swim* highlights the skills and strategies in supporting a visual approach to the performance and is worth exploring in detail.

An early scene in the narrative hears a detailed description of the college the student narrator rarely attends and sets up the audience for the kind of comic world typical of *At Swim*. The focus on the external world is encountered by the student's drifting around the building and beyond the apparent academic environment:

> The College is outwardly a rectangular plain building with a
> fine porch where the midday sun pours down in the Summer
> from the Donnybrook direction, heating the steps for the
> comfort of the students. The hallway inside is composed of
> large black and white squares arranged in the orthodox
> chessboard pattern and the surrounding wall, done in an
> unpretentious cream wash, bears three rough smudges caused
> by the heels, buttocks and shoulders of the event. (8)

Of course the humour in this passage lies less in the academic
knowledge acquired from being in college and more in the students'
preferences for lounging around the steps outside the building or in the
sexual encounters that leave their marks in its hallways. Indeed such
detail sets the audience up for the kinds of encounters with the
environment the characters have as well as indicating the sorts of
characters they are. Here, during the description of the college,
O'Malley as the unnamed student narrator stands still and blank-faced,
looking out to the audience while the passage is narrated about him by
another narrator (Hughes) from the side of the stage, giving context to
his idleness.

The 'drunken scene' is one example of the ways in which humour
generally works throughout the performance. It takes the student
narrator and his drinking friend, Kelly (McGeown), around the south
part of Dublin city, 'through Stephen's Green on a Summer evening [...].
[Kelly] was a coarse man but he was lacking malice or ill-humour. He
suggested that we should drink a number of jars or pints of plain porter
in Grogan's public house (5)'. Hughes narrates this part of the narrative
standing upstage left of the playing space in a circus ringmaster's outfit
– black pants, white shirt and a red velvet coat trimmed with golden
lapels – while the student narrator and Kelly – dressed in black suits,
trousers and flat caps – act out the dialogue. The student narrator walks
confidently around the stage, his self-assurance accompanied by lively
1930s music. He is met by Kelly who comes through the closed red
curtains upstage, unaware of the student narrator when he first enters;
he then suddenly and exaggeratedly sees him. His first gesture enacts a
crude spitting action, assuring the audience as to his coarseness of
character; the action inspires a call for a pint done in mime to his friend
and they both saunter downstage towards the audience, as if to
Grogan's pub, each one wearing a frozen smile. A barman (John Carty),
dressed like a French waiter and sporting a toothbrush moustache,
holds a tray carrying two pints of porter and does a fast-paced walk
round the stage towards them. They each take their pint, salute good

health to the waiter, who exits the same way he enters, and as the student narrator tells us, both 'adjust the glasses [of porter] to the front of us and reflect on the solemnity of the occasion (5)'. The audience are told that this is the student narrator's first taste of porter. The student narrator lifts the glass to his mouth and slowly begins to drink. Comically, sombre music of a male choral choir comes on when the student narrator is a third of the way through his pint as he continues to drink it in one go. When finished, the music stops, he takes his emptied glass, holds it up and looks out asking, 'Who are my future cronies, where are the mad carousals? [...] (6).'

The humour of this routine uses quick-paced lines, sound over-determining the mood and maniacal movements sometimes bordering on slapstick. The routine elaborates on the narrative with a physical contrariety, embodying a comic principle advanced by Andrew Stott: '

> At the heart of slapstick is the conceit that the laws of physics are locally mutable, that the world can rebel against you, or that the person can be suddenly stripped of their ability to control their environment or anticipate how it will behave'.[6]

Yet the experiential nature of viewing the humour of *At Swim* belies an indebtedness to the concept of 'outlining'. Weitz extrapolates the concept from Maurice Merleau-Ponty's essays on painting to show how an object in performance might be transformed from perception to reception, referring to 'the artist's use of line to mark the outer contours of objects in space and the meeting of one texture with another, even though "there are no lines visible in themselves" for someone perceiving the same object(s) in the real world'.[7] Enhanced outlining, reminiscent of the movement in silent movies, is indeed a prominent feature of *At Swim*, accounting for the various visual strategies which orchestrate the perception or attention to its theatrical images– both at one time and/or in succession.

The following scene draws attention to the idea of outlining for comic effect, revealing the actor's costume, voice, action and body consciously organised through subversion and defamiliarization, throwing into relief, in particular, the body's knowledge of its conditions of orientation in actions such as walking, talking and swaying. The narrator says:

> I was down in Parnell Street with the Shader Ward, the two of us drinking pints. Well, whatever happened to me, I started to puke and I puked till the eyes nearly fell out of my head. I made a right hames of my suit. I puked and puked till I puked air.

> [...]. I thought my stomach was on the floor. How I got home at
> all I couldn't tell you. (6)

O'Malley as intoxicated student narrator enables the audience to see
and feel the state of his predicament – the swirling walls of the
environment and the difficulty of getting into bed in such an inebriated
state. The sound of undulating music accompanies the scene and
emphasises how out of his mind on alcohol he is, as he struggles to cope
with the regular tasks of walking home and getting to bed. Here the
casual order of the world no longer works. Like the dialogue which
describes the intense feeling of what it is like to feel sick and then
vomit, so too O'Malley embodies the physiological experience of the
drunken walk together with the impulses of and reactions to the
vomiting body. Struggling to keep hold of his coat which he carries
home (we presume he is unable to put it on), the student narrator
finally arrives at his bedroom where he wipes his drooling mouth with
his sleeve and wraps himself slowly and protectively under his
bedclothes (his coat now becomes his bedclothes). The clarity and
delicacy of O'Malley's skill in outlining enables the audience to get a
greater sense of the student narrator's drunken world in terms of
'holding' and 'seeing' the pint glass, 'feeling' his stomach pain, 'feeling'
the cold, 'seeing' his bedroom, experiencing the swirling ground and
walls and so on.

There are further devices the company employs to support the visual
schema of the production. The 'ambush scene' led by Shanahan, an
American cowboy, seeks revenge on Red Kiersay, the notorious cattle
raider, for stealing his livestock. The scene betrays comic intent by
overlaying well-known urban Dublin locations with the frame of a
nineteenth-century cattle war from the American West, mythologised in
fiction and film.

The drifting begins with Shanahan's recruitment of Red Indians,
who are camped in Phoenix Park. Later, the characters move from The
Red Swan Hotel in the city centre to Mountjoy Square to Drumcondra,
and later that night from The Red Swan Hotel to Ringsend to Irishtown.
The drifting moves to a full-drawn battle scene, complete with the genre
soundtrack of arrows, bullets and broken glass. The frenzied event
imposes geometric shapes upon the performance space, including
circles, diagonals and lines. Those configurations achieve a busy
activeness that gives the illusion the stage is more populated than it is.
The performers must then negotiate the ambush, moving through
'crowds' and 'obstacles' typical of nineteenth century street traffic.

The audience's attention is drawn between one thing and the next by a mix of dialogue, sound and movement. The movement and sound in particular add to the frenetic nature of the scene, affecting a comedy of disorientation. Contrastingly, the actors' facial expressions during the actual battle add to the humour, as though they are not fully aware of the mayhem going on around them. The use of the ensemble here provokes a multifaceted, open perception of the scene resulting in multiple points of interest before Kiersay is captured. And, of course, the actors' playfulness in the scene engenders in the audience the ways in which to see and experience the characters' revolt against their author.

Indeed Blue Raincoat's use of sound, lighting and movement contributes to the visual strategies employed to direct the audience's attention to its theatrical images. The use of multi-cut scenes, for example, remains a constant motif throughout the production, a device that embodies the theme developed by the dialogue. Multi-cuts can be described as a series of short scenes shifting quickly amongst upstage, downstage and/or offstage areas using spotlight, sound, and/or the stage-within-a-stage curtain opening and closing. Certain scenes and actions are emphasised over others using sound and/or lights, or by moving the action around the stage, or both. Some guidance is given to the audience by the dialogue, which may direct the path they are supposed to follow. The actors' roving movements promote the kind of drifting attention which the narrative expresses, remaining wide open to the host of ridiculous humorous moments which the dialogue and performance suggest.

Indeed, the instability of the stage world is highlighted in the courtroom scene, containing numerous multi-cut scenes, further demonstrating Blue Raincoat's comedy-friendly physical style. The scene sees layers of the story's narrative intertwine, revealing in particular a humorous take on the intersection between the non-natural and the everyday. The courtroom plot exploits the story within a story for comic effect, poking particular fun at the politics involved in writing a story, amusingly debating the responsibility the author has to his fictional characters, as well as raising issues of plagiarism. The scene presents fictional characters frustrated by their fictional author, who has abandoned them in his original storyline. They bring the fictional author to court where he must account for the many allegations heaped upon him.

This scene can easily be read as a satire on issues of 'authenticity' surrounding an author, his material and copyright laws. The concerns are reminiscent of Flann O'Brien's targets in his satirical column in *The Irish Times* under the pseudonym Myles na gCopaleen, which included the Dublin literary elite, Irish language revivalists, the Irish government, and the 'Plain People of Ireland'. A brief description of the courtroom plot is necessary, which will highlight how it facilitates humour, followed by a synopsis of its expression in performance.

The unnamed narrator's fictional writer, Trellis, has a son Orlick, after forcing himself upon one of his own fictional characters Sheila Lamont. Orlick creates a scene using Trellis's characters and persuades them (among them the Good Fairy, who does not appear to be that 'good', a Pookah – i.e., ghost – and a talking cow) to bring Trellis to trial for his mistreatment of them.

In one of the first cross examinations, another fictional author, Mr Tracy, alleges that Trellis created or borrowed characters from his writings that were either not needed or were mistreated by his pen. Taking off his hat, Mr Tracy (Ciaran McCauley) in a working-class Dublin accent accuses Trellis of stealing one of his characters and returning her pregnant, thereby forcing Tracy to change the path of his original story. Trellis and Tracy share a spotlight centre stage and as the accusations get more heated and the dialogue increases, they separate left and right. The spotlight now moves over and back from one to the other eventually 'getting confused' and losing pace. The scene is broken by the spotlight which moves quickly upstage right and off the central performance space when Trellis's character, Shorty, interrupts the scene asking, 'What is a potato peeler? (38)' The next witness is promptly called by the sound of crashing cymbals.

The actors assist or enhance comic effect by enacting the fictional characters with great sincerity. Other fictional characters become engaged in the exchange, interrupting with their concerns about the allegations, adding to the 'seriousness' of the situation. The aforementioned 'confused' spotlight indicates that the scene cannot be taken seriously, because of its inane and speedy dialogue, emphasising the extent to which the argument has lost its logic.

When the talking cow (John Carty) comes through the proscenium curtain in a fully lit stage, wearing what looks like an adult fancy-dress cow outfit, she moves assertively downstage lamenting how she was left unattended for long periods of time. Her sincerity about the pain she endured is entertainingly enhanced by the use of flailing legs (arms) and saggy udders; the cow's head nods and moves about in sincere defence. A character of Trellis's, Anthony Lamont asks, 'Can you not milk yourself?', to which she replies, 'No', explaining that she has no hands and even if she had arms they would not be long enough (53). Carty performs the cow's body comically, with human feelings and rational argument. The dialogue is sped up during moments of tension and the physical interaction between costume and human bodies combine to make the interplay of movements onstage comical through misshapen variations on 'real' behaviour.

Throughout the courtroom trial, the actors play two characters (O'Malley, three) indicated by the use of a hat on or off or in O'Malley's case also a red nose. Cross-gender and role play is a natural part of the production on the whole, adding to the potential humour. The trial is another example of how the production gives snippets of information to the audience conveyed through a string of scenes. The trial is ended abruptly by Anthony Lamont, who exclaims, 'I think the time has come for the black caps', followed shortly by Orlick who states, 'We will have one more witness for the sake of appearance and then we will get down to business (54)'. Four knocks on a door and the sound of a gong moves the courtroom scene back to the student narrator's uncle's house and on to the final scenes of the play. In foregrounding the visual experience of the play, Blue Raincoat recreates highly determinate compositional patterns which promote for the audience the perception and visual strategies as a series of theatrical pictures above anything else. The narrative is served via physical techniques that support one another for enhanced comic effect. The use of repetitive structures throughout the production afford the audience a better grasp of the ridiculousness of the situation as articulated through the speedy narrative amidst the embodied visual palette. The audience is thus prompted that pertinent events happen (student narrator with no name rarely goes to college/drinks too much/composes a second rate novel whose fictional characters revolt against him) and to see some kind of logic to an already convoluted text. The result is a production that facilitates a non-naturalistic perspective on the flux of the playful, the bizarre, the fantastic and the surreal – in short, an embodied comedy of literary disorientation.

[1] Guy Debord, 'Introduction to a Critique of Urban Geography', trans. by Ken Knabb in Harald Bauder and Salvatore Engel-Di Mauro (eds.), *Critical Geographies: A Collection of Readings* (Praxis (e) Press, 2008): 23.
[2] Guy Debord, 'Preliminary Problems in Constructing a Situation' in Knabb, Ken. (ed.) *Situationist International Anthology* (Berkeley, CA: Bureau of Secrets, 1995): 45.

3 Debord, 'Introduction to a Critique of Urban Geography', 23.

4 Jocelyn Clarke, unpublished script of *At Swim Two Birds*, property of Blue Raincoat, Sligo, 2009: 9. All subsequent citations from the script appear as page numbers in parenthesis following the quoted passage.

5 Eric Weitz, *The Cambridge Introduction to Comedy* (Cambridge, Cambridge University, 2009): 29.

6 Andrew Stott, *Comedy* (London and New York, Routledge, 2005): 23.

7 Weitz, 96.

5 | The Joyful Mysteries of Comedy

Bernard Farrell

Comedy is full of mystery. And that is why psychologists can spend years trying to discover why we laugh and how we laugh. Retired comedians can make money teaching would-be comedians how to tell jokes. (Trevor Griffiths had fun with that in his biting play, *The Comedians*). Theatre managers sit scratching their heads as they stare at empty seats when another sure-fire comedy mysteriously fails. And dramaturgs persist in trying to crack the code and teach aspiring playwrights how to write these sure-fire comedies. All fruitless exercises because, I would suggest, comedy defies theory, experience or education. Instead, it relies on Instinct, Attitude and Inspiration. And can anything be more mysterious (or mercurial) than these three, strange bedfellows?

Many years ago, when I decided to write a play, I wrote a comedy. I don't know why. To me, there was no option. I had a story to tell, a story that, at times, angered or intrigued or puzzled me and the only way I could tell that story was to lace it with laughter. And so I have continued in my career, dealing with my frustrations in play after play, sometimes lacing them with lashings of laughter, sometimes with less. But never with none.

In 1978, at the rehearsals of my play, *I Do Not Like Thee Doctor Fell*, I overheard one of the actors saying to another, 'You know, I think there could be a few laughs in this'. This was the first play that I had ever written and, by good fortune, it had been accepted by the Abbey Theatre and was due to open in three weeks. When I heard that comment, far from being encouraged, I was immediately plunged into a silent whirlpool of panic. This was not only because the actors in question were actors of some experience and reputation – the cast included Liam Neeson, Tom Hickey, Garrett Keogh, Billie Morton – but also because, while the play was indeed very serious, it was also intended as a comedy, and would be nothing if it didn't have a lot more than 'a few laughs'. Clearly, from the unperformed script that they still held in their hands, there was little to indicate much laughter.

If I knew then what I know now (twenty plays later), perhaps I would not have been so worried. I would, at the very least, have recognised the process. The play, as written, does not have any obviously funny lines. There are certainly no jokes. And the issues that hold and harness the drama – betrayal, bullying, suicide, attempted murder – are more the stuff of tragedy than comedy. And presented with this subject matter, the play's first director, Paul Brennan, gave the play what I would in later years recognize as his precise, analytical exploration of each character, each sub-plot, each action. Thus the play was rehearsed in an atmosphere of forensic examination, truthful seriousness, with little hint of comedy.

The actor's comments, therefore, clearly reflected the mood of that rehearsal room, and it was not until the first preview in the Abbey's Peacock Theatre that the play was allowed to reveal its true self. Then, in presenting the characters' anguish, terror and dilemma with absolute seriousness, the story mysteriously emerged in all its hilarious glory.

So Paul Brennan's astute method of telling the story through laughter – and not *for* laughter – allowed this, my first play, to make its mark, attract its audience, please the critics and keep the Abbey box office ticking over nicely. And the lesson for me was: The darker the play (and *Doctor Fell* is dark) the more light it will require. But the secret is that this light (the comedy) should be subtle, allowed almost to emerge unannounced, never to dominate – in short, it should be (that word again) 'mysterious'. And if the playwright has done his/her work in the writing, the laughter will enhance – but never unbalance – the drama, and nothing will be lost.

If, in 1979, the reaction of the audience took some of the actors by surprise, it was nothing to the surprises that awaited me, following that opening. Many of my friends, who never imagined that I could write a play, were astounded by my theatrical emergence and often, out of desperation, asked which parts did I write and which parts were written by the actors. One friend – desperately trying to solve the mystery of me – earnestly asked which came first, 'the gags or the story'. Indeed, some of my neighbours – many of whom never bothered to see the play anyway – took a curiously dim view of what I regarded as Comedy.

The most memorable example of this was my chance meeting with a rather supercilious lady whom, for simplicity and out of respect, I will call Mrs Haughty. She had lived nearby for almost all of my life but, with her perennial air of superiority and entitlement, had always managed to ignore me. But on one particular day, shortly after the play opened, on a road in Glenageary, she not only engaged me in conversation, but even called me by my name! Our exchange went something like this:

> **Mrs Haughty**. Bernard, I understand that you have written a play?
> **BF**. Yes I have, Mrs Haughty.
> **MH**. And I understand that it is in the Abbey Theatre?
> **BF**. It is indeed.
> **MH**. And I believe that it is a comedy?
> **BF**. Yes it is.
> **MH**. And I understand that, in this comedy, there is a boy who throws a cat under a train?
> **BF**. Ehhh – yes, that is true, Mrs. Haughty.
> **MH**. And you think that is funny, do you?

With that, she disgustedly turned and walked away, never giving me a chance to reply. But if she had, what would I have said? Perhaps, if I had waited a few weeks, the reviewers would have told me that what I had written was a Black Comedy. That might have helped in explaining its comedy to Mrs Haughty. However, a few weeks later, when the play transferred to the Abbey main stage, it was then referred to as 'a Biting Satire', and, in varying productions in the months and years that followed, I have seen it become 'an Absurd Drama', 'a rollicking send-up' and 'a side-splitting night'!

So I could never have really explained the comedy to Mrs Haughty or to anyone. To me, it was not a style or a title or a brand of comedy – it was simply a play that I had to write. At times, it became absurd, at times terrifying and sometimes frivolous – but, put together in the right, instinctive order, all these elements performed their function of telling the story in its most powerful way and, mysteriously, it worked!

Then, in the hiatus that followed the celebration of *Doctor Fell*, a fresh set of questions began to emerge, many of them harbouring thinly disguised challenges and others the dimly recognised traces of treachery.

The most common question was the harmless, 'And what's next in the pipeline?' But, occasionally, came the warning, the shot-across-the-bow: 'It's not going to be another comedy is it?' Probably the most threatening was one that was always asked in hushed tones, with a wink of the eye and the mischievous appearance of ill will parading as undying support: 'That *Doctor Fell* will be a hard act to follow, won't it?'

Each time I heard any of these questions, I was reminded of Brian Friel's masterpiece, *Faith Healer,* in which Francis Hardy, the faith healer of the title, performs a magical feat of healing and is at once commanded by admirers and naysayers alike, to do it again and do it better! The play itself is written in a masterly blend of tragedy and comedy but, at its core, it is – I would suggest – Friel writing about the creative process: its mystery, its triumphs, its falterings, its recoveries and, principally, its unpredictability. Whether this is true or not, I do know that with each demand and question to me, I had many a 'Francis Hardy moment', and, every time, I prayed that what happened to him would not happen to me!

I know now, in hindsight, that what was critically expected of me at that time was another black comedy. However, the Abbey, in commissioning a new play made no such stipulations. Joe Dowling, then the Abbey's Artistic Director, just wanted a new work, to be delivered in my own time, in no specific style and in no particular hurry.

The play I wrote was a satire on the way the Irish behaved abroad – an opportunity for me to voice, and an audience to share, a 1980s mirror image of ourselves, as we all availed of cheap travel and rushed to holiday abroad, away from the squinting windows of home, finding freedom in the company of strangers and free to pose as anything except what we really are. It was a play of pretence and pretentions, of snobberies and selfishness, it was a reviewer and a revealer of our hidden vices – and certainly not a black comedy.

The broad reaction to this play was interesting – and made me realize that, as in the theatre of the Greeks and the Romans, comedy will always be seen as the poor cousin of tragedy. Moreover, even within the genre of comedy, there is a hierarchy of 'types', against which each is critically judged, identified and then neatly slotted into its box. Black comedy – possibly because of its proximity to tension and tragedy – is probably the most respected. Satire and parody remain high and the *commedia dell'arte* style has enjoyed a revival (possibly because experts like to both explain it and pronounce it). After that, the status and appreciation levels drop sharply. Eventually if a work is even suspected of being farce or 'boulevard' or burlesque it moves into the danger zone of critical dismissal.

Canaries – for such was the name of my second Abbey play, so named because it is set in the Canary Islands – was indeed a satire, with serious undercurrents and, to contrast the light and shade, I occasionally applied dollops of farce. Once again, for me, this form (or selection of forms) was dictated by nothing more than the demands of how best to tell the story.

The play opened at The Abbey for the 1980 Dublin Theatre Festival and was a popular success. Critically, however, there were murmurings that, after *Doctor Fell* (and presumably having got black comedy out of my system), I should have moved onwards, and upwards, and closer to tragedy. Instead, in their view, I had dodged the challenge and gone for 'easy laughs'. And I thought – ah, if only that were possible.

Unfortunately, in theatre as in life, there are no easy laughs. Ask any poor devil who ever had to make a Best Man's speech or any of us who ever tried to chat up an out-of-our-league stranger at a party, and prayed for laughs. We would be contented to see a smile, or half-smile. Now, put that same challenge to a playwright who sets out to extract laughter from a crowd of strangers, sitting in the darkness, probably in from the cold night, perhaps having spent twenty minutes trying to find a parking space and now angrily aware that, with the price of tickets and the cost of a baby-sitter, this night has cost them a lot of money and therefore, it better be good! Easy laughs do not come easily.

Canaries, I would suggest, was not a success because it had layers of farce, but because it was a stinging satire that hit its targets accurately and, in doing so, earned its laughter through an audience's recognition of what was onstage and their sheer relief that they were not in the same humiliating predicaments. In the glow of the play's success, I never tried to make these points nor did I even try to defend the legitimacy of farce. Instead, when I was commissioned to write a new play for the Abbey, I did write a full-blown, indisputable, unrepentant farce!

This was almost inevitable as I have to admit to a real affection for farce – even if I always find it extremely difficult to write, and to get right. In later years, in plays that were regarded as my 'darker' and 'more serious' work, there is always more than a sprinkling of farce. My influences (those I blame!) are essentially the French masters – Molière (whose *Don Juan* I later adapted for the Abbey Theatre), Eugène Labiche, Georges Feydeau – and certainly Dion Boucicault (whose *Forbidden Fruit* I refashioned as *Petty Sessions* for the Abbey). In Britain, I point the finger at Ben Travers, Arthur Wing Pinero, Alan Ayckbourn and Joe Orton – but, at the root of my appreciation for the relentless, logical lunacy that is the essence of good farce, I look no further than Stan Laurel and Oliver Hardy.

From my childhood, I – like many others who work in comedy – have regarded Laurel and Hardy, at their best, as the masterminds of everything perfect in this genre. This was perhaps never better demonstrated than in the thirty minutes of their 1932 film, *The Music Box*, a simple story of them trying to deliver a crated piano up 131 concrete steps. Here we witness again their perpetual battle against an unsympathetic world, whether in human form (a nursemaid, a policeman, a postman, an outraged professor) or inanimate objects (prams, pens, steps, a piano) which seem, in turn, to assume the personalities of their vexing, human counterparts. Expertly woven into this comic extravagance is a verbal array of malapropisms, mispronunciations and witticisms, all underscoring their bewildered alienation in a society they do not understand and that will never understand them.

So it would not surprise me if there are elements of the comedy of Laurel and Hardy in my third play for the Abbey. However, *All In Favour Said No!* was not written as farce for the challenge, nor as an homage. Again, for me, it was the only style that suited a play about the ridiculousness of head-office hierarchies and the posturing of factory-floor unions when faced with the threat of a strike. Its success brought me great personal joy (as it got a lot out of my system) – and, I think, also granted me much comic confidence in having managed to write a full-blown farce where, throughout, when the comic buttons were pressed, the audience appropriately erupted.

Many of these comic buttons, of course, do not always come directly from the script but rather evolve from rehearsal-room decisions – where the director, the playwright or an actor may occasionally make an assured declaration that if a particular word is stressed or a certain action is taken, the audience will certainly explode into laughter. It is a risky business and, at that early point in my career, I seldom attempted it, choosing rather to make quiet, tentative suggestions to the director during coffee breaks. However, in the rehearsal for this play, I remember hearing myself confidently informing the entire room that, for better comic effect, a line should be directed to a different actor, in a different direction, at a lower tone. I then added that this would result in prolonged laughter before another line could be spoken. This was received in silence and then questioned by seasoned actors, but I remained adamant. At the first preview, before our first audience, (the acid test of comedy), I waited in trepidation for the moment and, thankfully, when it came I was proven to be right. It was a small victory, probably long forgotten by everybody involved but, for me, it remains a turning-point: the moment when, instinctively, I knew I was right and had the confidence to proclaim it.

Subsequent plays moved me through varied and different moods of comedy, from uproariously comic work to dark plays that provoke the kind of laughter an audience will guiltily question themselves about on the way home. Moving from Dublin premieres of the plays at the Abbey and the Gate Theatres, to Red Kettle Theatre in Waterford, to the Laguna Playhouse in California, brought different demands, new freedoms, changing styles and constant challenges... but always presenting new opportunities to explore varying aspects of comedy and, occasionally, to encounter comedy in many, unsuspected cultural flavours.

In various translations of the plays, I have sat in foreign auditoriums, not knowing a word of the language but hearing the laughter and the silences come at the right moments and knowing that this new audience was solidly in tune with the play. This, in itself, is wonderful evidence that, internationally, we have a broad, comic alignment – that what is funny and ironic in one country, one culture, can find an exact replica of that reaction in another. However, there can be exceptions to this – and these are often comical in their own right.

I remember seeing the German premiere of *Doctor Fell*, which opens with a caretaker sweeping a room while idly singing a song. This sweeping continues until the second character arrives onstage and the play begins in earnest. In Ireland, audiences always delighted in the humour of how the caretaker, without supervision, haphazardly swept the room, pushing dust under rugs and hiding debris behind radiators. In Germany, however, the play began with the caretaker diligently sweeping the room, inch by inch, carefully collecting all debris and putting it into small sacks. This continued for perhaps two minutes, then four minutes and, at six minutes, he was still sweeping. My fear, as I watched, was that very soon the audience would begin to leave, one by one, not having paid to see a man giving them a masterclass on how to sweep a room.

However, the audience stayed and the sweeping (eventually!) ended and the next character appeared and the dialogue began. At drinks after the play, the director asked me if I had any notes, comments, reactions. I said – truthfully – that it was an excellent production – but wondered at the length of time the caretaker took to sweep the room. The director was puzzled. 'But,' he said, 'this caretaker is a sympathetic character and, for the play and for the comedy, we must ensure that the audience likes him, so we show that he works hard, is a trusted employee and does his tasks perfectly.'

I, of course, agreed. But this was clearly a cultural difference, in which comedy clashed with comedy. In Ireland, we admired the caretaker for cutting corners; in Germany, for that, he would never have been 'a sympathetic' character. He would have been a dosser ... and immediately disliked ... and the comedy would have suffered. Hence, the sweeping marathon!

Years later, I told this story to Alan Ayckbourn – and he responded by reducing me to tears of laughter with even funnier cross-cultural experiences from his own career. The occasion of our meeting was my visit to Scarborough where my play, *Happy Birthday Dear Alice,* was about to open at his Stephen Joseph Theatre. Over some days, I had the privilege of spending many hours and many meals in the company of this man who, for years, I have idolised as a Master of Comedy.

We talked about his wonderful play, *A Small Family Business,* which I had seen at the National – and, to the best of my knowledge has never been produced in Ireland. By Ayckbourn's own admission it is a play about organised crime, greed, sexual deviation, murder and drug-taking – and yet it is hilarious. Its gory murder scene had, on the night I saw it (and I presume every night), the audience in shrieks of the uncontrolled laughter of surprise, fear and relief.

Ayckbourn explained the process delightfully – quoting our need to laugh in the face of hopelessness and then, in the writing, how it falls to the playwright to gently coax the audience to see the correct aspects from the correct angles and to firmly establish the comic context in both action and reaction. When I was not immersed in his theatrical experiences, his hospitality and his self-deprecation, we (as playwrights do) bemoaned the lack of appreciation for the art of comedy.

I used regularly to have these same conversations with Hugh Leonard (or 'Jack', as he liked selectively to be known) and, almost as a game, we used to exchange examples of how comedy as an art form is so poorly regarded. I would cite how Molière was never admitted to the Académie Française in his lifetime and Jack would trump that with how Laurel and Hardy, in over twenty-four years of great comedy, only got a Lifetime Achievement Academy Award when Hardy was already dead and Laurel was too ill to accept it. Ayckbourn tells the story of how a critic (in a clearly positive review of one of his plays) wrote that he had laughed shamelessly throughout. 'Why "shamelessly"?' Alan wryly wondered. And Hugh Leonard was forever amused at how producers, directors and actors all try desperately to forget that Chekhov was essentially a self-confessed comic writer and insisted that his major, revered works were comedies. 'But nobody believes him', Jack would say, with that knowing twinkle in his eye, 'because they realize that there are no awards going for turning tragedy into comedy – it is the opposite that will have them applauded to the awards podium – even if their tragedy was a comedy in the first place!'

I have often regretted that, in the time since Jack died, he missed seeing at least two productions that would have pleased him greatly. He would certainly have revelled in the 2012 Sydney Theatre Company production of *Uncle Vanya* (with Cate Blanchett as Yelena) which, amid the tragedy of the play, didn't ignore or dilute or diminish the comedy. In his review of the Broadway production in 2012, Ben Brantley of the *New York Times* wrote of the play's climax: '... that scene is as rowdy and demented as anything out of a Marx Brothers movie and as utterly despairing as a choral lament from Sophocles'. Jack would have felt vindicated!

I have also wished that he had lived to see The National Theatre's version of Goldini's often neglected, *A Servant of Two Masters*, in a sparkling new production and retitled, *One Man, Two Guvnors*. This had wowed London audiences for months before transferring to Broadway where I saw it with, once again, James Corden in the lead. This was farce at its most brilliant, most assured, most accomplished, in a production that was fast-paced and ruthlessly pared down to its comic essentials – to the hysterical delight of New York audiences.

Jack would have loved that – and indeed, I know that he would have seen in it the essential comic truth of how hard work makes the art of comedy look easy. And even now, I can almost hear him repeating one of his favourite anecdotes, popularly attributed to the dying words of Edmund Kean. Visited by an acquaintance, the great actor was asked if his illness was very difficult to endure. 'Dying is easy', he is reported to have said, 'it is comedy that is difficult'.

That difficulty, however, is often relieved by sheer Good Luck – the good fortune of being able to assemble a perfect cast, production team and director who recognise, understand and appreciate comedy. I have been fortunate in the premieres of my plays in being coupled with directors such as Patrick Mason, Ben Barnes, Paul Brennan, Pat Laffan, Mark Lambert, Jim Culleton and Andy Barnicle who have nursed these first outings into existence with a firm appreciation of the seriousness of comedy and an understanding of its power and, in each case, taken the work to areas far beyond what I would have envisaged.

The payoff, of course, is the exhilaration of hearing an audience respond, on cue, to created comic action, in waves of (controlled!) laughter. The downside is the heart-breaking sense of confusion and mystery when the comedy doesn't work – when the sense of failure screams out in the silence of the audience. In tragedy, the silence of a bored audience can be excused as 'rapt attention'. In a comedy, there is nowhere to hide – and all escape routes are closed. The best we can do, in that nightmare silence, is to accept the mystery – and pray for less mystery and more hope in the next one.

For this, we rely again on our comic instincts – and those who will write comedy are born to do that. How do they know they possess these mysterious instincts? They don't until (and unless) they test them. Are there any signs that a comic instinct for storytelling lies within us? I expect that it is different in each of us.

For me, I remember my father having a wonderful sense of humour – not in the telling-of-jokes sense, but in his ability to observe both the peculiar and the mundane ordinariness of life and to reframe it in a comic way that managed to engage us, his children, as much in our childhood years as through our adolescence and into our adulthood. Thus, he was flexible in his humour, he could adjust –and he knew his audience.

If that was the source for me, I am very grateful. But how did this manifest itself in me – in the days before I started writing publicly?

Well, perhaps a hint of my attitude to the world and my need to reframe it in a comic way was perhaps shown in a cartoon that I saw many years ago, that I cut from the paper, pasted to cardboard and hung above my writing desk, maybe as a reminder or maybe as an encouragement. It is by Bill Tidy and was first published in *Punch* magazine in May 1968. As mysterious as comedy itself, it became my talisman, my influence, the manifestation of how (unbeknownst to many and maybe to me) I see the world.

The cartoon shows the headquarters of what I presumed to be The White Star Line just after news of the sinking of the Titanic had been announced. We see the crowds, now moving away, broken-hearted, lovingly comforting each other. The high-ranking official who imparted the news is still on the steps of the building and about to go inside. But his attention is drawn to a man who is approaching him, out of the departing crowd. This man is holding a rope which secures a polar bear, standing high on its hind legs. And the man – on behalf of the polar bear – is anxiously asking the official: 'Yes, but is there any news of the iceberg?'

Now, why have I always thought that cartoon was so funny? I don't really know – but, without analysing the humour out of existence, is it perhaps because it tells us to see the alternative point of view, to comically flip the situation over, to dig deeper... and not to be afraid to be a little bit subversive. And maybe, for me, that is the root of comedy. Or maybe it's not. Maybe it is better not to ask – and just to accept it as a joyful mystery... and get on with it.

6 | The Dublin Dame: From Biddy Mulligan to Mrs Brown

Ian R. Walsh

From Jimmy O'Dea's beloved Biddy Mulligan to Brendan O'Carroll's increasingly popular Mrs Brown, we can chart one of the most enduring comic creations associated with Dublin city in the caricature of the proud working-class woman played by a male comedian. For the purposes of this essay I have called this figure the Dublin Dame. It is hoped such a title stresses the importance of the Irish city (Dublin) and of the British pantomime and music-hall tradition (Dame) in this creation. It is my intention to investigate why the Dublin Dame has such humorous appeal for Irish and British audiences and how this figure performs the city of Dublin, in the sense of both showing and creating the city.[1]

Jen Harvie, in her recent book, *Theatre and the City*, suggests, 'theatre is a part of urban process, producing urban experience and thereby producing the city itself'.[2] She elaborates, 'how the theatre does this is implicit and everyday: city people work in, make and go to the theatre; it is their urban experience'.[3] However, while theatregoing may be part of an urban experience, it is the rural representation of Ireland that has been perceived to be dominant on Dublin stages. Indeed, Declan Kiberd argues cogently in his essay, 'The City in Irish Culture', that in Irish literature Dublin is continually represented in rural terms. He even suggests Sean O' Casey's most famous Dublin plays present the city's tenement dwellers as a community of intimate villagers. Reasoning for such recourse to the rural is given by Thomas Kilroy who comments that, 'within metropolitan centres there is always nostalgia for cultures which are untouched, untainted by ennui, the busyness, the crowdedness of the centre'.[4] However, in Ireland the repeated recourse to the rural and indeed the pastoral is overdetermined, as it is bound up with the homogenizing tendencies of nationalist artistic endeavour. Here, the pastoral offered a fixed, unifying image of Ireland that allowed for a representation that could be grounded in authenticity. This was most important in a postcolonial nation, for as David Lloyd suggests, 'it is the inauthenticity of the colonized culture, its falling short of the concept of the human that legitimates the colonial project'.[5] Therefore, in terms of identity the rural pastoral allowed for an authentic consensual Irish identity that presents Irishness in terms of stability and legitimacy.

Lionel Pilkington has suggested how Ireland and its people have been characterized paradoxically as being 'essentially performative: possessing a core of being that is inherently theatrical'.[6] It was such characterisations of the Irish that the revivalist project wished to distance itself from, presenting Ireland as not the home of 'buffoonery and easy sentiment' but one of 'ancient ideals'[7] – an essentially romantic rural country of peasants with a long tradition and a noble history.

What this perception of a recurring rural ideal on city stages does not consider is the popular theatre in Ireland, which would have accommodated much larger audiences of city dwellers contributing to Harvie's concept of the theatre and urban process. Upon examination of the popular theatre in Ireland, the recurring figure of the Dublin Dame emerges as giving representation to an Irish urban experience. The Dublin Dame as a figure and the various sketches written around this character escape the reduction of urban process to rural fixity as Kiberd identified recurring in Irish literature and drama. It does this through its 'essential performative'[8] nature, for the comic appeal of the pantomime Dame is its ambivalence. The Dame never makes any pretension to identify himself as a woman. Lawrence Senelick proposes: 'Gender illusion played no part in this line of business; the Dame was always a clown in petticoats, and if her false hips or breasts fell down, she would pull them up and get a laugh'.[9] The Dame's distinctive quality is its play with duality.

The origins of the Dame can be traced to folk and carnival performances shared by both Britain and Ireland, of men dressing as 'unruly women' types during religious festivals.[10] In terms of the more formal theatrical tradition, men have been garnering laughter dressing up as women from the medieval pageant plays onward through the Elizabethan era and the Restoration, and then later in the Harlequinade which evolved into the modern British pantomime form. The roots of the modern incarnation of the Dame figure are found in the British pantomime tradition and the Victorian Music Hall. It is in the figure of Dan Leno that these two things come together. Leno was an immensely popular star of the Victorian music halls, who performed many different recognisable comic types, such as the shopkeeper, the lodger and the landlady. In the music halls he appeared alone onstage speaking and singing directly to the audience.

Leno was quickly adopted by the pantomime, where he was especially suited to the traditional Dame role, in which he had license to speak directly to the audience and perform comic set pieces that had no role in the plot. Leno's great innovation as a Dame figure was his emphasis on pathos. For Max Beerbohm, he was 'so put upon' but yet 'so plucky' and was 'incarnate of the will to live in a world not at all worth living in – surely all hearts went out to Dan Leno with warm corners in them reserved to him forever and ever'.[11] Leno's Dame was presented as a working-class elderly woman who appeared in 'a plain skirt, an apron or shawl, sturdy boots and her hair parted severely in the middle, drawn ruthlessly back behind the ears and decorated perhaps with a top-knot or stray ringlet'.[12]

Leno's creations laid the template for many female impersonators to come, including Dubliner Jimmy O'Dea, who was to be declared 'The Irish Dan Leno' by the *Daily Mail*. In partnership with Harry O'Donovan, who wrote most of his material, O'Dea created Biddy Mulligan, the first Dublin Dame. The origins of the character are found in a song written by W.S. North for a Gaiety theatre pantomime, *Taladoin or the Scamp With The Lamp*, which opened on December 26, 1889. The song was at that time entitled, 'Queen of the Coombe', and was sung by Richard Purdon, playing the Widow Twankey. The song tells of a widow from Dublin's Coombe who makes her living by selling fruit, sweets, clothes and fish from her stall on the street. It was later adapted by Seamus Kavanagh and became, 'Biddy Mulligan, the Pride of the Coombe', and was a popular ballad even before O'Dea famously recorded it and embodied its titular character. O'Dea biographer Philip Ryan writes of Biddy Mulligan in terms redolent of Leno's sympathetic 'put upon' but 'plucky' Dames:

The character he portrayed was the typical Dublin shawlie, witty and sharp-tongued though she could assume an air of gentility with a quasi-refined accent until, goaded by her errant husband, Mick, her mood and accent suddenly changed and she poured on him a torrent of unrestrained invective. She had a genuine dignity in the face of adversity and was ever optimistic.[13]

This quote from Ryan also draws attention to the fact that the character of Biddy Mulligan was drawn from observation of the real Dublin street dealers.

Dublin has been characterised by its streets and the galaxy of eccentric characters that have made it their stage. Indeed Dublin's quintessential street figure is that of Molly Malone, immortalised in the eponymous ballad where she hawks her cockles and muscles along the streets 'broad and narrow' (interestingly Biddy Mulligan first appeared in 1930 in a show entitled, 'Alive, Alive O!'). Following the famine and a mass exodus of rural families to Dublin, the number of street dealers grew significantly. These dealers were comprised of predominantly destitute widows with children to feed. Their daughters then grew up to become dealers themselves, and a tradition of female street traders was established and accepted as a part of Dublin city life.

Oddly, these marginalized figures have since become representative of an urban authenticity: they are often categorised as the 'real' Dubliners. But as representative figures they are curiously marked both by their difference and similarity to the dominant national Mother Ireland figure. They are maternal, and thus associated with nurture, fertility and sacrifice, but unlike the iconographic figure these women are active participants in the public sphere of commerce and dwell in the public place of the street. Their home is not the cosy domestic cottage, but their stall on the street. Indeed, in interviews collected by Kevin C. Kearns in his oral history of Dublin street life and lore we learn that families were reared on the street with children trading alongside mothers and babies sleeping in fruit boxes alongside the stalls. In these interviews the street sellers also reveal the performativity of their lives on the street. One oral testimony speaks of the women as all 'being characters who sold here'[14] and another reveals that, 'if there wasn't much selling they'd dress up for a bit of a laugh. Dress up like they were somebody else'.[15] Several of the accounts mention the women singing and dancing, and one oral testimony speaks of the street dealers in terms particularly redolent of the Dame figure in their mannishness and their benevolence: 'And I'll tell you, the women long ago were fine, big women. Hefty, big women maybe fifteen or sixteen stone. And the women were tough ... And they had big hearts. Oh their hearts were as big as their muscles'.[16]

Biddy Mulligan cut a grotesque mother figure onstage – mannish, uncouth and anarchic – but also sympathetic. In this the Dame figure may have allowed Irish people the comic relief of being able to mock the overdetermined figure of Irish mother without feeling they had betrayed such a figure. Roger Baker suggests this dual positioning of the audience offers a safe transgression, and is one of the great appeals of the Dame figure:

> ... this is one of the secret powers of the Dame, she is the vicious agent of lethal dreams. Appalling and humiliating things happen to her which her audience (perhaps shamefully) would like to see happen to a real woman – but it's alright, really because we know that they are only happening to a man. That teasing duality ... provides a distancing effect ... the Dame is kinder – to us, to herself and to her targets. Once more we are reminded that while the drag queen inevitably focuses on women, all the forces that created that particular woman are also under attack.[17]

Interestingly, O'Dea's performance of the Dublin street dealer did not emphasize or rely on the caricature of the woman as harridan for its humour, and according to Ryan this was something O'Dea consciously resisted. Biddy Mulligan never revealed her bloomers or displayed an avaricious sexual appetite as O'Dea's contemporary proponents of the Dame tradition such as Arthur Askey, Douglas Byng and Frankie Howerd did on the British variety stages. In fact, this convention is played with in the 'Biddy Mulligan in Court' (1939) sketch. Mulligan is describing to the court how she met her husband and as she does so the barrister proves overly eager to know more and more details of her courtship revealing his prurient interest in the tale. Mulligan, recognising this, stops the telling to exclaim with exaggerated prudishness: 'Ah, you dirty old man!'

As is evident in this sketch, the comedy of Mulligan's masquerade relies on exposing the civilized modernizing mask of the rising middle classes, uncovering their ridiculous self-importance, haughtiness, cruelty, and base desires. Mulligan aims to pull up official Ireland's alluring gown to reveal the dirty underwear beneath. The audience is always positioned as sympathetic to the Dame. Typically the Dame figure is larger than those who challenge her, but Mulligan was always smaller, due to O'Dea's height. Biddy Mulligan was often paired with the comedian Noel Purcell, playing various figures in authority that Mulligan was challenging (such as judges, tram drivers and bookmakers). Purcell was over six feet tall and would thus cut a giant mock-Goliath figure to a dwarfed but heroic David-like O'Dea. Harry O'Donovan, in writing the sketches, also seemed to make the woman dealer from the Coombe particularly sympathetic.

In all the sketches, Mulligan enters a space, disrupts, and then is either forced to leave or fails in her planned endeavours. This is evident in the early Mulligan sketch, 'Sixpence each way' (1930), which remained ever popular. Mulligan here enters a bookmaker's office and wishes to place sixpence each way on a horse called 'Water Sprite', but doubts her choice after the bookmaker is dismissive in his attitude toward her. She then spends the rest of the sketch continually changing the horse's name on her betting slips, as various characters enter and place bets on different horses. Eventually, the result comes in and the winner is 'Water Sprite'; Mulligan misses out because she changed her bet.

In 'Mrs Mulligan on the Tram' (1939), the widow gets on a city tram with her odious-smelling fish and the passengers and the tram driver spend their time trying to get her off the tram, which they eventually succeed in doing. In both these sketches the audience are invited to side with Mulligan. Both the Bookmaker and the tram driver are rude, impatient and dismissive. One sketch, entitled 'Buying a turkey'[18], goes so far in its courted sympathy as to be redolent of Charlie Chaplin's mixture of pathos and comedy, in which laughter gives way to tears. In this sketch, due to penury, Mrs Mulligan is forced to buy a small, miserable-looking turkey for her Christmas dinner, but due to a mix up by a messenger boy she is presented with a large succulent turkey. The stage directions read:

> *Mulligan is about to call him back. He is off. Music plays softly. She moves towards the turkey. Puts out a hand gingerly and takes it. Turns slowly and walks a couple of slow steps ... suddenly makes a dash and runs off. (Blackout)* [19]

The Biddy Mulligan sketches perform Dublin in the sense of showing the city – giving it representation. All the sketches take place in locations associated with city life – trams, courthouses, bookmakers offices, and specific areas and landmarks are referenced throughout the sketches. Ryan reports:

> The Mrs. Mulligan records, as a collection, vie with Joyce's *Ulysses* for the frequency of their reference to Dublin streets from the Liberties to Grafton Street; to characters ranging from well-known bookies to Alfie Byrne and now defunct institutions such as the Royal Iris and Williams and Woods.[20]

In this regard the sketches, following Michel de Certeau's language,[21] help to transform specific places into social spaces, that is, into environments marked by the actions, movements and daily practices of inhabitants. The popularity of the Mulligan character throughout the 1930s and up to the 1960s meant that an urban experience was given representation in a period historically renowned for its fidelity to a rural ideal promoted by the state and cultural institutions. This era is often described as De Valera's Ireland and is marked by his famous 1942 St. Patrick's Day speech, in which he gave a specifically rural vision of Ireland with 'cosy homesteads' and 'comely maidens dancing at the crossroads'. But the period is also characterised by a conservative and consensual society dominated by the Catholic Church. The Mulligan sketches never challenge the authority of the church, and despite the anarchy created by the character, it would be wrong to think that such performances were in some way radically threatening to social orders and cultural hegemonies.

Mulligan's humour functioned similarly to that of Arthur Lucan's Mother Reilly (another Irish Dame figure) in British films of the 1940s and 1950s. Jeffrey Richards writes:

> ... the humour is not based on making her [Mother Reilly] seem out of place, uncomfortable or intimidated, it is with her all the way in deflating pomposity, subverting the rules of middle-class decorum and triumphing in her anarchy. But she does so within a framework which makes it clear that society as presently structured is basically sound.[22]

Here, then, the mockery of hierarchy through type does not destabilize, but re-affirms such structures and clichés. However, I would argue that the comic appeal of the Dame does not lie in either superiority or revolt but rather in its mode of address through its self-reflexive framing. It is also in this concentration on the process of performance that the Dame figure replicates the urban process of the city. Ryan suggests:

> To Jimmy, Biddy Mulligan was a real character, in the theatrical sense, and rather than give the usual superficial performance of a Dame comedian he played her as a real woman, drawing on the reserves of the femininity in his own nature. And he drew a fine line between a recognisable comic creation and the overblown reality of the real thing. Jimmy was aware of the trap of being too perfect and never lost touch with his personality.[23]

This rather confusing quote with its casual mixing of terms such as 'real' and 'theatrical' points to the complexity of the Dublin Dame figure, but more importantly foregrounds the issue of O'Dea's personality. In his recent book on the history of British variety, Oliver

Double points out that an understanding of 'personailty' is a key to unlocking the appeal of variety acts. Double suggests for variety artists the success of an act was not solely dependent on the quality of their material or skill, but in the development and presentation of an onstage personality that generated a familiarity and 'warmth' between audience and performer. He writes of such warmth: 'It implies likeability and an ability to make the audience feel affection. ... What was achieved was a very personal relationship between performer and audience – an imagined friendship in which the audience felt they knew the performer personally'.[24]

O'Dea had such a warm personality on stage, and much of the success of Biddy Mulligan depended on the distance created between the performer and the role. Biddy Mulligan was always the roguish, popular Jimmy O'Dea playing an elderly woman street dealer. Indeed, in pictures of O'Dea as Mulligan it is clear that little effort was made to disguise O'Dea's recognisable male and comically malleable face. Another distinctive quality of Mulligan was that she spoke not like the dealers she was modelled on but like O'Dea himself. There is no pretence of a female voice and Mulligan's Dublin accent is one very much inflected with O'Dea's own unusually distinctive accent. The poet and theatre critic, John Jordan wrote:

> Off-stage his accent was certainly Dublin, but just as certainly it had been vamped as are vamped the accents of all actors. On-stage even when he aimed at the broadest kind of Dublin accent, he retained to superb effect, some of the actor's voice intonations. The result was a heady blend of the hilarious and the immutably dignified. I think it was partly due to his retention of at least an echo of polite actor's speech that not one of Jimmy's personations ever became truly ridiculous. The fortunes of the Widow Mulligan were generally in decline. But miraculously the throwing of an extra bit of vocal refinement convinced us that these near disasters were mere briars in the path of an indestructible *grande Dame*.[25]

It is thus the performativity of O'Dea's voice, its deviant and ludic quality that made sound recordings of the Mulligan sketches such a success. It meant that the duality of the visual stage figure of the Dame was translated for an audience of listeners.

As suggested by Jordan in his comments regarding O'Dea's vocal performance, the notion of a genuine intimacy with the variety performer is itself another illusion. Double comments: 'This idea of personality is nothing if not ambiguous. The variety artiste appears as him – or herself, but it is a projection of self, and as such larger than life'.[26] But this distancing of the performer from the role reminds the audience of the artifice of the performance and of their importance in the creation of the theatrical event. They are intimates of the performer and they are co-conspirators in the theatrical world created. This type of performance mirrors the urban experience as a process that its citizens help to create. The contestation, ambivalence, and process associated with the city are performed by the Dame figure in its distancing and 'teasing duality'[27]. Thus the Dublin Dame performs the city in the sense of creating the affect of the city.

I wish to conclude by examining a contemporary example of the Dublin Dame in Brendan O'Carroll's creation, Mrs Brown, and in such an investigation offer a reason why this figure has had such lasting comic appeal. O'Carroll's Mrs Brown was first popularised through a radio sketch, then the character was the subject of three books that proved to be bestsellers. One of these books, *The Mammy*, was adapted into a film by Angelica Huston entitled *Agnes Browne*; sell-out stage shows then followed with O'Carroll playing the Dame role of Mrs Brown. Most recently O'Carroll has made his character the subject of a television sit-com, co-produced by RTE and BBC, *Mrs Brown's Boys*, for which he both stars in the role and writes the material. This television show won the BAFTA for best new comedy in 2012 and it is this sit-com which I will address briefly at this point.

O'Carroll's Dublin Dame shares many of the same characteristics as Biddy Mulligan – she is a widow and she is a street dealer by profession. This Dublin Dame no longer lives in the tenements of Dublin's inner city, but now resides in the predominantly working-class suburb of Finglas, where many of the tenement dwellers were relocated to council housing after the 1960s. But what has changed significantly in O'Carroll's contemporary Dublin Dame is the return of the British conception of the Dame as an uncouth, foul-mouthed harridan, who gets laughs in showing her knickers. This humour can be read as inviting derisive laughter at the perceived incongruity of post-menopausal women delighting in anything and everything that can be construed to be sexual. This would perhaps explain the appeal for a younger generation, who are rarely given any representations of older women as sexual beings, with youth consistently idealized on television. It could also be read that the older Irish and British audience, who grew up in a more sexually repressed era can identify with Mrs Brown, who struggles with adapting to a contemporary, sexually liberated world.

Here, they grant O'Carroll comic license to utter and act out many of their own fantasies and thus achieve some comic relief. However, such readings do not sufficiently take account of the self-reflexive aspects of the show and O'Carroll's use of distancing in the performance of Mrs Brown. These features are characteristic of the established conventions of the British pantomime form. Millie Taylor explains:

> In pantomime the Dame and comics, and to a lesser extent the immortals [conventional panto characters], are positioned between the world of the audience and the world of the story, interacting with both, forming a link between the two, and constantly altering the distance thus created between audience and performance. This position allows these characters to exist both within and without the story, to comment on the story, and reflexively to draw attention to the theatricality of the pantomime event.[28]

The space created by the duality of the performance world of pantomime wherein the performers (and the audience through them) can both dwell in the world of the story but also step out of it to comment on it, is entitled 'pantoland' by Taylor. Sketches involving the Dublin Dame character create and inhabit such a 'pantoland'. As already mentioned, this is evident in the Biddy Mulligan sketches, through O'Dea's personality and costuming, but it is also applicable to Mrs Brown. O'Carroll repeatedly uses distancing techniques in *Mrs. Brown's Boys* to create a type of 'pantoland' performance for the studio audience as well as for the viewers at home.

In each episode of *Mrs. Brown's Boys*, O'Carroll as Brown makes direct address to the audience and the camera through an opening prologue and closing epilogue. Throughout his performance, he nods to the audience (and camera) to acknowledge their presence, raises eyebrows and often comments to them on the story as it unfurls.

In the first episode of the television series O'Carroll walks through the set to get a prop left in another TV stage set and, as he does, so the camera follows him, showing other cameramen, sound operators, etc. Here, the constructed nature of the piece is deliberately revealed. At another point in the same episode Mrs. Brown elicits a large 'ah' of sympathy from the audience after a short speech about the trials of being a mother. O'Carroll reacts to this response by turning to the audience and shouting at them, incredulously, 'it's a man in a fucking dress!' Again, in this instance the audience is shockingly reminded of the artifice of the show. The use of such devices could be said to produce a postmodern, knowing, self-reflexive commentary on tired conventions of television sit-coms of the past, whilst performing within such conventions. But such techniques do not originate from experimentations based on contemporary philosophical theories, they are long established comic conventions rooted in British pantomime.

Taylor views such self-reflexivity as being essential to the enjoyment of pantomime events in which 'performer and audience are joined in a complicitous act of laughter towards the production'. For her the use of such distancing effects 'sets up the two myths of pantomime: that the performance is rubbish and anyone could do it; and that the performers are having great fun, enjoying themselves in a free-flowing, anarchic way'.[29] Such myths are actively promoted in *Mrs Brown's Boys* in the already mentioned effects, but also most obviously in the continual laughing of the cast while delivering their lines. Unlike Mrs Brown, the rest of the cast are not given the power to directly address or acknowledge the audience (camera). However, they are often seen laughing while delivering lines. This corpsing is not edited out or presented as a blooper reel after the credits, but is made part of the show. In this laughter the cast deliberately shows their complicity with the audience: In their laughing at O'Carroll's performance as Mrs Brown they are showing the audience that they are having great fun and invite the audience to enjoy themselves just as much as they are doing onstage.

In Biddy Mulligan and Mrs Brown a 'pantoland' is created in performance, a shared space between audience and performer through which they can enjoy shifting positions of being committed to the success of the story and entertained by the failures of its presentation. Such a communal ludic space offers temporary pleasing connections and distances between the performers and the spectators. The Dublin Dame figure in its duality not only mirrors the urban process in terms of ambivalence and contestation but its appeal would also seem to be that of the city where one can be at once connected and removed.

Mrs Brown's Boys has proven an enormous popular success for both British and Irish television networks, attracting viewers in their millions. The Dublin Dame is proven to be possessed of an enduring appeal. Indeed, it is the character's own ability to endure in the face of adversity that has led to such appeal. Susanne Langer writes:

> It is true that the comical figures are often buffoons, simpletons, clowns: but such characters are almost always sympathetic, and although they are knocked around and abused, they are indestructible, and eternally self-confident and good-humoured.[30]

The Dublin Dame presents such an indestructible comic figure and it is its celebration of survival against the odds which would seem to have spoken to a people in the uncertainty of a newly independent, modernizing Ireland and that now speaks to a contemporary British and Irish audience living in the precariousness of present global economic uncertainty.

---

1 This follows Richard Schechner's concept of performance as consisting of being (or doing), showing and showing doing. See Richard Schechner, *Performance Studies: An Introduction* (London: Routledge, 2002): 22.

2 Jen Harvie, *Theatre & the City*, (Basingstoke: Palgrave MacMillan, 2009): 7.

3 Harvie, 7.

4 Thomas Kilroy, 'A Generation of Playwrights', *Irish University Review 22-1-2, (Spring-Summer 1992): 141.*

5 Lloyd is quoted in Colin Graham, *Deconstructing Ireland: Identity, Theory, Culture*, (Edinburgh: Edinburgh University Press, 2001):132.

6 Lionel Pilkington, *Theatre & Ireland,* (Basingstoke:Palgrave Macmillan, 2010): 2.

7 These terms are from the often quoted section of a letter composed by Lady Augusta Gregory to potential financial backers of the Irish Literary Theatre. The full quote reads: 'We will show that Ireland is not the home of buffoonery and easy sentiment, as it has been represented, but the home of an ancient idealism'. Augusta Gregory, *Our Irish Theatre: A Chapter of Autobiography by Lady Gregory*, (Gerrards Cross: Colin Smythe, 1972): 20.

8 Lionel Pilkington, *Theatre & Ireland,* (Basingstoke:Palgrave Macmillan, 2010): 2.

9 Laurence Senelick, *The Changing Room: Sex Drag and Theatre* (New York; Routledge, 2000): 242

10 See, Natalie Zemon Davis, "Women on Top: Symbolic sexual inversion and political disorder in early modern Europe", in Barbara Babcock, *The Reversible World: Symbolic Inversion in Art and Society* (Ithaca; London: Cornell University Press, 1978):147-190.

11 Quoted in Alison Shaw and Shirley Ardener (eds.) *Changing Sex and Bending Gender* (Oxford: Berghahn, 2005): 125.

12 Roger Baker, *Drag: A History of Female Impersonation in the Performing Arts* (London: Cassell, 1994): 177.

13 Philip Ryan, *Jimmy O'Dea: The Pride of the Coombe,* (Dublin: Poolbeg, 1990): 74.

14 Kevin Kearns, *Dublin Street Life and Lore: An Oral History*, (Dublin: Glendale, 1991): 105.

15 Kearns, 115.

[16] Kearns, 117.

[17] Baker, 162.

[18] I have been unable to find out when this was first performed but the full sketch was published in Harry O'Donovan, *O'Dea Laughs: A Selection of Sketches* (Dublin: P.J. Bourke, 1944)

[19] Quoted in Ryan, 75.

[20] Ryan, 69.

[21] Michel de Certeau, *The Practice of Everyday Life*, trans. Steven Rendall (Berkeley: University of California Press, 1984): 117.

[22] JeffreyRichards, *The Age of the Dream Palace: Cinema and Society in 1930s Britain*, (London: I.B. Tauris, 2010) :298

[23] Ryan, 74.

[24] Oliver Double, *Britain Had Talent: A History of Variety*, (Basingstoke: Palgrave Macmillan, 2012): 118.

[25] Quoted in Ryan, 80-81.

[26] Double, 122.

[27] Baker, 162.

[28] Millie Taylor, 'Distance and Reflexivity: Creating the Stage World of Pantoland', *New Theatre Quarterly*, 21 - 4, (2005): 333.

[29] Taylor, 337.

[30] Susanne K. Langer, *Feeling and Form* (New York: Charles Scribner's Sons, 1953): 342.

7 | 'Still getting above our stations': Slagging as national pastime and the cultural body in the comedy of Samuel Beckett and Marina Carr

Sarah Jane Scaife

> ...To say that humour is universal is, of course, to say almost nothing or very little.'[1]

SIMON CRITCHLEY *FROM THE INSIDE*

As a practitioner and sometime lecturer I have had the experience of teaching American drama students who have come to Ireland to learn about Irish theatre and culture. One of the very first things I introduce them to, in my role as acting teacher, is the culturally embedded, Irish tradition of 'slagging'. I explain to the visiting actors that in Ireland, rather than praise the child unreservedly, telling them how brilliant they are, the Irish style of guiding the child into the cultural norms that they will find themselves encountering and negotiating throughout their lives, is to develop the ability to 'slag' and be 'slagged' without getting unduly upset either way. Slagging thereby serves as a national pastime. But even more so, it is an ingrained response to the sociocultural environment, within which we find ourselves as Irish. To 'slag' someone is to ridicule them, to point out something they are doing that reflects that they are possibly 'getting above their station'. The expression, 'who does he/she think he/she is!', forms the underlying question covered by the particular slag in operation and is rooted I assume in our postcolonial past. An important aspect of slagging is to explain to the person being slagged, if it is to their face as opposed to behind their back, that you were 'only slagging' them, thereby relieving you as 'slagger' of any responsibility for offence to the 'slagee'.

Although this introduction has been more than slightly tongue in cheek, I will try to impart a flavour of how slagging is reflected within our drama and daily life. There is a black humour embedded within the *re*presentation of Ireland as text. No doubt it comes from a societal self-consciousness or insecurity, embodied by a country that hasn't quite come to terms with the disparity between its reflection on the world stage and its secret insider knowledge that this international mirror does not reflect their reality. Philosopher and humour scholar Simon Critchley argues:

> Humour is a form of cultural insider-knowledge, and might, indeed, be said to function like a linguistic defence mechanism. Its ostensive untranslatability endows native speakers with a palpable sense of their cultural distinctiveness or even superiority.[2]

In terms of slagging as a form of humour, I believe it certainly acts like a 'linguistic defence mechanism' reflecting a lack of self-esteem on a national level, more than a sense of superiority. Nevertheless, it also provides a rich seam of humour for the majority of the country on a daily basis, as there is always someone or something to slag. It is important for the aforementioned American students to accept this national pastime before they begin to read the plays they are about to learn about, as it provides the key to much of the meaning within our drama, and to the disjunction between the words they read and the performativity of those words embodied through character. In other words, I am trying to set a level playing field of performative interpretation for the students, otherwise plays which are of an hilarious darkness or scathing humour for 'us', become tragic dramas imbued with pathos and sentimentality in performance, for 'them'.

I mention this national pastime in order to introduce the plays of Marina Carr in particular, which are saturated with cruel, cutting slagging, and often have me and other Irish audience members crying with laughter, though sometimes conscious of embarrassment and shame at what it is we are laughing at. In her play, *The Mai* (1994), two older women, Julie and Agnes, are discussing – or slagging – their niece, Beck:

> **Julie.** I wish to God she'd take that peroxide out of her hair.
> **Agnes.** She's a holy show in those tight black pants.
> **Julie.** I hope she's not pregnant.
> **Agnes.** Glory be, I never thought of that.
> **Julie.** (*proud she's thought of it*) Oh you have to think of everything.

Agnes. She'd never have it.
Julie. God forbid! A divorcee with a child, born after the
divorce.
Agnes. She'd never go for an (whisper) abortion, would she?
Julie. We'll find out if she's pregnant first and, if she is, with
the luck of God she'll miscarry.
Agnes. Poor little Beck, she was always so nervous.[3]

Carr takes as her starting point a recognizable scene of two women
discussing a younger woman, their niece. The full hypocritical paradox
of Irish, religious and cultural norms are displayed within this short
extract, in which slagging turns into something on the cusp of humour
and horror. The idea that it would be better for all that a miscarriage
take place rather than have to do something socially abhorrent, such as
abort the child, is bad enough, but that this provides us with an
opportunity for laughter seems even worse to me. Critchley writes:

> There has to be a sort of tacit consensus or implicit shared
> understanding as to what constitutes joking 'for us', as to which
> linguistic or visual routines are recognised as joking. That is in
> order for the incongruity of the joke to be seen as such, there
> has to be a congruence between joke structure and social
> structure – no social congruity, no comic incongruity.[4]

It is impossible to ignore what is being exposed within this and
many Irish plays, which centre around abuse of power and hypocrisy
within the body politic of Ireland, represented as a rather large but
dysfunctional family. The destructive nature of the family as a unit
within an unhealthy alliance of church and state provides for a darkly
comic reveal when embodied on stage. In one of Carr's earliest plays, an
absurdist comedy, entitled *Low in The Dark* (1989) Binder is
introducing Bender to an unseen stranger, in the explanation of her
name:

> **Binder.** Wait till he hears it.
> **Bender.** My name? Well now, when you translate it...
> **Binder.** (*pushing Bender aside*) Her name is Bender and
> when you translate it, it still means Bender!
> **Bender.** Stop it!
> **Binder.** Because she is a bender! All her life she's done
> nothing but bend! She bends over, she bends back, she bends
> up, down, under and beside. She is Bender! ...[5]

Bender represents the 'typical' Irish mother of my childhood as she
was portrayed in Irish drama, without, perhaps, the eulogising of her
role that would have been there had she been imagined by a male writer

– the long-suffering but noble mother as represented purely by her function within Ireland as 'family'. Carr takes this representation and pushes it into black comedy as she does with religious hypocrisy and social pettiness and greed. As Irish we share this understanding of the mother and the religious and social hypocrisy in a collective, somatic and psychic way; we wouldn't be inclined to laugh so hysterically otherwise. Eric Weitz puts it so well when he writes: 'At its most spectacular, laughter simulates a sort of bodied earthquake, which lays momentary waste to our encrusted psychic patterns'.[6]

Weitz goes on to argue: 'Every comic moment in the theatre draws upon a deep, dense root system of experience, which the spectator brings to the theatre event.'[7] The more ingrained a behaviour is in relation to its social congruity, the more hilarious and immediate its comic release can be in its *in*congruity; comedy is born from this everyday recognition.

An embodied version of this effect occurred to me a few years ago, as I sat with my husband and children in the local church for the confirmation mass of my youngest child. At this stage the reams of reports into child abuse resulting from the collusion of Church and State had already been exposed through the Ryan Report. Every day the revelations were becoming more appalling and the cover-ups and unwillingness to accept culpability by many concerned was harder and harder to listen to. I had, at this stage lost all belief in what up until then had been presented by the clergy as the possibly misguided but ultimately benevolent aspect of the Church, and could only consider the whole institution as ridiculous. As we prepared to put money in the second collection basket I caught a glimpse of the mother of one of my daughter's classmates. She had been caught out without money for the second collection, as she obviously, like me, didn't attend anymore. This had happened to me at many previous masses so I knew what she was going through. The look of fear on her face as she saw the basket approaching was just comical. That visual allied to the thoughts going through my head as I listened to what the priest was saying, and the incongruity of my private experience in this most public of events, caused me to laugh. My daughter's look of horror when she realized what was happening, coupled with the years of ingrained behaviour of churchgoing, made me laugh even more; I attempted to cover it by kneeling down and placing my head in my hands on the pew in front of me, but didn't succeed. I was experiencing 'a sort of bodied earthquake'. My daughter started hitting me as my shoulders began to shake, and tears poured down my cheeks at the absurdity of it all. I had an image of myself just lying down on the ground of the church and crying loudly with laughter at the hypocrisy of it all (but I didn't). I wanted everyone to acknowledge the enormity of what was taking place in the church, almost as if it was a play; I felt the whole congregation should have been howling with laughter. My daughter never forgave me for embarrassing her.

This personal experience returns me to *Low in the Dark;* in it Carr highlights the relationship between mothers, their sons and the Catholic Church. The play opens with Bender and Binder (mother and daughter) in the bathroom. Bender is in the bath, drinking and smoking; Binder is standing on the toilet looking out the window for possible suitors. Bender has given birth to a virtually impossible number of babies; there are babies everywhere, colour coded, but she is looking for the baby she calls the Pope:

> **Bender**. I want the Pope! Get me the Pope!
> **Binder**. (*Flings the Pope at her*) He's not Pope yet!
> **Bender**. Woe betide you when he is! Neglecting him like that! (*She gives reverential and preferential treatment to the Pope.*)
> **Binder**. You fed him already! (*Exits.*)
> **Bender**. I'll feed him again. I want him fat and shiny. Holy Father, (*bows to the baby*) you'll pull your auld mother up by the hair of her chinny chin chin, won't you? We'll have tea in the palace and I'll learn Italian and the pair of us side by side, launching crusades, banning divorce, denying evolution, destroying the pill, canonizing witches. Oh a great time we'll have, you singing the Latin with a tower of a hat on you, the big stick in your rubied fist and them all craw-thumping around the hem of your frock and whispering for miracles. And me sitting there proud as punch in the middle of the incense and the choir. Oh, a great time we'll have, the pair of us, we will surely.[8]

This scene is hilarious to me as an Irish woman born in the late 1950s. I can imagine that Irish mother of my youth, who literally brought her son up to be a priest, with all of the disturbing psychic questions of why she would want that for him. I once served food at the ordination ceremony for a priest; it was to all intents just like a wedding, his mother holding pride of place at the head of the table. It could have provided the inspiration for the wedding scene in Act II of Carr's *By The Bog of Cats...*, in which the bridegroom's mother, Mrs Kilbride, enters the scene to greet her son Carthage on his wedding morning, wearing:

> ...what looks extremely like a wedding dress, white, a white hat,

with a bit of a veil trailing off it, white shoes, tights, bag, etc. ...
They pose like a bride and groom, Carthage glaring at Mrs.
Kilbride.[9]

In Ireland, it seems we laugh at the Irish mother, religion,
drunkenness and 'rude' things, almost like children, with whom I
sometimes think we are on a societal level. Bisi Adigun in his essay, 'An
Irish Joke, a Nigerian Laughter', speaks of this childish humour, which
my sister calls the 'pooh, fart, bum' humour of young Irish boys. Adigun
writes:

> Take farting as a typical example. On many occasions, I have
> had the misfortune to be around people who find farting openly
> really funny. And for some strange reason, this 'joke' never fails
> to generate laughter among Irish lads. ... The act of
> drunkenness is another example that readily comes to mind.[10]

When I returned to Ireland from five years in America in the late
1980s I could not understand how it seemed as if all you had to do to
make an Irish audience laugh was to: slag a priest, portray someone
drunk, say something 'rude' or laugh at an old Irish woman. I now
wonder if it was a nervous laughter, a shared realization that we don't
have to be afraid of the forces that controlled our country and lives
anymore; that we have 'grown up'. It represented a mocking of taboos.
Critchley, in a section marked, 'Having the courage of our
parochialism', sums up his argument with the following: 'So, humour is
what returns us to our locale, to a specific ethos which is often
identified with a particular people possessing a shared set of customs
and characteristics'.[11] Even more interesting is what follows: 'If humour
returns us to our locale, then my point is that it can do this in an
extremely uncomfortable way, precisely as thrown into something I did
not and would not choose'.[12]

FROM THE OUTSIDE: BECKETT

Our homegrown love of humour through slagging was driven home
when in 2006 I spent much of my working year abroad. What I
appreciate about working outside Ireland, particularly in Asia, is that I
am constantly reminded of the cultural specificity of how I think, how I
interpret the phenomena around me that I normally take for granted. In
2006, I was invited to the Central Academy of Drama, Beijing, China, to
conduct a residency on the drama of Samuel Beckett with the acting and
directing students there. I had previously worked on Beckett's shorter
plays in countries both in Asia and Europe, and was fascinated by how

the different world views affected not only how the plays were read from the page, but also how they were translated into another language. Whole sections of plays were totally changed as to meaning being released through performance, due to misreading of how Beckett plays with the image onstage, language and writing in relation to form and meaning. Pronouns were added in *Catastrophe* (Mongolia*)*; movement sections without words were taken out in *What Where* (China); pauses and stage directions were amended or ignored in *Waiting for Godot* (Mongolia), all in attempts to 'correct' mistakes perceived as a result of translation. This was very interesting for me, as there was an acceptance that whatever was written or read was interpreted as 'meaning something', just because it was under the literary banner of Beckett. Mistakes were given a level of intellectual coherence that was not at all intended as part of the original work. Most importantly, humour was at risk all the time – in China the lexical text was interpreted literally and not in juxtaposition to the image onstage.

For instance, in the play, *Catastrophe*, there is a very dark humour present, which arises from a sense of moral absurdity when a director attempts to create the perfect visual image of 'Catastrophe' for his audience. The director controls his Assistant psychologically, who in turn controls and manipulates a live body onstage, forming his limbs into the perfect sculpture to embody 'Catastrophe'. Beckett is playing with the form itself within the use of language in a metatheatrical way, by lampooning himself indirectly through the role of 'Director', as he carries out the creation of his theatrical image onstage. Beckett is, of course, renowned for the prescriptive element contained within his stage directions; this can take up the same amount of space as the text. In this section the Director is instructing the assistant in minute detail to find the most abject of positions for his sculpture onstage; after a while she attempts a suggestion of her own:

> A. [*timidly*] What about a little ... a little ... gag?
> D. For God's sake! This craze for explicitation! Every i dotted to death! Little gag! For God's sake!
> A. Sure he won't utter?
> D. Not a squeak. [*He consults his chronometer.*] Just in time. I'll go and see how it looks from the house.[13]

One would have to assume an element of caricature involved in this instance, but it is of such a subtle nature that it would be very difficult to trace without a detailed study of Beckett the artist and his scrupulous attention to detail. Later on when the image is almost complete she asks:

A. [*timidly*] What if he were to ... were to ... raise his head ... an
instant ... show his face ... just an instant.
D. For God's sake! What next? Raise his head? Where do you
think we are? In Patagonia? Raise his head? For God's sake!
[*Pause*] Good. There's our catastrophe. In the bag. Once more
and I'm off.[14]

Once again an Irish/American audience usually will laugh at this
section. I am never sure if it is because of an implied reference to civil
rights, or to the original image of the Patagonian people by the
explorers from Europe, such as Darwin's Beagle expedition, as giants.
Both of these sections use black comedy as a way of looking at the
action on the stage; they enable the piece to avoid tipping into pathos,
and instead to straddle the line between tragedy and comedy in a
similar way to Carr. For instance, our assumptions are constantly being
upended in terms of the use of religious language; it is nearly always
used in juxtaposition to what is being said by the characters. When
someone uses the name of God, it is nearly always to underscore the
lack of religious empathy being demonstrated by that character, which
in turn provides a commentary on the social relationship to religion.

When we rehearsed *Catastrophe* in Mandarin, there was no hint of
irony or comedy in the presentation of the Director, only the
presentation of absolute autocratic power. At one stage the Director
actually stubbed out his cigar on the hand of the Protagonist,
representing 'Catastrophe' (the actors had bandaged the Protagonist's
hand prior to this, so it would not hurt him). He threw wads of money
at the Protagonist as a complete sign of disdain; the Assistant flung
herself to the floor crawling on her belly to the Director as a sign of
submission. From our reading of the translation into Mandarin there
was no sense of irony, however, through actually embodying it in
rehearsal over time we found a point of understanding between us.
Later, when we discussed the process, the students explained to me that
after 1945, unlike in Europe where I had explained that the general
feeling among artists was one of despair following the atrocities of the
war, the Chinese were, ideologically speaking, in a very upbeat and
positive state of mind, looking forward as a collective to the
improvement of their lot. Cao Bo, an academic from the University of
Hunan and Chinese translator of Beckett, explained to me that for the
Chinese, 'humour and ideology are connected, especially dark
humour'.[15] He told me that '... in Chinese literature the emphasis is
more on the external journey of man in *relation to* society not the

internal journey that Beckett takes [italics mine]'. Cao argues that Chinese writers:

> mostly stick to the neo-classical principle of didacticism with a socialist touch; few are as experimental as western avant-garde writers. When humour is too dark, they won't take it as humour. To them, humour almost equals light amusement. The reason why Chinese readers as a whole can't appreciate western dark humour lies probably in our cultural unconscious.[16]

It wasn't until later that I came to any real understanding of the above; in fact I had not identified 'humour' as a culturally specific problem at that time. Much of the humour within a Beckett piece is of a darkly comic nature, (I would say akin to slagging) and is based on undermining or ridiculing the very structures of epistemology and meaning through the institutions of western science and religion.

FROM THE OUTSIDE: CARR

During my time at Central I found an operatic intensity about the work we did with Beckett, and that led me to look at Marina Carr's *By the Bog of Cats...* as a possible vehicle for a co-production. As the play is based on the classical texts of *Medea*, I believed it would have enough of a shared understanding of the structure underlying it. It is full of symbolism, colour and drama. White dresses, the black swan and the trailing blood in the opening scene of the white bog covered by snow, evoke a gothic fairytale. I am aware that classical Greek tragedy is not natural to the Chinese Four dramatic tradition, as the idea of the individual pitted against the gods does not sit easily in Chinese culture. However, as this was an academy of drama I was sure that the directing students would have a firm grasp of the form itself. At that time, I was contemplating how to negotiate the 'tragic' elements within the play, paying no real attention to the issues of humour or of how the tragic is communicated through a shared understanding of humour. Andrew Stott writes that Aristotle noted, 'we are the only creatures who feel compelled to laugh'[17]; we also have the distinction of needing some kind of ideology in our lives with which to create 'meaning' for ourselves. This ideology is often translated as religious belief; it can take the form of a shared vision for humanity as in socialism, communism, humanism – an 'ism' of some kind seems to be a prerequisite for human social or cultural life. Stott argues:

> Even though comedy often seems to be suspending, inverting,

or abandoning dominant norms, these inversions are produced
in relation to the cultural orthodoxies from which they must
always begin.[18]

I decided to translate two scenes from the play in order to explore
practically whether the play would read in its cultural resonance for a
Chinese audience. Chia Hsin Chou, a Taiwanese research student at
Trinity College at the time, agreed to translate two scenes for me before
she left Ireland. I tried out both scenes in Mandarin and in English with
students from the Beijing Foreign Studies University in another
residency, which culminated in a 2009 presentation of the scenes to
celebrate St. Patrick's Day in Beijing. It was interesting in retrospect,
that the scenes we picked were both serious ones. We picked the scene
between Hester and the ghost of her brother Joseph, in which Hester
berates Joseph for stealing her mother away from her. The scene
explores the abandonment of Hester by her mother and the resultant
ruination of her life caused by this abandonment. The Chinese girls
identified greatly with this notion of the daughter being cast aside for
the son and the pain and emptiness ensuing from this unrequited love.
The one-child policy in China seemed to highlight thematic issues of the
family and thus looked like the ideal text to work on together.

It was only when the official translator from China, Li Yuan, came to
Ireland to help her understand the cultural issues surrounding the
translation of the full play that the enormity of the differences in
cultural understanding rooted in humour took place. Stott writes:

> Jokes therefore emerge from within the social framework and
> necessarily express the nature of their environment, which
> means that all jokes are necessarily produced in a relative
> relationship to the dominant structures of understanding and
> the epistemological order.[19]

Li Yuan and I met to read through the play word by word for
meaning. As we read through, I explained specific areas of cultural
difference – religion, the communion dress and money were of
particular interest, why there were so many white dresses, why the
characters spoke such a strange dialect, what a 'traveller' and 'the bog'
were, and many more issues she had not been able to comprehend fully.
These were all straightforward enough areas from my perspective, as
they were so specific to Catholicism and to Ireland. However when Li
Yuan told me she had not found any humour in the play I was shocked.
Later on when Cao Bo said the same with regard to the three novels of

Beckett he had translated I felt a similar shock. Mrs Kilbride and Josie are playing cards together in this scene:

> **Mrs Kilbride**. Snap −snap! Snap! (*stacking the cards*) How many games is that I'm after winnin' ya?
> **Josie**. Five.
> **Mrs Kilbride**. And how many did you win?
> **Josie**. Ya know right well I won ne'er a game.
> **Mrs Kilbride**. And do ya know why ya won ne'er a game, Josie? Because you're thick, that's the why.[20]

How can one translate something faithfully without its humour remaining intact? Li Yuan just didn't believe me when I told her that the audience would find a grandmother cruelly 'slagging' her grandchild funny. Similarly, the translators did not believe someone would laugh at the mocking of a priest and of religion that takes place at the wedding ceremony, nor the hinting of incestuous behaviour between Mrs Kilbride and her son, my favourite of these being when Mrs Kilbride in her 'mother of the bride' speech tells of Carthage's greatness as a son:

> **Mrs Kilbride** ... When his father died he used come into the bed to sleep beside me for fear I would be lonely. Often I woke from a deep slumber and his two arms would be around me, a small leg thrown over me in sleep –
> **Catwoman**. The craythur
> **Mrs Kilbride**. He was always aware of my abidin' love for our Lord, unlike some here (*Glares at the Catwoman*) and on wan occasion, me birthday it was, I looked out the back window and there he was up on the slope behind our house and what was he doin'? He was buildin' Calvary for me. He'd hammered three wooden crosses and was erectin' them on the slope Calvary-style. Wan for him, wan for me and wan for Our Lord. And we draped ourselves around them like the two thieves in the holy book, remember, Carthage?
> **Mrs Kilbride**. ...And we draped ourselves around them like the two thieves in the holy book, remember, Carthage?
> **Carthage**. I do not, would ya ever sit down.
> **Mrs Kilbride**. Of course ya do, the three crosses ya made up on the slope and remember the wind was howlin' and the pair of us yellin' 'Calvary! Calvary!' to wan another. Of course ya remember. I'm only tellin' yees this story as wan of the countless examples of Carthage's kind nature and I only want to say that Caroline is very welcome into the Kilbride household. And that if Carthage will be as good a son to Caroline as he's been a husband to me then she'll have no complaints. (*Raises her glass.*) Cheers.[21]

Each time I explained that the audience would be laughing at something I could tell that Li Yuan just didn't believe me. I began to wonder if I had got it wrong and that the audience would not be laughing. Adigun identifies this response when he writes about the audience reaction to Martin McDonagh's *The Beauty Queen of Leenane*:

> ...one thing that I found deeply unsettling was what most people in the audience found really funny about the play. Most of the time when the audience laughed, it was when something funny was said or done at the expense of the powerless, senile old woman, who is trying desperately to hang on to her daughter, who should have been married a long time ago.[22]

For Adigun this was culturally unacceptable and for Li Yuan also; there is a respect given to age in both Adigun's Yoruba culture of Western Africa and Li Yuan's Chinese culture – in short, no slagging elders. In Li Yuan's case she was translating the actual meaning of the words Mrs Kilbride said in isolation from the culturally comic set-up of the action within the play.

I brought Li Yuan into the Abbey Theatre archive to watch the original performance on video, for myself also, as I was beginning to question a culture that found the slagging of old women and ideological knocking the main source of comedy. We watched the video of the performance together and Li Yuan wrote furiously, noting everywhere that the audience laughed. Two things happened here, the first being that I realized the words themselves didn't necessarily translate the embodied version that the Irish reader would subconsciously understand. In retrospect this seems naïve; however I do not think anyone who is writing can be aware of just how much every single detail of how they perceive the world within a culture is reproduced when they write, and again when that writing is performed and brought to life. Stott cites Andrew Horton in claiming that,

> like language, and like "texts" in general, the comic is plural, unfinalized, disseminative, dependent on context and the intertextuality of creator, text, and contemplator.[23]

In other words, when Carr was writing the characters she had the traces of voices and bodies in mind, saying the words; subconsciously, the director and the actors also understood this unwritten body and voice of the hypocritical Irish grandmother. The shared cultural and social history of church, family and social circumstances of a small island community such as Ireland was just twenty-five years ago, allowed the Irish audience a very fast reading of the text into its full embodiment onstage. I recognized this in the body of Mrs Kilbride and heard it in her voice. Bernadette Sweeney in her essay, 'Form and Comedy in contemporary Irish Theatre', writes about this. She argues:

> The comic value of dramatic material can be measured most clearly in performance, and can lend an audience an element of complicity, a permission to play, which has on occasion, pushed the boundaries of theatrical form in Irish theatre.[24]

The second thing that happened was that while we watched the video together, I mistakenly thought that Li Yuan also saw and heard what I did and understood the humour once she had watched it in action, embodied on the stage (albeit, via video). It was not until later that I realized that she still did not find it funny, per se, but could see that the audience did. When I worked on a full staged reading of the play with the students of the Beijing Foreign Studies University, I came to a greater understanding about the humour in the play. This was partly because we worked through it dramatically and whenever something provoked laughter or failed to provoke it, we took time to analyse why. Ma Dan Ning, the young woman who played Mrs Kilbride, spoke both Mandarin and English. She investigated the part in English first, discussing with me what each element meant and how its humour played out for an Irish person, before she could then find a corresponding type of Chinese woman who was full of pride and hypocrisy. She recorded an interesting memory of the experience as it played out for her:

> For the role I played, Mrs Kilbride, I can absolutely picture a vivid image of such kind of women in China. But one interesting thing I feel is that the images I have for Mrs Kilbride in two languages are different. In fact there are some big differences between them.[25]

Ma Dan Ning's interpretation of where comedy comments on the culturally shared recognition of the religious aspects in the play underscored the enormous part that religion plays within the piece. So much of the whole play is tied in with what it means to be Irish, which in turn is connected to religious ritual, the four white dresses in the play conveying the symbolism of religious ritual in our culture. The christening dress, communion dress, wedding dress and shroud are all white, a sign of purity, and are so much a part of our daily imagery that they provide the perfect symbol for a comic 'incongruity' and the corresponding tragic dénouement, in which Hester in her ragged

wedding dress slits her daughter Josie's throat while she sits on her lap
in her communion dress. This scene, coming after the hilarity of the
comic set-up of the four white dresses for the wedding party is cruelly
dark. The black comedy within the play pivots on this religious
sensibility, which would have been indelibly inscribed in an Irish
audience of the time. Interestingly white in Chinese culture denotes
death and mourning, red denotes luck and happiness and is used for
weddings. Ma wrote:

> One thing that really amazes and attracts me in *Bog* is the
> religious element. I mean unlike what the western media
> usually describe, there actually are many extremely pious
> religion believers in China, too. But when I really see some
> people praying to God from the bottom of their heart, I think
> it's a feeling that the generally atheistic Chinese people will
> never understand. Maybe Communism in China is something
> similar to religion, but the situation now is that it is more like a
> symbol of the regime than the ideal people share. Most Chinese
> people now don't believe in anything, not even Communism, so
> for us it's very difficult to understand the role religion plays in
> the play, not to mention sense the sarcasm to the Church.

In Chinese performance, there was sometimes laughter where I
would not have expected it, nor would most people from Ireland, I
would say. These parts were always very melodramatic moments and
required a heightened dramatic tension on the part of the actors. From
what the students told me it seemed due to the formality of the
language used in translation, which is different to the language used
everyday in modern Chinese culture. They told me that it happens a lot
when movies are dubbed in cinemas, at which everyone is laughing at
completely inappropriate times. Nie Ao Heng, the Chinese student who
played Monica in the staged reading wrote about this:

> In the very last part of this journal, I want to share my
> observation on the 'laughability' of some lines in drama. Well,
> speaking of this I have to confess my misconduct, that is I can't
> help laughing when some serious lines of Carthage are
> delivered, "The cattle! The calves! Ya burnt them all, they're
> roarin' in the flames! ... A' ya gone mad?" I think it has a lot to
> do with the translation and if it was in English, I am pretty sure
> that I wouldn't behave this way. Even if the lines are translated
> into Chinese, they still sound very English. But then I asked
> myself why I find those Chinese lines funny, after all, if the
> lines are meant to be amusing, having people laugh is of course
> a good thing. But what if the lines are serious? (Some of

Carthage's lines are really not meant to be amusing!) In that case, seeing people laugh is just tragic, which is why I want to sew my mouth every time I can't help laughing at those serious lines.[26]

It would be impossible for me to make any deep analysis of how a Chinese audience would read comedy in *By the Bog of Cats...* It is only possible to read, through my Chinese students' and colleagues' eyes, how much our own Irish sense of humour is so tied to our cultural norms, such as slagging and religion. Both of these areas are rooted in our cultural ideology, our history of being colonized and of our national identification of ourselves as Catholic. It is interesting to note that Hungarian poet and translator Andres Imreh, says that Beckett is 'comprehended as an author of hilarious sense of humour by the Hungarian public'.[27] When I asked him why he thought that Hungarians would share his sense of humour he wrote that, along with poverty and religion, '... being a small country and consequently having a long experience of oppression. This is at least at the root of Hungarian humour: a kind of resistence, mocking the world (and the self), a way of survival'.

It will be very interesting to see how much will change in terms of an Irish sense of the comic, now that the institution of the Church is no longer a central presence in everyday thought, especially within the daily lives of young Irish people, with the role of the mother dethroned and the removal of taboos regarding sex and the institution of marriage in general. I already find that I have to explain to Irish students how it was growing up under the regime of the Catholic church in Ireland as they do not have the embodied experience of it that my generation did. Maybe the future audiences of Ireland will read the play, in a similar way to the Chinese student, Li Shang Chen, who wrote in response to the reading:

As I read the play more and more times, my understanding of the play is much simpler and simpler. At last I understand its theme as maternal love, Hester's longing for love from her mother and her love for Josie. Maybe this is the part that can touch the bottom of people's hearts.[28]

As tropes such as the Irish Mother and the Catholic Religion begin to fade from their dominant positions within the social norms of our society, the humour which was predicated on these tropes and norms also changes and adapts itself to the new social order. Whether the habit of slagging continues as a national pastime, drawing other cultural and religious norms into the comic mix or not remains to be seen. However the shocking resonances of humour rooted in these tropes do not now operate with the same visceral experience of release through laughter for the younger audiences as they did for my generation. It's time for a new order.

WORKS CITED

Adigun, Olabisi, 'An Irish Joke, a Nigerian Laughter' in *The Power of Laughter: Comedy and Contemporary Irish Theatre*, ed. Eric Weitz (Dublin: Carysfort, 2004)

Beckett, Samuel, Samuel Beckett: The Grove Centenary Edition, (New York: Grove, 2006)

Carr, Marina, *Marina Carr: Plays*, (London: Faber and Faber, 1999)

Critchley, Simon, *On Humour* (Routledge: London, 2002)

Stott, Andrew, *Comedy* (New York: Routledge, 2005)

Sweeney, Bernadette, 'Form and Comedy in contemporary Irish Theatre' in *The Power of Laughter: Comedy and Contemporary Irish Theatre*, ed. Eric Weitz (Dublin: Carysfort, 2004)

Weitz, Eric, 'Introduction' in *The Power of Laughter: Comedy and Contemporary Irish Theatre*, ed. Eric Weitz (Dublin: Carysfort, 2004)

PERSONAL CORRESPONDENCE

Cao Bo, interview, Dublin: October 2012

Ma Dan Ning, personal notes: 14 November 2010

Nie Ao Heng (Gloria), email: November 2010

Imreh, Andres, email: 26 January 2012

Li Shang Chen, personal notes: 14 November 2010

---

[1] Simon Critchley, *On Humour* (Routledge: London, 2002): 66.

[2] Critchley, 68.

[3] Marina Carr, *The Mai* in *Marina Carr: Plays*, (London: Faber and Faber, 1999): 136.

[4] Critchley, 4.

[5] Marina Carr, *Low in the Dark* in *Marina Carr: Plays* (London: Faber and Faber, 1999): 65.

[6] Eric Weitz, 'Introduction' in *The Power of Laughter: Comedy and Contemporary Irish Theatre*, ed. Eric Weitz (Dublin: Carysfort, 2004): 1.

[7] Weitz, 2.

[8] Carr, *Low in the Dark*, 54-55.

[9] Marina Carr, *By the Bog of Cats...* in *Marina Carr: Plays* (London: Faber and Faber, 1999): 303.

[10] Bisi Adigun, 'An Irish Joke, a Nigerian Laughter' in *The Power of Laughter: Comedy and Contemporary Irish Theatre*, ed. Eric Weitz (Dublin: Carysfort, 2004): 77.

[11] Critchley, 73.

[12] Critchley, 75.

[13] Samuel Beckett, *Catastrophe* in *Samuel Beckett: The Grove Centenary Edition*, (New York: Grove, 2006): 487.

[14] Beckett, 488.

[15] Quotes from Cao Bo come from the transcript of a personal interview, conducted in Dublin, October 2012.

[16] Ibid.

[17] Andrew Stott, *Comedy* (New York: Routledge, 2005): 2.

[18] Stott, 8.

[19] Stott, 10.

[20] Carr, *By the Bog of Cats...*, 277-78.

[21] Carr, *By the Bog of Cats...*, 310-11.

[22] Adigun, 77.

[23] Stott, 7.

[24] Bernadette Sweeney, 'Form and Comedy in contemporary Irish Theatre' in *The Power of Laughter: Comedy and Contemporary Irish Theatre*, ed. Eric Weitz (Dublin: Carysfort, 2004): 8.

[25] Ma Dan Ning's personal reflections, noted November 2010. Also the following quote.

[26] Nie Ao Heng, personal email to the writer, November 2010.

[27] Andres Imreh, personal email to the writer, November 2012. Also the following quote.

[28] Li Shang Chen, personal notes: November 2010.

8 | 'The problem with laughter': The clown as double agent in Barabbas' *City of Clowns*

Eric Weitz

The clown persists as an interesting creature in today's world. With bloodlines to the medieval Vice figure, popular entertainers, and the *zanni* of the *commedia dell'arte*, the clown habitually throws the invisible lines of socio-cultural convention into relief by playfully, naïvely or foolishly failing to observe them. The clown or clown-like figure often becomes a child's escort across the verbal divide to a grown-up grasp of approved comportment and the ways of the world.[1] In recent times, a broad school of clowning practice has turned the trademark red nose into a studio technique for self-discovery, a way of exploring one's individuality beneath our encrusted public faces. This association by the clown or clown-like figure with cultural inscription and subjectivity invites inspection in biopolitical terms as established by Michel Foucault and Giorgio Agamben.

I have suggested elsewhere that the prototypical clowning engine derives historically from the figure of the country bumpkin, who does not know some of the more obvious rules of society, and sometimes even fails to grasp some of the basic principles of physical being.[2] *City of Clowns* premiered in 2010, featuring Raymond Keane plus a host of local performers. The production opened at The Complex, in the Smithfield area of Dublin, and went on to play elsewhere in the country, drawing upon local performers to populate the titular city. It inspired two student productions (*College of Clowns* and *Academy of Clowns*, in 2011 and 2012, respectively), directed by Keane, at the Samuel Beckett Theatre, Trinity College Dublin.

The piece comprises of two sections, the first a seemingly conventional clowning turn by Keane as a character he calls Fibrils, grounded in his Raymond Clown persona, itself born almost twenty years ago at the dawn of Barabbas Theatre Company's existence (with fellow performers Veronica Coburn and Mikel Murfi). For this first part the audience sits in a customary head-on configuration; the second half sees them ushered into an adjacent space, in which they are allowed to roam amongst thirty or so red-nosed performers, caught up in loops of activity, which they have discovered, explored and shaped under Keane's guidance. Although the unspoken theme of the evening resides in the body blow absorbed by those on the ground – especially those who fell prey to Arts Council cuts – in post-bailout Ireland, the piece also presents itself as an interrogation of the clowning project itself, from two salient perspectives.

Clowns are what I have come to call laughter-centric figures (among others, like tricksters and jesters), who seem to attend human lives across cultural boundaries. While sometimes operating under prescribed or ritual mandates, laughter provocation tends to be a featured discursive strategy. Under scrutiny laughter reveals itself as an ambiguous human response, primed by a feeling of superiority even as it renders the body temporarily powerless. *City of Clowns*, in fact, allows excavation of some of these sunken conduits of political force beneath the site of mainstream comic performance, with particular regard to notions of biopolitics.

Michael Billig unpacks the social provocation of laughter in his book, *Laughter and Ridicule*, building upon work by Henri Bergson and Sigmund Freud: 'It suggests that ridicule lies at the core of social life, for the possibility of ridicule ensures that members of society routinely comply with the customs and habits of their social milieu'.[3]

This calls attention to the fact that all jokes are made at someone's or something's expense, even if the butt is so widely accepted or seemingly ineffectual as to seem negligible. Billig proposes that the wiring for such a behaviour-modification effect is installed in us as children. He describes how grown-ups teach children the rules of language and conversation at least in part through 'disciplinary laughter', inscribing the feeling we know as embarrassment – albeit in a benificent manner. (A small child, for example, who has misidentified one of the farmyard animal sounds in a book may meet with some kind of soft-edged laughter from the parent or carer.) Billig suggests that this way of imparting some of our cultural basics informs uses of laughter later in life: 'What is embarrassing is typically comic to onlookers.

Social actors fear this laughter. Accordingly, the prospect of ridicule and embarrassment protects the codes of daily behaviour, ensuring much routine conformity with social order.'[4]

There is a co-present flip side to this effect, which stems from a sense of social reification *also* at the heart of humorous laughter; as Bergson observed more than a hundred years ago, 'laughter always implies a kind of secret freemasonry, or even complicity, with other laughers, real or imaginary'.[5] Scientists now suspect that the body is neurologically wired to respond to the sound of others' laughter.[6] One can see, then, how the humour mechanism trades upon a division of the world into in-groups, the invited laughers, and out-groups, the proposed targets or 'butts' of the joke, the objects of ridicule. This leads in biopolitical terms toward fields of thought developed by Giorgio Agamben with regard to the 'logic of exclusion' he takes to underpin the wielding of sovereign power through history.

Agamben observes in *homoSacer*, 'One of the essential characteristics of modern biopolitics ... is its constant need to redefine the threshold in life that distinguishes and separates what is inside from what is outside.'[7] And this is exactly the sort of fulcrum exploited by humorous laughter. With an impetus toward consensus, the socially galvanizing aspect of mainstream humorous laughter is always going to favour the projects of normalizing society.

In the same essay, Bergson confirms laughter's part in behaviour modification around some approved centre:

> Laughter is, above all, a corrective. Being intended to humiliate, it must make a painful impression on the person against whom it is directed. By laughter, society avenges itself for the liberties taken with it. It would fail in its object if it bore the stamp of sympathy or kindness.[8]

Three-quarters of a century later, Michel Foucault located the rise of biopower in just this transition from the state exerting a direct bodily threat to keep its population in order, to the care and maintenance of a human population from within by various biopolitical 'technologies': 'a power whose task is to take charge of life needs continuous regulatory and corrective mechanisms'.[9] Well, there is no better example of herd instinct marshalled to self-policing effect than that which underpins social laughter, supplying fear of embarrassment to keep *oneself* in line and the pleasure born from ridicule to shape the behaviours of *others*.

Which brings us to the clown figure. Anyone of a certain age in western culture knows in their bones Wolfgang Iser's characterisation of clown metaphysics: 'Everything he does goes wrong but he persists, as if the repetition denotes constant success'.[10] Clowns teach us what to do and how to do it by inviting our laughter at what *not* to do and how *not* to do it. The clown assists in formatting the body of the entry-level spectator with the mechanism that springs the humour trap, installing notions of ridicule at the expense of deviant or incompetent thought, feeling and comportment. It is true that *any* position can elicit laughter from its in-group audience by ridiculing an 'other' – but mainstream comic performance by definition seeks a broadest possible confirmation of thought and prejudice, and is therefore likely to trade on reification of values, attitudes and stereotypes carried by the broad centre of the population (up to and including false senses that we are actually challenging the status quo by making fun of it).

Agamben, in *The Open: Man and Animal*, concludes in part: 'In our culture, the decisive political conflict, which governs every other conflict, is that between the animality and the humanity of man. That is to say, in its origin Western politics is also biopolitics'.[11] This conceptual tandem is defined in Agamben's *homo sacer*, which details the ways in which sovereign power has opened a point of leverage between the biological life of the human, *zoē* in the Ancient Greek conception, and the social subject's political viability, *bios*. Agamben traces to Roman origins the case whereby a criminal could be considered insufficiently pure for sacrifice, while at the same time unprotected by society's injunction against murder. This model has been invoked through history and across cultures to allow the state to reduce some of the human animals within its borders to the state of a 'bare' or 'naked life', doubly excluded, and open to ostracization, isolation and the ever popular extermination, with the concentration camp its perversely definitive achievement.

Enter the clown figure, which, as noted above, derives historically from the country rustic or bumpkin, and often was occupied with the simple bodied projects of animal needs and desires – eating and drinking, sleeping, excreting – a human animal with the emphasis on *zoē*, ever shy of the threshold to *bios*. Susanne K. Langer identifies in the clown-like figure the sense of a body excluded from socio-cultural matrices: 'in fact his whole improvised existence has the rhythm of primitive, savage, if not animalian life'.[12] Through comic displays of failure and incompetence the clown often presents an image of an instinct-driven bare life, whose credentials for social viability are laughably suspect.

Clowns and clown-like figures are laid bare to extravagant comic humiliation, subjected to slapstick violence for an audience's entertainment. The clown may not be *homo sacer* himself, but he comprises a clever performative construction, a quasi-human provocateur who plays along the fault-lines of *zoē* and *bios*, sacrificing dignity at the altar of laughter. Clowns show us how to think playfully, but conventionally serve the social structures of the status quo if only by pointing to them.

It is therefore my pleasure to point out that the ingrained templates of clowning practice can be deployed in adult contexts to help theatre-makers swim upstream against the biopolitical current. In *City of Clowns*, generic markers and strategies of clown performance have been invoked to unsettle the traditionally conservative inflection.

As suggested at the outset, *City of Clowns* premiered at The Complex in Dublin, a reclaimed industrial location, which, at the time, accommodated both a conventional stage configuration, with rows of chairs for spectators facing a playing area, and an adjacent warehouse-like space without seating. The incoming audience was met by a wall of cardboard boxes, along with other seemingly disused objects on the periphery, such as a mannequin and ladder. It is also worth revising the fact that Keane has acknowledged that the show emerged as a personal response to the effects, both psychological and pragmatic, of the merciless budget cuts enacted by successive governments, and their onerous effect on established companies like Barabbas.

When the lights go down, the stage appears unoccupied by actors – until activity can be detected in one of the cardboard cartons. The box shudders and shifts with clear evidence of something living inside causing it to alter its positioning and eventually to move, at one point threatening to bump into the front row of spectators. This segment goes on for a few minutes, until Keane's character, Fibrils, breaks open the top of the carton, to peer out at the audience.

One might ask, what everyday object better represents contemporary commercial culture than the cardboard box, the all-purpose shell for a million mass-produced products? We can see, hear and feel something within the box, pressing, straining against its cardboard sides. These first few minutes of performance show a bodied being, confined and reduced to a state of bare life. It is, in fact, possible to read this runup to Fibril's emergence as a sort of egg laid carelessly by late-capitalist culture, struggling to hatch. And it is not so far a leap to overlay this image with biopolitical resonance, the bare life of the clown/artist (evocative of the homeless subject, disused by the system) fighting to break free of some inhuman personal prison – a stark embodied metaphor for the sense of entrapment exacted by austerity measures and opaque government practices masquerading as free and open democratic process.

These opening minutes of performance show a human, physically contained and reduced to a state of bare life, yet framed theatrically by the title and a performer's body marked as clown by red nose. Fibrils finally bursts through the top of the box and drapes himself over the side in semi-exhaustion. He then comes to register the presence of an audience with slack-faced fear and panic. This is not the kind of jack-in-the-box greeting we might expect (e.g., 'Hello boys and girls, I'm Google the Clown!'). Neither is it the ingenuous self-deprecation sometimes adopted as a performative strategy to gain sympathy from an audience.

Fibrils apparently wants no part of the clowning mandate, nor the spectators; he desperately tries to extricate himself from the situation, breathing like a cornered animal. Stepping out of the box and inadvertently crashing into the stacks of boxes would amount to a vintage slapstick opening under other circumstances; here he apologises profusely in panicked whispers of, 'Sorry, sorry'. He declines the usual privileged connection between clown and audience and tries to escape out a back door beyond our sight. We hear audible reports of his panicked efforts to escape the theatre event itself, rattling of doors and chains and a terrified cry of, 'I want out! I just – want – out!' The customary clowning responses would involve inquisitive looks to the audience or takes to uncooperative props. Here, he is simply desperate to extricate himself from the audience gaze. The activities retain the bare shapes of clown-related patterns, but the generically default joking permission has been disabled, and most laughter has the hollow ring of habit. Fibrils looks like a clown and does clown-like things, but his body exudes unhappiness from a world without laughter.

Fibrils eventually puts on the mannequin's jacket thereby literally assuming a new and sunnier outlook, engaging with the audience and becoming the kind of clown the red nose generally signifies. A few more conventional clowning numbers restore something of his comic soul, whereupon he finds a small 'baby' box, which he takes wholly to heart – only to have it become gradually sick and die. Fibrils tries in abject desolation to end it all by setting fire to his world – and fails. This Tragedy for Clown finds little emotional lift from poor Fibrils' inability to obliterate his pain.

In biopolitical terms, the show has eschewed a simple reversal of the bodied charge from laughter to non-laughter. It has instead drained some of the pleasure, the key to laughter's bodied convincing that supplies its power to control. This animal, portrayed to touching effect through Keane's emotional integrity, will not surrender its personhood, despite the generic trappings that commission the psychic distance required for unfettered laughing to take place.

At this point in the performance, a child clown appears from the offstage area, a sort of *deus ex machina* sent to airlift Fibrils from his psychic pit of despair. She (or he, depending on when and where you saw it) beckons Fibrils to follow her, and both lead the audience to an adjacent space – a large, warehouse-like room – a commercial-industrial box writ large. The space is inhabited by some thirty-plus clowns, each occupying a patch of the room and engaged in a repeating fragment of activity Keane calls an 'obsession'.

In the original run, one clown stood in a corner, beginning to write something very important on a post-it note, then stopped, crumpled it and dropped it to the floor – to begin again. A rolling stair unit had clowns with suitcases queued on each step, with the topmost clown periodically rotating to the end. One clown surrounded himself with single shoes; another stood on a ledge shifting back and forth between, 'Will I?' and 'Won't I?' The circular form of these obsessions evokes a machinelike repetition. In a later incarnation a clown moved through the space with bicycle handlebars held in front of him, giving a sense of unending travel; another clown flips through a rack of clothing, and another persists at painting the same abstract design at the base of a structural column.

Interestingly, Bergson has something to say about people, machines and laughter: 'The attitudes, gestures and movements of the human body are laughable in exact proportion as that body reminds us of a mere machine'.[13] The behavioural loops in the city of clowns approximate machine-like repetition, but human feeling is in no way denied. In fact, feeling seems to breathe through the skins of the clowns even as they remain trapped in their travails, filling the industrial space with a halting sense of the bare lives soldiering on. Here arises another interesting angle upon Foucault's thought. He describes how power over life evolved in two basic forms: 'One of these poles ... centered on the body as a machine: its disciplining, the optimization of its capabilities, the extortion of its forces, the parallel increase of its usefulness and its docility...'.[14]

This part of the piece incarnates a sense of bodies used and worn by the machinery of late-capitalist, faux-democratic culture. At the same time these bodies, given a disarming sense of a clown's naïveté by their red noses, cycle bravely through the same strips of gesture and feeling whether because or in spite of the sovereign power's relentless attack upon the human spirit itself. These furtive descriptions do not afford a full-bodied sense of the spectator's experience, but I do believe that the slowed pace of the city's inhabitants tended to affect the collective heartbeat in the room, a bio-performative achievement out of the ordinary. This city of clowns incarnates Agamben's cautionary claim, delivered in the third part of *homo sacer*: 'Bare life is no longer confined to a particular place or a definite category. It now dwells in the biological body of every living being'.[15]

The show is built for travel, and at any geographical stop, Keane runs a day of workshops for local volunteers to cultivate clowning loops for the night's performance. In a similar, yet extended fashion, Keane worked with second-year Drama and Theatre Studies students at Trinity College Dublin for several weeks, guiding them toward discovery of a personal clowning loop (sometimes in pairs or threesomes). In these two productions, Keane fashioned the student's confections into hour-long pieces that occupied the Samuel Beckett Theatre for several performances. In *College of Clowns*, the first incarnation, spectators were led into and around the space as a group, the order of viewing prescribed. A year later, in *Academy of Clowns*, the production awarded the audience freedom of the space, which was populated by both stationary 'acts' and a handful of roaming clowns.

In this creative model the workshopping through which each performer finds and sculpts a performance loop enables a one-by-one appropriation of the clown persona for individual expression and *without* an obligation to cause laughter, the bringer of conformity. Once again, if we laugh it is a different kind of laughter, together with the attending clown at our collective predicament. In Fibrils' segments before he puts on the uniform and after his 'baby' dies and in the performance of these obsessions, the effects may not amount to actual reversals of sovereign power, but they do stake out spaces for so many points of resistance, for the moment reversing the polarity on conventional technologies of laughter, and temporarily revealing these clowns as double agents in the biopolitical scheme of things.

WORKS CITED

Agamben, Giorgio, *homo sacer: Sovereign Power and Bare Life*, trans. by Daniel Heller-Roazen (Stanford: Stanford University, 1998)

---------- *The Open: Man and Animal,* trans. by Kevin Attell (Stanford: Stanford University, 2004)

Bergson, Heri, 'Laughter' in *Comedy,* ed. Wylie Sypher (Baltimore: Johns Hopkins University, 1980)

Billig, Michael, *Laughter and Ridicule: Towards a Social Critique of Humour* (London: Sage, 2010)

Foucault, Michel, 'Right of Death and Power over Life', from *The History of Sexuality, Vol. 1* in *The Foucault Reader: An Introduction to Foucault's Thought,* ed. Paul Rabinow (Harmondworth: Penguin, 1984): 258-72

Iser, Wolfgang, 'Counter-sensical comedy and audience response in Beckett's *Waiting for Godot*', *New Casebooks*: Waiting for Godot *and* Endgame, ed. S. Conner (Houndmills: Macmillan, 1992): 55–70

Susanne K. Langer, *Feeling and Form* (New York: Charles Scribner's Sons, 1953)

Weitz, Eric, 'Failure as Success: On clowns and laughing bodies', *Performance Research: A Journal of the Performing Arts*, 17:1, (2012): 79-87

---

[1] It is true that many grown-ups admit to not actually liking red-nose, baggy-pants clowns, or at least find them creepy, frightening, and otherwise unappealing. The birthday-party clown performer represents a fairly recent incarnation in broad historical terms, and may not always succeed in putting his audience at ease (the character of Cam, played by Eric Stonestreet on US television's *Modern Family,* has in a few episodes offered a deft caricature in his clown persona, named Fizbo). We are still more likely than not to have come under the influence of figures in television and film, performers who employ clown-like bodied styles and humour patterns in teaching the world by making entertaining mistakes.

[2] Eric Weitz, 'Failure as Success: On clowns and laughing bodies', *Performance Research: A Journal of the Performing Arts*, 17:1, (Feb. 2012): 79-87. The article eventually works its way round to consideration of *City of Clowns*, upon which this essay extends.

[3] Michael Billig, *Laughter and Ridicule: Towards a Social Critique of Humour* (London: Sage, 2010): 2.

[4] Billig, 202.

[5] Henri Bergson, 'Laughter' in *Comedy*, ed. Wylie Sypher (Baltimore: Johns Hopkins University, 1980): 64.

[6] Robert R. Provine, *Laughter: A Scientific Investigation* (London: Penguin, 2001): 150.

[7] Giorgio Agamben, *homoSacer: Sovereign Power and Bare Life*, trans. by Daniel Heller-Roazen (Stanford: Stanford University, 1998): 131.

[8] Bergson, 187.

9 Michel Foucault, 'Right of Death and Power over Life' (from *The History of Sexuality, Vol. 1*) in *The Foucault Reader*, ed. Paul Rabinow (Harmondworth: Penguin, 1984): 266.

10 Wolfgang Iser, 'Counter-sensical comedy and audience response in Beckett's *Waiting for Godot*', *New Casebooks*: Waiting for Godot *and* Endgame, ed. S. Conner (Houndmills: Macmillan, 1992): 56.

11 Agamben, *The Open: Man and Animal*, trans. by Kevin Attell (Stanford: Stanford University, 2004): 80.

12 Susanne K. Langer, *Feeling and Form* (New York: Charles Scribner's Sons, 1953): 133.

13 Bergson, 79.

14 Foucault, 261.

15 Agamben, 139.

9 | 'Talk about laugh': Why is the Irish personality renowned for being so funny but Irish comedy on television somewhat less so?

John Waters

On television one evening during the days of post-Christmas torpor that accompanied the death rattles of 2012, I caught one of those reviews of 'Irish comedy on television', which we are periodically offered as an alternative to new comedy shows. It was called, *Having a Laugh! Great Irish Comedy*. As these things normally go, it was quite diverting in its own way, because it seemed to cover most of the relevant territory, evoking that strange brand of nostalgia that, when watching television, we seem readily disposed to confuse with being entertained.

It had the lot: bits of *Hall's Pictorial Weekly*, *Nighthawks*, Twink, *Leave it to Mrs O'Brien*, Tommy Tiernan on the *Late Late Show* and, of course, *Father Ted* – all the stalwarts of the previous 40 years of Irish comedy on television. (Interesting that such programmes are always fashioned as 'Irish comedy on television', rather than 'comedy on Irish television' – clearly a device to permit the inclusion of *Father Ted*, pretty universally acknowledged as the jewel in the crown, but unfortunately produced in and broadcast from another country.)

Another thing that strikes you about such programmes is that they are almost entirely of an historical character and construction. There is no programme or comic talent of the moment that qualifies for inclusion, or – one is moved to suspect – any that would make the cut for some such retrospective in the foreseeable future – for anything other than reasons of sentiment or curiosity value. This is remarkable in itself. Never before has Irish society been so obsessed with laughter, so self-conscious of its need and capacity for laughter, so intent upon seeing laughter as a moral force – and yet, judging by much of what passes muster in television comedy at least, the evidence of the kind of creativity capable of provoking such laughter is lamentably sparse. The impression, watching such retrospectives, is that we Irish are capable of being successful at generating comedy, but that this capacity is sporadic and erratic.

Yet the 1990s is seen as a veritable golden age of Irish comedy, especially in the category of stand-up. Before that, the legend has it, Irish comedy, as perhaps best exemplified by the Jury's Cabaret phenomenon, was directed at enabling outsiders – tourists in particular – to have a laugh at our expense. In the 1990s, we learned that the things we laughed at among ourselves could make for an even better comic formula, a discovery that launched a host of careers, including that of the late Dermot Morgan, who had discovered this truth ten years before anyone else. But this Irish comedy of the '90s, for all its strengths and strides, was not underpinned by the kinds of energies that those who speak about its merits tend to imply.

Ireland presents a profoundly comedic landscape as an inevitable side effect of its past. In Ireland for historical reasons, the 'joke' has an unusual pathological dimension, arising in part from the pratfalls inflicted on us by history, and inviting us to laugh at ourselves as an alternative to tears. There is a neurosis at work at the heart of Irish life, from which we protect ourselves with laughter. In the works of Samuel Beckett, for example, there is a quality of truth which is far more real than outsiders comprehend. Because his plays in particular have acquired the label, 'absurdism', it is assumed that the characters are in some sense akin to cartoons. In fact, the men Beckett depicts are people he actually observed, refugees from a catastrophe that became a slapstick. We natives watch them with two sets of eyes: the eyes of the outsider, contracted by dint of literary education, and the eye of the insider, which sees what is actually there.

The joke that is intrinsic to Ireland and its people gravitates around the idea of a culture, truncated by interference, suddenly rebooted and beginning to behave as though it had never been disrupted. Irish reality turned into something utterly different to what might have been imagined as a logical progression from what had come before. Everything that was previously forbidden – sex, movement, flamboyance, passion – was suddenly possible, and this made people different from what they might (notionally, which is as far as one can go) have become had history unwound in a different way. For all the nostalgias we engage in, we've never really got to the truth of all this, but surrounded it with false meanings, both positive and negative.

One of the problems with such an arrested culture is that it has no way of growing organically, or even of imagining how this might have happened if the interruption had not occurred. And so there are only two ways of responding culturally, one being fossilization, the other a process of lurching forward in jumps and starts, reacting neurotically to developments elsewhere, imitating, rejecting and trying to unbecome what you have been given as a self-description. Because of the fragmentation of original meanings, and the consequent development of multiple versions of itself, Ireland has always combined a strong sense of nostalgia with a desire to escape its past and become something other than it actually is. Those who remain in this culture are trapped, therefore, between an out-of-date version of Ireland – existing largely in the imagination of its exiled millions but reflected in, for example, the kind of kitsch iconography aimed at tourists – and their own yearning to escape, perhaps to some idealized notion of what Ireland might have become with a different history. Our aunts and uncles went off and built Manhattan, while we who remained continued to live in cosy homesteads but watched our children acquire the sensibility of skyscraper dwellers and pursue doctorates in the absurdist drama of Samuel Beckett. Thus, poverty and kitsch came to have the same face, and history lurked like a custard pie to take the fun out of modernity.

This is the mainspring in the work of the playwright, Martin McDonagh, who took the world by storm (more or less parallel to Irish stand-up in the 1990s) with plays like *The Beauty Queen of Leenane* and the *Cripple of Inishmaan*. McDonagh's plays made the world laugh without quite knowing what it was laughing at. Many of the jokes relate to the imprisonment of his characters in one world upon which another world seeks to encroach. The existence of familiar items of modern living, like potato crisps and Australian soaps, in the sub-modern lives of people who seem reluctantly to belong to a different version of history, creates a tremendous poignancy and pathos. This model of comedy, interestingly, appears – on the surface at least – to become equally funny to both insiders and outsiders, who share the same universal cultural ideals and therefore perceive the pathos behind the lurch towards the modern.

For the insider Irish, however, the laughter is shot through with sorrow. To some degree, the insider laughter is exaggerated in an attempt to bury the sorrow and conceal its existence, and this renders the laughter of the insider pretty much indistinguishable in terms of volume and duration from that of the outsider who has no stake in the pathos. But, in part at least, the laughter of the insiders is provoked because the world these characters inhabit is saturated with nostalgic meanings, both for those who stayed and those who have gone away, while imprisoning those who have had to stay in a cartoon world which remains uncannily real. McDonagh's characters remain in poverty, but occupy a place which, in the memories of the departed, has a connotation of Paradise. We, the 'objective' insiders, laugh to protect ourselves from the psychic disintegration that might follow from a genuine encounter with a sense of the sadness they must experience. To avoid entering the darkness their existences imply, we turn them into comic figures. To enjoy the kind of laughter which emanates naturally from the stuff of Irish life, we have to withdraw sympathy from ourselves. It seems somewhat indecent voyeuristically to enjoy that humour, deprived of its catastrophic context, but a joke is a joke and we can't help laughing. 'What is humour after all', asked the French writer Michel Houellebecq in one of his published letters to the philosopher Bernard-Henri Lévy (*Public Enemies*, 2011), 'but shame at having felt a genuine emotion? It's a sort of tour de force, a slave's elegant pirouette when faced with a situation that under normal circumstances would evoke despair or rage. So, yes, it's hardly surprising that humour is these days rated very highly.'

We laugh, then, not to mock those who become the butts of the jokes but to protect ourselves from what we imagine must be their griefs. Laughter is like a layer of gristle between bones which would otherwise grind into one another to the point of seizure. It is a kind of self-protection, a philosophical response born of the need to maintain a blinkered outlook in the face of a calamity which is inevitable and inescapable.

Like Flann O'Brien, Martin McDonagh looks at Ireland through a filter of irony, which reduces its inhabitants and their locations to cartoons. But whereas in, say, *An Beal Bocht*, O'Brien's purpose is to mock and deride his own characters' attachments to misery, McDonagh creates a sense of the forlorn nature of his characters in the midst of their wretchedness. The humour is always fragile and under threat from a dark sorrow. Yet, in the bleakness of McDonagh's visions is a profound comedy, which works precisely by squeezing the laughter out between our desire to protect ourselves from the abyss that threatens these characters at every turn and the necessity to cut them loose in case they drag us down also. McDonagh is deeply funny but ultimately saddening in a way Flann O'Brien's writing is not. *The Poor Mouth* pulls its punch by leaving open the possibility that its characters are distortions. McDonagh's characters are only in the slightest degree caricatures of real people – i.e., of us and all belonging to us. Only by virtue of this mercy are we spared their despair, from which only our laughter separates us, as though a partition made of feathers.

It's always dangerous trying to talk about humour, because, while you can laugh about talk, you can't really talk about laughter. This isn't just because the nature of a joke is elusive (though it is), but also because we live in an age in which humour has mysteriously acquired a quasi-moralistic significance. Someone who makes people laugh is regarded as a kind of modern-day prophet, and the only way to grapple with this phenomenon without becoming the butt of the joke is to compete with such maestros for the laughter of your audience. And since it's almost impossible to say anything relevant or constructive on the subject of humour in this way, most people tend to say almost nothing about a particular piece of comedy except that they did or did not find it funny. This is not merely prone to tautology, but also risks giving rise to a kind of 'laughter fascism', whereby the funnyman or funnywoman becomes virtually unassailable, immune from critical commentary or analysis. The result is not merely a growing misunderstanding of the nature of laughter, but an escalating denial about the conditions to which our laughter should be drawing attention.

This in part explains the peculiarly erratic character of Irish comedy, evident yet again in the documentary referred to above. What is most strange is that when Irish comedians talk about comedy, they always assume that the nature of their craft and function is both self-evident and self-evidently virtuous. They speak about their achievements, or those of their fellow comedians, as though of heroic exploits, with occasional mentions of honourable failures. Always there is this sense of a lengthy battle to overcome vaguely intimated dark and oppressive forces which – it is implicitly suggested – have conspired to prevent people laughing as is their entitlement. It seems almost invariably to be implied also that these forces are by definition either political or religious.

Thus, in attempts to discuss recent Irish comedy, there is inevitably an encounter with vainglory. Invariably, the retrospectives include tacit celebrations of the daringness of the stand-up comedian, – for example, Tommy Tiernan, in provoking the wrath of Catholic Ireland by his appearances on the *Late Late Show* – what in that TV documentary he called 'clench-holed people' and 'crawthumpers' who are easily upset by what he called 'stupid stuff'. Or, there will be references to *Father Ted* as an example of the increasing 'maturity' of Irish culture in relation to Catholicism as the twentieth century drew to a close. And so forth.

I'm not necessarily disputing anything in such characterisations, but I would prefer the discussion to go a little deeper. Participants in such retrospectives always assume that laughter is essential, but they never say why. They always seem to suggest that humour offers some kind of irreplaceable social benefit, but they never spell out what that benefit might be, or even to be aware that this is what they are suggesting. At the end of the particular documentary I watched, there was a clip of the late comic actor, David Kelly, quoting what he described as an old Dublin saying: 'You have to laugh... or cry'. From the way he said it, or the way what he said was edited, it seemed he was suggesting that the basis of laughter was already obvious and agreed. What might we cry at or because of as an alternative to laughter? In all such treatments, the nature and benefits of laughter are invariably taken as existing in their own right – which is to say that humour is placed in an ideological frame, and this frame which sees the context of comedy as existing wholly in the social dimension. Humour is, by this outlook, a satirical instrument rather than a symptom of something that, emanating from man, has its consequences in a fundamental human response to the contradictions and indignities imposed on the soul of man by socialisation. Humour, in other words, becomes political as opposed to being an existential protest against social reality.

Don't get me wrong (he said defensively): I think I agree with the proposition (that we 'have to laugh'). But I would love to watch just one programme about comedy in Irish society or on Irish television that addresses the idea: *why* (do we have to laugh)? Why do we tend to assume that laughter is essential to a society and why, therefore, is the freedom achieved by comedians considered important beyond the fact of causing people to experience muscular spasms as a result of encountering incongruous or irreverent ideas or being told things which conform to their existing prejudices? Why does it continue to represent some kind of achievement when a comedian on the *Late Late* causes a bunch of elderly ladies to ring up RTÉ and complain? The answer to this question, if it could be arrived at, might go a long way towards explaining why it is that Irish television comedy has been as inconsistent as it has.

One theory about this is that the literary manifestations of Irish humour (Beckett, O'Brien, McDonagh, etc.) tend to look inwardly for their jokes, whereas modern Irish comedy, especially in its televisual manifestation, has become caught between the UK and US models of humour, which are fundamentally divergent. British humour is generally class-based and highly politicized, whereas the American kind is, indeed, essentially existential. You can get the distinction pretty clearly by contrasting the styles of John Cleese and Woody Allen. Cleese, in *Fawlty Towers*, for example, rails against the toffs who he imagines look down upon him, whereas Allen contemplates the inevitable pratfall of his existence, worries that the universe is expanding and wonders why his life is naturally shit. 'I never regard any woman as perfect unless she rejects me,' he says, leading us toward the abyss of self-apprehension that allows no social excuse.

Eoghan Harris, the newspaper columnist and screenwriter who wrote sketches for Niall Toibin's highly successful TV shows of the late 1970s, appears to have given more thought to these matters than most commentators of our time. For an article I wrote about Irish comedy in 1989, he told me: 'You only have to fade up someone speaking in an upper-class accent, and straightaway nine-tenths of the British population are already beginning to smile. From Spike Milligan, through *Python*, Hancock, Cleese, right through *Spitting Image*, and including *Yes, Minister*, you will find the whole basis of British comedy rests fundamentally on British class structure. This poses a huge problem in Ireland, where there is no class structure'.

We have become even more confused, Harris pointed out, by virtue of our exposure to the American brand of humour, courtesy of movies and TV shows like *Taxi*, *Cheers*, *Frasier* and, latterly, it occurs to me, *Curb Your Enthusiasm*:

> The American tradition is basically a pure capitalist tradition, whereby there's no market mediating. There's only the individual soul – Woody Allen wandering in Manhattan – and God up there. It's self-deprecating, deep into the human psyche – very, very black, Freudian, very psychological humour: 'Why did you make hamburgers, God?' and 'Why did you make an aeroplane?' and 'Why is my dick so small?'

Man's attempt to escape his nature ultimately supplies the raw material for the comic, and this idea unites the British and American models. The British class system is a construct in which man's vanity becomes magnified by virtue of his attempts to escape his solitary smallness; America, a much younger society, places its individualized citizens in the open, their humanity caught in God's searchlight as well as that of their own self-doubt. Ireland, caught wandering in the precincts of globalised Anglo-Saxon culture, has become confused concerning what should be most fundamental to its self-understanding.

Having lost sight of its essence, it generally opts to create laughter by a process of mimicry.

You could take this further and say that, whereas British comedy addresses itself to the group concerning its own preoccupations, American comedy speaks to the group about the individual, and is in this sense closer to the dramatic function of tragedy than to the conventional notion of comedy as 'light relief'. Patrick Kavanagh said that tragedy is merely 'underdeveloped comedy', perhaps an encapsulation of an aspect of the Irish outlook in this regard that has, rather emblematically, been interfered with by a rather narrower British tradition beaming in for more than half a century from across the Irish Sea.

Most Irish comedy of the modern kind works on the principle of imitating something that has been successfully executed in either the US or UK. Because we have been exposed to both models, and have failed to distinguish between them, we don't really have access to a core attitude out of which a successful and consistent model of television comedy might grow. More precisely, Irish comedy has fallen continually between trying to imitate the structure of British comedy and trying to get at the things that seem to relate to ourselves and our own particular experiences, which might align us more closely with the personality of the American comedy we see in the movies and on TV. We can get it right 'accidentally' by means of a good joke, but rarely on the basis of a coherent plan. Thus, we can do it, occasionally, but can never say what it is exactly we have done. Irish comedy essentially succeeds by putting imported ideas into an indigenous key. It lacks the fundamental self-knowledge essential to the consistent and reliable creation of successful, indigenously truthful humour.

There is a further problem in that the core root of inherited Irish comedy is already a convergence of two disparate indigenous traditions: a conventional Dublin music-hall model and the aforementioned comic literature, perhaps the most celebrated in the world. Long before television, Wilde, Beckett and O'Brien had created some of the most perfect comedy ever put down on a page, invariably taking inspiration from the reality of life in the Dublin all three came to know at different times. All three were comedians in the purest degree, all drawing their raw material from a society in which talk always aspired to the condition of comedy, and life had a pronounced knack for playing tricks on the natives. But the twin-tracked tradition of stage and page has presented problems in the modern era, with regard to translating the natural themes of Irish society into jokes for the modern medium of television. Techniques that work on the stage – improvisation, projection, streams of consciousness – are usually death on television, whereas the wordiness of literary comedy is difficult to translate onto the small screen.

One of my favourite comic sketches on television is the one in which Ali G confronts the DUP big cheese Sammy Wilson across the latter's desk in Belfast. It's hard to say whether Sammy knows it's a wind-up or not. You suspect he must, although the exchange gives no sense of being rehearsed:

> Ali asks Sammy: 'So is you Irish?'
> Sammy jumps and grabs the bait: 'No, I'm Bratish'.
> (Translation: British)

Ali's timing is immaculate:

> 'So is you here on holiday?'

It's a great joke, but, for reasons to do with the mystery of laughter, difficult to explain to anyone who doesn't know the politics from the inside out. Superficially, you might think the gag a straightforward stab at Sammy's air of loyalist pomposity, but it's a little more complicated. The 'sting' of the joke is to be located somewhere in the region of Sammy's passionately felt identity, and the ludicrousness – to outsiders – of him claiming the brand of a neighbouring island whose inhabitants regard him as a foreigner. But Sammy is not so much the butt of the joke as the instrument of its delivery. His 'Norn Iron' Unionist sense of being 'Bratish' stirs the memory of a long-running conflict involving many bloody calamities and brings a certain darkness to the undercurrent of the joke, giving the laughter a guilty edge which has to do with the fact that the joke risks excluding a whole tribe of people by virtue of offering them offence. The script is economical, just 13 words, which could scarcely be cut back any further.

It also has a clear point. Way back in the mid-1980s, long before he became a star through *Father Ted*, Dermot Morgan told me:

> Comedy, if it's good comedy, actually has an inbuilt point of view. I think when the writing gets to the stage where you can feel the cutting edge of it, then you're talking about some substance in the humour. How can you claim to be an observer of society if you don't formulate a point of view, if you're just bouncing from one joke to the next?

Eoghan Harris offered a similar analysis:

> Comedy is always serious. It is always bleak. There are no

neutral comedians. Whenever you get a person writing comedy which is allegedly non-political, it is always in support of the status quo.

Without such understandings, Irish comedians of the TV and stand-up varieties remain trapped in outmoded forms of kneejerk mockery and satire – ridiculing long dead institutions and offending the sincere beliefs of elderly spinsters, while the true rigidity of the present moment goes unremarked. Strangely, until *Father Ted*, Dermot Morgan himself seemed to be trapped in precisely such a rigidity, seeing Irish society through his political prejudices rather than through a purely comic viewfinder. His pre-*Father Ted* attempts to reinvent Irish comedy were decidedly mixed. His variety interjections on *The Live Mike* were diverting and highly watchable, but attempts to translate his vision into a show of his own fell apart on the sheer eclecticism of his targets and his desire to inflict a political wound. Driven by a profound artistic craving to address fundamental truths, but perhaps misled by the British model of comedy, Morgan could never quite work out who the enemy was. It wasn't until Graham Linehan and Arthur Matthews provided him with a script that allowed him to be himself that he came into his own as a comic genius. Linehan and Matthews were a generation younger than Morgan and therefore accordingly more detached from the things Morgan felt compelled to satirize. Father Ted, although ostensibly dealing in the same material as Morgan's early work as a stand-up (his Father Trendy character for *The Live Mike,* for example), was characterized by a sublimation of its inspiring rage that Morgan himself was unable to achieve as a writer.

Some years after *Father Ted* became a cult hit, I found myself discussing this subject with a group of colleagues from virtually every corner of the globe while attending a journalists' conference in Istanbul. Listening to British journalists expounding on the subject of TV comedy, I noticed two things: one, that they were claiming *Father Ted* as their own, and, two, that they regarded it as primarily a satire on Catholicism, Irish-style.

In fact, *Father Ted* works because it is fundamentally much closer to the American model, which places human beings outside politics and class structure. *Father Ted* is not a satire – it really operates on the basis of an implicit question: what in the name of God do priests do all day? The programme was so unmistakably Irish that it should have been made in Ireland, but wasn't and probably couldn't have been. If it had been tried at home, it might well have fallen flat in an attempt to make a point, which is perhaps related to why its success has not been exploited in the home territory. The problem is that, seeing its success through British eyes, we identify only those elements which correspond to the social revolution which coincidentally accompanied it, namely recent scandals enveloping the Irish Catholic Church. The conventional wisdom is that the point of *Father Ted* was to be 'daring', to heroically 'take on' a powerful institution. But this has relatively little to do with why *Father Ted* was funny, and remains so almost regardless of what happens in the social realm.

My favourite theory of laughter is that of the French philosopher Henri Bergson. In his essay on laughter, Bergson proposes that all humour derives fundamentally from rigidity in human behaviours and affairs. We find funny, he says, anything that breaks away from the natural patterns of human life, by becoming mechanistic and predictable. Fundamentally what makes people laugh is the absence of alertness and elasticity in the object of ridicule, which is to say forms of sclerosis deriving from the culture of the group. What we find funny, it seems, are those elements in each other which deviate from the law of life, which abjures rigidity and mechanization. This expresses itself in what Bergson calls 'absentmindedness' – which can embrace the concept of a man falling down a manhole, or the idea of a Catholic priest who thinks the story of Jesus is 'mad, Ted'.

Adapting Bergson's thesis, we might say that *Father Ted* was funny because it placed its characters in an apparently rigid lifestyle and uniform – that of Catholic priests – and then allowed their lives to proceed in a manner which constantly defied and indeed transcended this inflexibility. Or, to put it somewhat theologically: comedy occurs with the insinuation that, in spite of whatever certainties we may hold to on this score, we do not have free will, but are mere puppets on wires being pulled by heavenly – or hellish – forces.

There was an interesting moment in the TV documentary I referred to above in which one of the participants commented on a prior attempt at comedy involving priests which featured on RTE television back in the 1980s. That sit-com, *Leave It to Mrs O'Brien*, has become, for Irish comedians, almost iconic in its indisputable unfunniness. Oddly, in its essentials it exhibited a number of remarkable similarities to *Father Ted*: The Mrs O'Brien in question being a priests' housekeeper, and the 'joke', such as it was, centred on the idea of priests behind the closed doors of the parochial house. In fact, several contributors to that documentary referred to *Leave It To Mrs O'Brien* as though it represented everything that was wrong about previous Irish attempts to do comedy on television. This particular commentator, however, criticised it for a different reason: that it had given an entirely wrong impression of priests – as loveable, eccentric characters – when in fact, she appeared to imply, they were all awful paedophiles whom comedians should have been opposing and exposing with every fibre of their talent.

But you could make the same accusation against *Father Ted*, which is redeemed 'only' because it is funny, and is funny mainly because it manages to see beyond the ideological obsessions of the generation which has taken it to its heart without really asking why. *Father Ted*, no more than *Leave It To Mrs O'Brien,* does not take on the role of satirising or condemning – it simply plays situations for laughs, and by virtue of its success in this endeavour appears to acquire a sense of having succeeded as a kind of satire by accident. *Father Ted* is funny not because it exposed Catholic priests for what they were or are, but because it gets to something that nothing else has got to: the felt rigidity that bedevils the religious sense among believers and unbelievers alike. The religious question, more than any other, exposes the human vulnerability to the most fundamental fears and doubts. To hear even an obvious gobdaw like Father Dougal breathlessly express the same doubts felt by most people is a kind of liberation that transcends any political aspect. The laughter it provokes is personal, but has the appearance of being something else.

I have a certain fascination with the seeming insatiability of our modern appetites for humour. Everywhere you go, laughter-as-commodity is being peddled – on the TV, the radio, the newsstands, the internet. Since the start of the economic crisis, it often seems that the imperative to make one another laugh has grown in something like inverse proportion to the economic outlook. For a while there, my teenage daughter had a fondness for watching TV comedy panel shows back to back – those ones with Stephen Fry and Ian Hislop being so relentlessly clever that you think their jaws might fall off from laughing at their own jokes. I used to ask her: Do those guys ever cry? She said I wasn't funny.

Maybe not, but the point is that laughter should always arise from human situations, which implies spontaneity as a *sine qua non*. The industrial variety of laughter has in common with porn and prostitution that, being devoid of affection, it ultimately becomes reduced to spasm for its own sake. And, as my mother used to say, it's all great fun until someone loses an eye. With some honourable exceptions, Irish comedians tend to talk like prostitutes rather than lovers. They know about technique and position, but seem indifferent to the underlying energies. They are far too pleased with themselves, on far too little evidence. They exist by imitation and prejudice, and thus are evaded by the possibility of genius.

The sad reality of Irish TV comedy is that the most impressive success of recent years has been *Mrs Brown's Boys* – essentially an extended fart gag – which has become one of the biggest comedy hits on British television in decades, and has consistently topped the ratings in Ireland also. The brainchild of stand-up comedian Brendan O'Carroll, the show subjects highly conventional styles of humour – mainly toilet-based – to a postmodern twist. Although constructed to the rules of standard sitcom, it's played before a live audience, thus creating a secondary layer of humour which arises from the occasional breakdowns due to slips or corpsing, which are ignored or glossed over, adding to the 'joke'. The effect is a strange sense of knowingness, which implies that the nature of the humour, likewise, is intentionally 'ironic', thus giving it a veneer of respectability which elevates it slightly and gives the audience a license to enjoy it without qualms. This, after all the talk, is what Irish comedy – at its most successful – has come to.

There is a reason for this which has very little to do with comic talent. The real problem has to do with political *nous* and fear of venturing into unapproved areas. The failure to translate the essence of Irish humour to television is not a problem arising from the timidity of broadcasters – as is often implied by comedians – but from something else. It relates to Henri Bergson's notion of rigidities, but also to what true laughter might be about.

It is said that there are essentially three kinds of jokes: jokes provoking a release of nervous energy; jokes that engage joker and audience in a conspiracy of superiority and jokes that work off an incongruous combination of understandings. The Ali G gag described above is a great joke because it ticks all three boxes.

A good joke often brings the surprise of realising that we share with others perceptions and judgements we considered out of bounds, or perhaps have put down to what might be called our sense of our own unspeakable inner ecology and now discover are held in common with others. The joke, under the protection of the form, tells us that we are not alone in our guilty and irreverent thoughts. It brings out into the open what might otherwise stay festering inside. That's maybe why they call laughter 'the best medicine'.

But a problem arises when new forms of repression begin to exercise themselves in reaction to the old ones. Several generations of Irish comics have made copious hay from lampooning the picaresque figures of the recent social memory – Eamon de Valera, John Charles McQuaid, etc. – and ridiculing various aspects of Ireland's past – Catholicism, nationalism, and so forth.

Comedians, by and large, regard themselves as belonging to the more progressive movements in social thinking and action. This, indeed, is intrinsic to their function. However, a problem arises when a failure to achieve the natural, cyclical turning over of political and cultural change in a society causes public thought to become stuck at a certain point. This occurred in Ireland from roughly the end of the 1980s, when, apparently by process of osmosis, a consensus was arrived at concerning questions of progress, modernity and political/social virtue. By definition, artists, including comedians, signed up to this agenda, which would have been unproblematic if the cycle of culture had continued to operate normally, and that generation of comics has been succeeded by another, with new ideas. However, since the late 1980s, the needle of ideological consciousness in the public square of Irish self-understanding has remained stuck on the same concepts of what constitutes public good and bad (liberalism, leftism, and progressivism are considered self-evidently virtuous, whereas dissenting from them is regarded as by definition a reactionary activity). Hence, several generations of comedians have come and gone, making jokes about the same people and phenomena, by virtue of adhering to the same ideological blueprint.

The joke about a society – if we can reduce it like this for the purposes of argument – cannot remain constant. As change occurs, as power shifts, the joke should change, and with it the target of the comedian. If this fails to happen, comedy begins to contribute to the shoring-up of the cultural sclerosis which has invisibly stymied the society's capacity to see forward to the new joke that might help to provoke a fresher understanding. By now the target of comedians should not be the greybeards of the 1950s and 1960s, nor the hollowed out husk of the Catholic Church, but perhaps the faux liberalism which sustains itself by maintaining such scapegoats long after their power has ebbed.

In such conditions, most comics fail in their vocation not because of a lack of comic talent but because they can't see past the ideological phantoms blocking up the public square. But this, for the avoidance of doubt, does not mean that Irish comics are incapable of making people laugh. They are indeed capable of provoking the semblance of laughter in their like-minded audiences. They are good at provoking releases of nervous energy in their audiences, because this merely calls for a minor shock element. They are even better at nurturing conspiracies of superiority – generating gales of apparent laughter by affirming the assumptions of the group, as opposed to awakening individual souls to the possibility of a deeper layer of commonality. It's interesting to observe this kind of comedian at work: he (or increasingly she) tends to rely on extravagant movement and a disposition of feigned laughter which threatens to burst out of him/her and almost prevents him/her from speaking. This is all part of the weaponry the comic employs to draw his audience into the conspiracy. All comedy is about conspiracy between comic and audience, but this essential condition does not describe all that comedy is or could be. The true comedian goes deeper to unsettle his audience and its sense of self-satisfaction. The true comic risks alienating his audience by moving ahead of it.

What seems or sounds like laughter is not always about humour. If you listen to the sound of laughter in any conventional context and look then to the spark that set it off, you will begin to notice that most of the responses are no more than reflex signals unconsciously calculated to smooth the course of human interaction and communication. The audience is signalling by its laughter that it approves of what the comedian is saying. In fact, if you pay close attention to the audience in attendance at this form of comic performance, you'll notice that many people who appear to be laughing are actually going 'ha-ha-ha', as though they've suddenly manifested in a frame of a cartoon.

One of the symptoms of a cultural sclerosis such as I've outlined is a kind of manic obsession with laughter directed at the imagined enemy by those seeking to persuade themselves that they remain a beleaguered opposition to some tyrannical and systematic imposition upon their freedoms. The fact that their cultural enemies are long dead does nothing to inhibit them. The laughter created by comedians in such a context, therefore, is really the laughter of solidarity and common purpose, a conspiratorial hilarity directed at the imagined ogres who bear down upon the huddled group of comic and audience. Without a broader vision, comedy tends toward laziness, and becomes content with obvious targets, of whom there is no shortage in the recent history of Irish life. The present, however, tends to decant comedic opportunity under the most rigorous scrutiny only, requiring comedians to cleanse themselves of prejudices and assumptions, which always involves the risk that they may lose their existing audiences. This is why, more and more, comics rely on passable imitations of political and other figures, getting tame laughs for accuracy rather than insight. And this is why celebrations of Irish comedy tend increasingly to be retrospective. We thought we had found our laughter mojo, but then the moment passed when our comics became too pleased with themselves on account of their upholding of the beliefs and ideas of right-thinking people. Generally speaking, contemporary Irish comics have succeeded at the level of nurturing groups of like-minded souls whose laughter is generated out of their beleaguered, rageful sense of fellow feeling arising from cultivated remembrance of selected episodes of oppression in the past. This is partly why *Father Ted* has become a sacred cow of Irish comedy – not just because it is funny (though it is) but because it draws its audience together in a gleeful huddle at the idea of Catholic priests being taken the piss out of.

Comedy should be a moral force. Bergson said that laughter is above all a corrective, and that what it corrects is men's manners. This, clearly, is what Irish comedians have in mind when they praise their own achievements in the laughter trade, but they rarely reflect upon what their denunciations imply or what improvements they might propose. They assume that it's all obvious on the basis that right-thinking people – who also happen to be the people with the right sense of humour – appear to share their prejudices.

Since all humour is group-based, the things that are regarded as funny tell a great deal about what the group considers to be in need of changing. But there is a difficulty, as Bergson outlines: Society, in order to effect its own efficient operation, imposes a certain degree of automatism on its individual members, seeking to reduce everyone to an approximate common mentality, agreeing broadly on things and seeing things broadly in the same generalized way. This is regarded as a necessary element of communal living. And yet, taken beyond some unspecified point, this automatism rightly becomes the target of the laughter of the group, as though some architect of human society has contrived this device to prevent the necessary process of homogenization from going too far. Thus, humour plays a vital role in the operation of society, though not exactly the kind of subversion often fondly imagined by many modern comedians. Instead, humour becomes the instrument for waking people up to that which is really oppressing them – or at least for preventing the sleep becoming too deep – providing a kind of controlled explosion of inner awareness as to the extent of the control outwardly exerted upon the individual in order to make him into a 'good' citizen.

In the documentary I referred to earlier, the comic actor – 'Father Jack' in *Father Ted* – Frank Kelly observed: 'After a revolution, the first people to be shot are the comedians.' This might be a comedian's self-aggrandizement, but there is also a core truth to it. The comic rightly regards his calling as a subversive one – that of undermining societal oppressions and tyrannies. In practice, however, the most effective comic often directs his fire at the individual, serving both to provoke the individual into wakefulness or, conversely, carrying out society's dirty work of keeping him in his place. Comedy intimidates, as Bergson says, by intimidating. It is neither compassionate nor just. It remorselessly seeks out the fear and the hidden secret. As Mel Brooks said: 'Tragedy is when I cut my finger. Comedy is when you fall down an open sewer and die'. In all but the most rudimentary jokes, there is a withdrawal of affection. Even the chicken crossing the road is subjected to mockery for its absence of ambition.

From the viewpoint of the powerful, comedy can assist the maintenance of the balance of societal control by providing a kind of cultural inoculation – against both any separatist tendency of the individual and the unexploitable sleep of the sheep. From the viewpoint of the powerful, the ideal situation is to have people laughing (though not at the aforementioned powerful). Inadequate comedy – i.e., comedy that falls short of its highest calling to subversion – becomes most deeply reactionary when it hunts people into the centre, where they become least dangerous to the establishment. It achieves this by alerting the individual to the existence of 'types' who have fallen into the conditions inviting mockery, and placed him on guard against the possibility that such eccentricities may become detectable in themselves. Thus, the paradox: the 'rebel' comic is capable of becoming essential to the survival of the system – by providing forms of deterrence against true forms of rebellion. Thus, as Eoghan Harris warned, comedy can be called into the service of the status quo – albeit here an unacknowledged liberal establishment, still pretending to be in opposition. It is arguable that, in the past twenty years or so, Irish comedy has been called into service by the new ideologies of liberal progressivism and that, far from serving to confront power, it has acted on behalf of the nouveau power-wielders in policing loyalty to the new orthodoxies.

What, then, are the 'rigidities', where the lack of alertness, besetting Irish society at this moment? Since, as Bergson puts it, 'comedy is a game, a game that imitates life', what are the elements of Irish life that we need to pay attention to – both for the purposes of producing a more truthful comedy and rectifying the rigidities that give rise to comedy in the first place? Given that Irish comedy has failed to enlighten us about the deeper nature of our actual culture, are there things we can learn from its failures that will lead us to the right answers?

The problem is that, if you approach these questions from an ideological position, you will almost by definition arrive at an answer that is out of date. An inferior comedian depends, essentially, on the current prejudices of the society. As these prejudices themselves become rigidified, outmoded, a problem arises: What, then, does the comic make his material from – the low-hanging fruit of the popular mentality or the stuff that cuts underneath to the subtexts to reveal what is really happening but remains unsayable? The best comedians are those who lay bare the inner turmoil held in place by society's conventions and protocols. But unless comedians are prepared to break out of their comfort zones, the rigidities remain undetected and everyone gets a pain in the face from laughing at the same stupid gags.

True laughter – that which touches on something hitherto unacknowledged but actually, really present – is comparatively rare. In fact, true laughter is impossible to fake or even to replicate without an authentic catalyst. Try to laugh, or reproduce in yourself the sounds and effects of laughter and you'll see how hard it is. Modern Irish comedians are not so good at jokes that work off the more furtive, surreptitious understandings residing behind the masks we sport in public spaces.

There have been a few great Irish comedians. Kevin McAleer, for example, who for a couple of years in the 1980s enthralled audiences with his strange, existential refractions of Irish reality – depicting his family, grandparents and all, on the cusp of a changing Ireland exposed to all kinds of new impulses and provocations. 'Ah now', he would reflect in a rumination about the pop singer Gary Glitter (later a convicted paedophile, which darkens the joke retroactively), 'the Glitters were all great singers'.

But there is nothing or nobody on the current Irish scene remotely approaching McAleer's level of playfulness. Most of the more successful comedians are merely impersonators, doing much the same thing as Frank Kelly and Eamon Morrissey on *Hall's Pictorial*, forty years ago. The laughter is far more frequently a signal of admiration for the accuracy of the mimicry, or an agreement with the implicit sentiment, than an involuntary response to an actual joke. Moreover, this kind of comedy doesn't operate primarily from the desire to generate laughter, but rather from a determination to continue repudiating what is held in common as the 'enemy' or the 'evil' bearing down upon us all.

Most modern Irish comedians cannot seem to get beyond the level of making their like-minded fellows laugh at a shared, if imagined, enemy. The problem is not that they are insufficiently 'funny', but that their politics do not permit them to penetrate the surface of things. They like to react, and to be seen reacting. But they are scared of taking the risk of ambiguity by abandoning the easy reflex offered by the collectivised 'memory' of a shared slight or offence, and asking their audience what they might be like underneath the detritus of commonly experienced culture or politics. They also lack the penetration and ambition of someone like Martin McDonagh, who as an 'intimate outsider' in Ireland was able to see things more clearly than the insider.

Irish comedy, then – in both its stage and televisual incarnations – fails to plumb the true comic depths of the Irish personality and experience for two reasons. One is that it simultaneously contrives to imitate two contrasting styles of comedy – US existentialism and UK class-based humour – resulting in a confusion of both purpose and outcomes. The other reason is more subtle: that Irish comedians tend to be people who do not take life seriously and are more interested in projecting attitudes than truly exploring reality. Indeed, many of them appear to go into comedy because they think it a suitable refuge from the gravity of reality. They think life a big joke and that mocking some received enemy is sufficient to qualify them as comedians. But their efforts rarely go beyond an invitation to the like-minded to engage in therapeutic exercises of call-and-response. And the laughter that ensues is rarely more than a chorus of complacent consensualism.

10 | 'Synge and "Protestant Comedy"'

Christopher Collins

> Humour is the test of morals.
> -J.M. Synge.[1]

Four out of Synge's seven full-length plays are comedies and many of his playlets are predicated upon a humorous clash of frames that elicit laughter. What predicates the elicitation of laughter in Synge's comedies is socio-political commentary; never should we mistake humour in Synge's plays as humour for humour's sake. These clashes of political frames can be explained by philosophies of humour and laughter such as the Incongruity Theory (*The Shadow of the Glen* [1903], *The Tinker's Wedding* [1909]) and the Carnivalesque (*The Playboy of the Western World* [1907]). However, there is one theory of laughter and humour that Synge's comedies appositely measure against: the Relief Theory. The Relief Theory postulates that laughter is elicited by a physiological approach to the identification of humour. When presented with the comic event, the reader of the comic frame engages in a social transaction between joker and listener, thereby relieving nervous or repressed energies, frustrations and anxieties. There is no manuscript evidence to suggest that Synge consciously orchestrated his comic dramaturgy in accordance with the Relief Theory because he believed that 'all theorising is bad for the artist'.[2] However, it is plausible to postulate that Synge considered laughter and humour from this philosophical persuasion because he maintained,

> the heartiness of real and frank laughter is a sign that cannot be mistaken that what we laugh [at] is not out of harmony with that instinct of sanity that we call so many names.[3]

For Synge laughter was cathartic, and his dramaturgy often attempts to exploit the gap between actions of amusement and reactions of laughter. Synge's comedies ask the spectator to create binaries between objects of ridicule and subjects of social sincerity. An avid reader of Molière and François Rabelais and a keen spectator of melodrama, Synge's comic strategies are marked by extraordinary situations, mistaken identities, ironies and reversals. But Synge wasn't simply a writer of farce. He was a ruthlessly caustic dramatist who could easily turn his hand to writing satire; his comedies are farcical but barbs of political commentary critically underwrite them. And so, if the efficacy of farce is in its ability to elicit laughter because the action is very much dependent on there being something at stake, then in Synge's comedies there is something doubly at stake: political intervention. Synge was intensely political and he used humour in order to provoke political reaction. Nevertheless, he is often considered to be a dramatist who was, in W.B. Yeats's famous phrase, 'unfitted to think a political thought'.[4] Synge was political; his closest friend Stephen MacKenna advocated that he would 'die for the theory' that Synge was intensely political 'but one thing kept him quiet – he hated publicity, cooperation and lies. [...] the lying that gathered round the political movement seemed to him to soil it utterly, and all that had part in it'.[5] By his own admission, Synge was unable to 'believe in trying to entice people by a sort of political atmosphere that has nothing to do with *our* real dramatic movement',[6] and so he channelled his political sentiments into comic plays. A salient dramaturgical motif in Synge's comedies is to ridicule Ireland's Catholic bourgeoisie and their unswerving adherence to Roman orthodoxy. Comic dramaturgy such as this is indicative of Synge's rearguard defence of Anglo-Irish sovereignty. Using Synge's unpublished manuscripts, this essay will consider how Synge wrote *The Well of the Saints* (1905) not just as a comedy that ridiculed Catholic Ireland, but also as a comedy that supported Protestant Ireland, by considering how the character of the Saint in the play is a Protestant tramp.

For Synge tramps and tinkers are comic devices with which he can facilitate political intervention by means of comic performance. Consider the dramaturgical role of the tramps and the tinkers in his other comic plays that contain tramps: *The Shadow of the Glen, The Playboy of the Western* World and *The Tinker's Wedding*. In all three plays, tramps and tinkers are anathema to greasy mercantilism that Synge associated with Catholic Ireland, and their comic plotting is humorous because it ridicules the mechanical lives that Synge considered to be commensurate with Catholicism. It is true that Synge mythologised his own life as a tramp of genteel poverty, choosing to sign off his letters to his fiancée, Molly Allgood, with the anonym of 'your old Tramp',[7] and while he lived a down-at-heel lifestyle, he certainly wasn't a tramp. At times, his Orientalism of tramps only serves to disclose his privileged position as a member of the Anglo-Irish Ascendancy:

> As he sleeps by Lough Bray and the nightjar burrs and snipe drum over his head and the grouse crow, and heather whispers round him, he hears in their voices the chant of singers in the dark chambers of Japan and the clamour of tambourines and [the] flying limbs of dancers he knew in Algeria, and the rustle of golden fabrics of the east. As the trout splash in the dark water at his feet he forgets the purple moorland that is round him and hears waves that lap round a boat in some southern sea. He is not to be pitied.[8]

The Saint-as-tramp in *The Well of the Saints* is Synge's fetishisation of a nomadic lifestyle, far removed from the demands of Irish modernity. Fetishisation such as this barely belies Synge's own insecurities of an Ascendancy class that struggled to orchestrate Irish capitalism: better to escape to the grime of the country, than to face the sweat of the city. Significantly, the similarity between the Saint-as-tramp and Synge-as-tramp, serves to suggest that the Saint's likeness to a tramp – just like Synge's – is a construct that is transmogrified in order to offer comic relief for the Protestant Ascendancy when clashed with a bourgeois Catholic frame of analysis. With this clash of frames there was also room for an intervention into the realm of the political; what was at stake was the relief of Roman Catholicism being ridiculed at the expense of Anglo-Irish Protestantism. Therefore, it was essential that Synge clashed two frames: the Saint as a Protestant tramp with 'worn feet' and 'welted knees' and 'dirty feet [that] is trampling the world'[9] and a gullible Catholic community. In order to make such an intervention, Synge's 'Protestant comedy'[10] as he called it, was very much dependent upon eliciting laughter in order to relieve Anglo-Irish social frustration and class anxiety. And in order to do that, Synge had to use farcical strategies in order to satirize a newly enfranchised Catholic middle class.

'THE HATE OF HIS MIND'[11]

In September 1889, Synge began to reject his mother's strict diet of evangelical Protestantism. In truth, Mrs Synge had expected the worst for quite some time; as early as April 1888, she had written a despairing letter to her son Robert in Argentina, maintaining that she could find 'no spiritual life in my poor Johnnie, there *may* be some, but it is not visible to my eyes, he is very reserved & shut *up* on the subject, & if I say any thing to him he never answers me, so I don't know in the least! The hate of his mind – it is a trying[,] state *very* trying'.[12] Something needed to be done. On 17 September, 1889, the Rev. John Dowse, curate of the church on Zion Road, Rathgar, Co. Dublin, knocked on the door of the family home. Rev. Dowse took his strict instructions from Mrs Synge in the drawing room before taking the younger Synge into the parlour, whereupon he advised him to accept the Lord as his saviour.[13] The precocious teenager held his ground and, in December, 1889 Synge informed his mother that he would no longer attend church or partake in Biblical study.[14] Synge's reading of Charles Darwin's *On the Origin of Species by Means of Natural Selection* at the age of twenty-four consummated his suspicion towards Protestantism[15] and after reading Darwin's implicit critique of the Lord as the Divine Creator he began to 'read works of Christian evidence at first with pleasure, soon with doubt, and at last in some cases with derision'.[16] Flatly refusing to even discuss Protestantism with his family, Synge was truly isolated not just from his family but also from his own class. However, while Synge claimed that Christianity remained 'a difficulty and occasioned terror to me for many years'[17] and that he had no time for talk of 'tedious matters of theology',[18] caution should be heeded over reductive claims that Synge completely rejected Protestantism. As Synge was dying on his own – albeit surrounded by his nurses – the Bible was firmly pressed against his chest and he repeated a mantra over and over again: 'God have mercy on me, God forgive me.'[19] Protestantism, then, was something that Synge played hide and seek with all his life, and as long as Synge held a lingering attachment to evangelical Protestantism, he also held an attachment to his Anglo-Irish Ascendancy upbringing.

Synge first began to write a comedy that strictly advocated Protestantism in 1903: *The Well of the Saints*. That Protestantism orbited *The Well of the Saints* can hardly be overstated. By way of example, Synge wrote an impassioned letter to Lady Gregory complaining that 'Miss Laird has been frozen out [of the company] because she is a Protestant'[20]; Miss Helen S. Laird (Honor Lavelle) was an original member of the Irish National Theatre Society and she played Maurya in the premiere of *Riders to the Sea* (1904), but she was afforded no place in *The Well of the Saints* cast. The play went through several drafts until its premiere in 1905 and, concomitant with this particular advocacy of Protestantism is his 1904 work, *Bride and Kathleen: A Play of '98*, a playlet that Frank Fay commissioned. Fay feared that the spectators at the Abbey Theatre were of the opinion that the company's theatre practice was 'irreligious and politically unsound'[21] and so, quite surprisingly, Fay asked the rock 'n' roll kid of the Abbey Theatre to allay his fears. Synge presented two women fleeing from rebels and English soldiers: Bride, a 'Papist Woman' and Kathleen, a 'Protestant Woman'.[22] Both women are on the run – Bride is fleeing the Republican rebels whereas Kathleen is fleeing the English soldiers. At this juncture, it is reasonable to postulate that Bride is, in fact, a supporter of Unionism (a political persuasion traditionally aligned with Protestantism) and conversely, the Protestant Kathleen is a supporter of Republicanism (a political persuasion traditionally aligned with Catholicism). Yeats, who was presented with the playlet, summarised the action between the two women as a 'quarrel about religion, abusing the Pope or Queen Elizabeth and Henry VIII, but in low voices, for the one fears to be ravished by soldiers, the other by the rebels'.[23] According to Yeats, the play ended with 'one woman [deciding to go] out because she would sooner any fate than such wicked company'.[24] That Synge would adopt such a political persuasion is not surprising, which is why the playlet ends abruptly with Kathleen's bitter defence of Protestantism:

> **Bride**. Heretic? What made them call you a heretic?
> **Kathleen.** What is it they call any good Christian Protestant but a heretic now?[25]

Synge is defending Protestantism against claims of heresy; sentiments in this playlet are thinly disguised as Kathleen's, especially when the dramatist was a staunch supporter of the Protestant Irish Nationalists: Henry Grattan, Robert Emmet and Charles Stewart Parnell.[26] The irony involved in such a comic exchange exploits the transaction between colonial dominance and postcolonial dissidence, precisely because Bride and Kathleen do not conform to stereotypical character types. This is a situation comedy that is very much dependent on mistaken identities; the dramatist thought that it would have been amusing to see a Catholic Republican fleeing from the 1798 rebels while a Protestant supports them. But the comedy is underwritten by sincerity: Synge's privileging of Protestantism. Eric Weitz has suggested that laughter 'offers a most dramatic way of subduing a group of people',[27] but the rebel Synge never got the chance to subdue his audience. Left unfinished in the archive, the playlet was never

performed because it was everything that Fay was looking to avoid: it
was irreligious and politically hostile to a predominantly Catholic,
bourgeois audience. This is why Gregory's summation of Synge's
political persuasion offers a greater degree of critical insight: 'he
seemed to look on politics and reforms with a sort of tolerant
indifference, though he spoke once of something that has happened as
"the greatest tragedy since Parnell's death"'.[28] Synge often intervened in
the realm of the political if he could support Anglo-Irish Protestant
rebels. Like Kathleen, Synge advocated for Republicanism with
Protestant hegemony, and he thought he could achieve such political
intervention by using comedy to demonstrate that Protestants could
lead Ireland's postcolonial project. *Bride and Kathleen: A Play of '98*
should be seen as a precursor to *The Well of the Saints*, because in that
play Synge uses farcical comic strategies in order to advocate for the
Protestant religion over Catholicism and, in the Ireland of Synge's time,
a satirical conceit such as this was extremely provocative. Not all
humour elicits laughter.

'CARELESS IRISH HUMOUR'[29]

The provenance of *The Well of the Saints* (hereafter, *The Well*) lies in
two sources, one primary and the other secondary. For the purposes of
considering Synge as a comic playwright, it is the secondary source that
is of critical concern.[30] The secondary source is Andrieu de la Vigne's
Moralité de l'aveugle et du Boiteux, which Synge read in Professor
Louis Petit de Julleville's *Histoire du theâtre en France: La Comédie et
les Mœurs en France au Moyen Age*.[31] Synge first began studying with
de Julleville in 1895,[32] but eight years later, when Synge began writing
The Well he returned to his former Professor's work and made notes on
the comic morality tale that was first performed in 1456.[33] Synge's
verbatim notes on "*Moralités Religieuses*" (Religious Morality) include
the following summary of de la Vigne's play:

> La moralité d'André de la Vigne s'ouvre au moment où le saint
> vient d'expirer. Son corps est resté exposé au fond du théâtre,
> et l'on va tout à l'heure l'emporter à l'église en procession
> solennelle. Deux mendiants sont en scène; l'un d'eux est
> aveugle, et ne marche qu'en tâtonnant, l'autre est boiteux, et gît
> au milieu de la route. Mais n'ayons pas trop grand' pitié d'eux.
> Ce sont deux paresseux, deux ivrognes; quoiqu'ils gémissent
> d'une voix plaintive; l'aveugle en disant:

> L'aumosne au povre disetteux,
> Qui jamais nul jour ne vit goutte.

et le paralytique:
Faites quelque bien au boiteux
Qui bouger ne peult pour la goutte.[34]

Clowning such as this runs right to the heart of *The Well* as Synge focuses his attention on the trials and tribulations of two blind beggars, Mary and Martin Doul, who are temporarily relieved of their blindness by a saint.

Identification of the Saint-as-tramp is dependent on Synge's unpublished musings on Irish hagiography in relation to his drafts of the play. It is true that individual saints first conducted the evangelisation of the Irish populace and, as J.N. Hillgarth has suggested, these saints were 'holy men who lived a life which alternated periods as hermits with periods as wandering preachers'.[35] This is precisely the character that Synge draws in *The Well*, where the Saint is characterised as 'a wandering Friar'.[36] However, the distinction between *The Well* and the material conditions of fifth century Ireland that Hillgarth describes is that Synge set the play in '*some lonely mountainous district on the east of Ireland, one or more centuries ago*'.[37] This is Greenane, near Ballinatone, County Wicklow (the play briefly held the title *The Crossroads of Grianan*)[38] and if the play was first performed in 1905 then Synge sets the play in the eighteenth century, a time when Popular Catholicism defined material conditions in Ireland.

The so-called Saint exploits the Catholic laity's residual attachment to Popular Catholicism. Popular Catholicism is not strictly syncretism between pre-Christian and Catholic beliefs but a substratum of Catholicism that authenticated pre-Christian cultural residue; as Michael P. Carroll points out, 'Irish popular Catholicism was in fact characterised by a set of emphases that were internally consistent but quite different from the emphases characteristic of official Catholicism.'[39] For example, in pre-Christian Ireland wells were considered to be sacred and the Catholic Church Christianised them through a process of dedication to a Saint; this is precisely what happened on the Aran Islands with what Synge refers to as the well of 'The Four Beautiful Persons',[40] which makes a guest appearance in *The Well* as 'a place across a bit of the sea, where there is an island, and the grave of the four beautiful saints'.[41] The Saint, then, arrives in Wicklow from the Aran Islands, a space and place where, as Synge admits, Catholicism is troubled by 'the cries of pagan desperation'.[42] Irish Popular Catholicism in the eighteenth century placed a strong emphasis on the lives of the saints, which is why Martin Doul says that he has 'heard the priests a power of times making great talk and praises of the beauty of the saints.'[43] However, while an emphasis was placed upon holy wells and saints, the efficacy of this belief was predicated upon a pseudo-mythology of saints in fifth-century Ireland not, as Synge dramatises, a saint that arrives in a community out of the blue; in essence, the saint is at least ten centuries too late. Synge's comic implication, then, is clear: the Saint in *The Well* is likened to (but actually is not) a wandering saint from the fifth century and his Saint is similarly faced with an Irish populace that gives considerable credence to those so-called backward pre-Christian sensibilities found in Popular Catholicism: the ability for holy groundwater to cure blindness. In this comic framing Synge exploits the implied efficacy of a Popular Catholicism ritual (that holy water can cure blindness) to satirize the orthodoxy of Roman Catholicism in the Ireland of his own time; Roman Orthodoxy was only achieved after the Devotional Revolution in 1875.[44] That this ritual of Popular Catholicism ultimately fails, and the Douls regain their blindness, allows Synge to demonstrate that the efficacy of contemporary Catholic ritual is predicated on spurious beliefs; in this clash of comic frames, the Saint may be implicit in the humour, but the satire is directed at the Catholic Church's appropriation of pre-Christian beliefs. The legitimacy of the humour, then, is very much dependent on Catholicism being the butt of the joke. However, the Roman orthodoxy of Synge's Saint is in considerable doubt; as Mary Doul suggests, the saint is 'a simple fellow, and it's no lie'.[45] The character of the Saint, then, has a mistaken identity and this mistaken identity is the fulcrum upon which humour in *The Well* balances because it affords Synge the opportunity to construct the Catholic community in Greenane as one that believes in the miraculous powers of a tramp disguised as a saint.

Timmy, a blacksmith who proves to be the Saint's closest ally throughout the play, heralds the Saint's arrival in Greenane. However, while Timmy may claim that the Saint is a servant of 'the Almighty God',[46] in an earlier draft of *The Well* these words are visibly struck out in pencil and right up until the penultimate draft of the play Timmy claims that the Saint is 'a holy man' and a 'sort of saint I think they call him'.[47] The Saint seems to be a precursor to the charlatan of *The Playboy of the Western World*. In that comedy, Christy Mahon is followed by a group of Mayo girls that are 'after walking four miles to be listening to [him]'[48] carrying presents such as 'a brace of duck's eggs', 'a pat of butter', 'a little cut of cake' and 'a little laying pullet' that was 'crushed at the fall of night by the curate's car';[49] in a similar fashion, the 'young girls' of Greenane are 'walking after the saint' while 'carrying things in their hands, and they walking as easy as you'd see a child walk, who'd have a dozen eggs in her bib'.[50] And just like Christy, who says that 'this is a fine country for young lovely girls',[51] the Saint believes that 'young girls' are the 'cleanest holy people you'd see walking the world'.[52] If the Saint has a mistaken identity, then commensurate with this farcical strategy is the comedy of the situation that Synge places his characters in. In this situation comedy there is something at stake: the efficacy of the cure for the Douls' blindness, which inevitably fails. And when the comedy of the situation is coupled with the Saint's mistaken identity, comic ironies and reversals are soon summoned to exploit humour.

The cure of the Douls' blindness may only be fleeting but it presents Synge with a frame in which he can present gags, jokes and routines that are indicative of situation comedy. According to Irish hagiography those members of the laity that offended a saint's honour either through the telling of lies or by the stealing of his or her crozier and/or bell were said to be struck down by divine power. Conversely, those that venerated the saint and his/her power were said to be miraculously cured of whatever ailed them. Irish folk belief attached considerable importance to the saint's Vestments, which were said to 'remain dry in a rainstorm or when thrown into water'.[53] However, the populace of Greenane fail to abide by this belief and Molly Byrne attempts to mock the Saint's divine power by asking Martin Doul to 'put his big cloak on you, the way we'd see how you'd look, and you a saint of the Almighty God'.[54] In a similar tone, the Saint admits that the only vestment he wears is a bunch of 'old sacks, and skin covering [his] bones'.[55] The Douls in particular are expected to offer their respect to the Saint's vestments because they are the Saint's supplicants, but they don't, thus offering comic irony. And so, if the Douls do not venerate the Saint's saintliness, and they are unable to be cured by the Saint's powers, the comic irony is furthered by the supposition that the Douls are just like the Saint: all three are Protestant tramps. A supposition such as this is given credence when we consider that Synge struggled to give saints the veneration that the laity gives them. Turning to his undergraduate notebook for Michaelmas Term 1899 at Trinity College Dublin Synge, who had been steadily reading Irish hagiography as part of his Gentleman's Degree, was finding the reading list less than interesting:

> *Nov. 23.* I am sick of the ascetic twaddle of the saints. I will not deny my masculine existence nor rise, if I can rise, by facile abnegation. I despise the hermit and the monk and pity only

the adulterer and the drunkard. There is one world of souls and no flesh and no devil.[56]

The character of the Saint in *The Well* is informed by this logic as Synge ridicules Catholicism. Synge's conjecture is clear, saints should not be seen (as they are in the Catholic faith) as canonised and virtuous figures that intercede through prayer, but everyday people. In this way *The Well* may appear to measure appositely against the Incongruity Theory of humour and laughter; to postulate a saint as not being commensurate with the saintly is incongruous. However, it is because Synge chose to clearly define the religious persuasion of the Saint, that the Relief Theory of humour and laughter can readily explain *The Well*'s comic dramaturgy. By means of comic performance, what Synge is relieving is his repressed desires that were founded on his own class anxieties and he does so by religious proxy: Protestantism.

'THE SAINT IS REALLY A PROTESTANT!' [57]

Reflecting on Dion Boucicault's stage-Irishman, Synge lamented 'how much the modern stage has lost in substituting impersonal wit for personal humour'.[58] It is not that Synge wanted a return to 'the careless Irish humour of which everyone has had too much'[59] but rather, he called for a return to the stock routines of situation comedy that marks Boucicault's melodrama. Placing ordinary characters in extraordinary situations was, in Synge's opinion, universally humorous because 'all decadence is opposed to true humour'.[60] And yet Synge also thought that 'no vice is humorous',[61] that is to say the object of amusement must force the spectator to question his/her coordinates of his/her moral compass. Martin Doul's slapstick clowning as he attempts to woo Molly Byrne is indicative of Synge's ability to allow his comedy to border dangerously on the immoral; Martin '*takes her by the arm and tries to pull her away softly to the right*', while Molly screams, 'leave me go, Martin Doul'.[62] Synge was fully aware that laughter is a social phenomenon and that his comic compass had immoral coordinates. But to Synge this mattered not. Above all else, Synge maintained that 'humour is the test of morals'[63] and he had come to this understanding after reading de Julleville's comic suppositions on "*Moralités Religieuses*". Comedy was at its most effective for Synge when humour questioned religious morals, and the legitimacy of humour in *The Well* was certainly a test of religious morals.

After the premiere of *The Well*, Willie Fay received a disapproving letter from Abbey actress Maire Garvey, who wrote to announce that

Synge's latest play was guilty of debunking Catholic priests. Fay subsequently passed on Garvey's sentiments to the dramatist, who took exception to sentiment:

> Dear Mr. Fay,
> I have just come home from a long day in the country and found your letter waiting for me.
> [...]
> In your letter you quote your objector saying *'these things are not true'*. What put the smile into my head was a scene I saw not long ago in Galway when I saw a young man behaving most indecently to a girl on the road side while two priests sat near by on a seat looking out to sea and pretending not to see what was going on. [...] The way the two priests sat stolidly looking out to sea with this screaming row going on at their elbows tickled my fancy and seemed to me rather typical of many attitudes of the Irish church party...the man in question – in my play – may have been a tinker, stranger, sailor, cattle-drover – God knows what – types with which no priest would dream of interfering. Tell Miss G. – or whoever it may be – that I write of Irish country life I know to be true and I most emphatically will not change a syllable of it because A. B. or C. may think they know better than I do.[64]

Synge readily admits that 'although the priests are learned men, and great scholars, they don't understand the life of the people the same as another man would'.[65] Synge understood that the mechanical rigidity of priests made them humorous and he exploited this in *The Well*. Six months before *The Well* opened at the Abbey, Synge was anticipating organised resistance under the guise of what he classified as 'a Neo-patriotic-Catholic clique'[66] and in anticipation of this resistance the dramatist made it his intention to satirize Catholic bourgeois sentiments towards priests:

> **Mary Doul**. let the two of you not torment me at all. [*she goes out left, with her head in the air*].
> **Martin Doul.** [*stops work and looks after her*]. Well, isn't it a queer thing she can't keep herself two days without looking on my face?
> **Timmy.** [*jeeringly*] Looking on your face is it? And she after going by with her head turned the way you'd see a priest going where there'd be a drunken man in the side ditch talking with a girl.

And so, 'on the spur of the moment', Synge told Miss Garvey 'that the said man in the side ditch was a Protestant and that if the priest had touched him he would have got six months with hard labour for common assault.'[67] Synge's jokes were falling flat. Shocked and appalled by Synge's suggestion that a priest would turn a blind eye to a drunk Protestant in a ditch with a (presumably) Catholic girl, Garvey 'seemed to have thought that [Synge] was sneering at the priest for not doing his duty', to which the dramatist replied that the very idea had 'never entered [his] head'.[68] However, to return to Synge's letter to Willie Fay, Synge pointed out that 'the man in question' in the ditch was a type 'with which no priest would dream of interfering,'[69] the suggestion being that a Catholic priest would not meddle in a Protestant's affairs. Joseph Holloway was also offended by Synge's disrespect for the Catholic Church and he failed to stomach the passage 'about the priest and the pair in the ditch'[70] because it contained 'more than a slight touch of irreverence'[71] and that was without considering the fact that Synge used language 'as freely as a coal-lever or a Billingsgate-fishwife'.[72] Willie Fay, the Abbey's resident producer, was in a tailspin. 'I realised', Fay writes in his dairy, 'that every character in the play from the Saint to Timmy the Smith was bad tempered', and so he asked Synge if 'the Saint might be made into a good-natured easy going-man' but 'Synge would not budge. He said he wanted to write "like a monochrome painting, all in shades of the one colour". I argued that all drama depended on contrast and on tension. All in vain.'[73] And the man in the ditch wasn't the only Protestant in the play.

Synge had mooted the Saint's religious persuasion as early as 1896. Between February and April of that year, Synge found himself in Rome and while staying in Rome he quickly adapted a daily routine: Italian language lessons with Signor Conte Polloni and Italian literature lessons at the Collegio Romano in the morning, before afternoon excursions to the Vatican to admire the Pietà, the Sistine Chapel and, on one occasion, the Pope.[74] The week before Synge quit Rome for Paris, his diary reads thus: 'Vaticano Statute & Sistina. Protestant comedy';[75] even at the spiritual home of the Catholic Church he was thinking of how to write a Protestant comedy and even though the diary entry is laconic and the Protestantism of the Saint is not directly alluded to in the play, Protestantism as subtext is mobilised because, as the dramatist admitted to his friend and walking companion, Padraic Colum: 'the Saint is really a Protestant!'[76] This is why Timmy the smith informs the Greenane parishioners that 'there's a holy man below';[77] according to the Protestant religion, saints are considered to be holy men and/or women; it is only in the Catholic Church that that they are revered through canonisation. Like Sean O'Casey, Synge was a satirist of pomp and while in Rome the dramatist became fascinated with the ostentatious ritual performances that mark the orthodoxy of Roman Catholicism. From that point on, it was only a matter of time before the dramatist would write a comedy that clashed Protestantism with Catholicism. Turning again to Synge's notes from de Julleville's *Histoire du théâtre en France: La Comédie et les Mœurs en France au Moyen Age*, it is reasonable to presume that Synge had been thinking about writing a comedy utilising Protestantism for quite some time because, as he recorded from de Julleville, 'theatre [can be] used by [a] Protestant to attack the Pope'.[78]

In *The Well*, the Catholic laity are held up for ridicule and satirised for believing in the comical powers of a Protestant tramp, saintly posing and posing saintly; the similarities to the life and times of what James Joyce nicknamed 'the tramper Synge'[79] are uncanny. Comic dramaturgy such as this allowed Synge to pay lip service to Protestantism as a religion, while at the same time advocating Anglo-Irish socio-politics. Just like Kathleen in *Bride and Kathleen: A Play of '98*, Synge was an advocate of the grammar of Nationalism only if his own class articulated its language. Synge's comedy, a seditious cocktail of farce and satire had succeeded in doing just that. At least Mrs Synge could take some comfort in her son's dramatisation of a Protestant saint-as-tramp and, as she remarked to her family, if holy water could be upset from the Saint's hands, then her son's 'associations with Nationalists had at least not brought him under the thumb of Rome.'[80] However, the humour inherent in Synge's dramaturgy was not conducive to laughter. Synge may have found relief, but his predominantly Catholic middle-class audience certainly did not. *The Well* failed to pull in the punters; the ridiculing of Catholicism at Protestantism's expense was no laughing matter.[81] But as Synge wrote to the Editor of *The Irish Times*, you were either laughing with him or at him: 'that is often the case, I think, with comedy'.[82]

WORKS CITED

Bourgeois, Maurice. *John Millington Synge and the Irish Theatre*. New York: Benjamin Bloom, 1913.

Carroll, Michael P. "Rethinking Popular Catholicism in Pre-Famine Ireland," *Journal for the Scientific Study of Religion* 34, no. 3 (1995): 354-65.

Fay, W.G. and Catherine Carswell, *The Fays of the Abbey Theatre: An Autobiographical Record*. London: Rich & Cowan, 1935.

Greene, David H. and Edward M. Stephens, *J.M. Synge: 1871-1909*. New York: Macmillan, 1959.

Gregory, Lady Augusta. *New York Public Library Manuscript*, Foster-Murphy Collection. TS Carbon (312), Box 5.

Hillgarth, J.N. *Christianity and Paganism, 350-750: The Conversion of Western Europe*. Philadelphia: University of Pennsylvania Press, 1986.

Holloway, Joseph. National Library of Ireland Manuscript: 1803.

Joyce, James. *Ulyssees*. London: Penguin, 2000.

Julleville, *L Petit de. Histoire du Theâtre en France: La Comédie et les Mœurs en France au Moyen Age*. Paris: Librairie Léopold Cerf, 1886.

Larkin, Emmet. "The Devotional Revolution in Ireland: 1850-75." *American Historical Review* 77, no. 3 (1972): 625-52.

MacKenna, Stephen. National Library of Ireland Manuscript: 13,276.

MacKenna, Stephen. "Synge." *Irish Statesman*. 3 November, 1928.

McCormack, W.J. *Fool of the Family: A Life of J.M. Synge*. London: Weidenfeld and Nicolson, 2000.

Masefield, John. *John M. Synge: A Few Personal Recollections, with Biographical Notes*. Dublin: Cuala, 1971.

Ó hÓgáin, Dáithí. *The Hero in Irish Folk History*. Dublin: Macmillan, 1985.

Roberts, George. 'Memoirs of George Roberts,' *The Irish Times*. 2 August, 1955.

Synge, J.M. *The Collected Letters of John Millington Synge*. Vol. 1, *1871-1907*. Edited by Ann Saddlemyer. Oxford: Clarendon, 1983.

Synge, J.M. *Collected Works*. Vol. 2, *Prose*. Edited by Alan Price. London: Oxford University Press, 1966.

Synge, J.M. *Collected Works*. Vol. 3, *Plays*, Book 1. Edited by Ann Saddlemyer. London: Oxford University Press, 1968.

Synge, J.M. *Collected Works*. Vol. 4, *Plays*, Book 2. Edited by Ann Saddlemyer. Gerrards Cross: Colin Smythe, 1982.

Synge, J.M. The J.M. Synge Manuscripts from the Library of Trinity College Dublin.

Synge, J.M. The Stephens-Synge Manuscripts from the Library of Trinity College Dublin.

Synge, Kathleen. The Stephens-Synge Manuscripts from the Library of Trinity College Dublin.

Yeats, W.B. *Essays and Introductions*. London: Macmillan, 1961.

Yeats, W.B. *Explorations: Selected by Mrs. W.B. Yeats*. New York: Macmillan, 1962.

Weitz, Eric. *The Power of Laughter: Comedy and Contemporary Irish Theatre*. Dublin: Carysfort Press, 2004.

---

[1] J.M. Synge, *The J.M. Synge Manuscripts from the Library of Trinity College Dublin*: 4405, f.10v. Hereafter quoted as *TCD MS*: and folio number. All quotes come with permission of Trinity College Dublin.

[2] *TCD MS*: 4405, f.4v.

[3] Ibid, f.10v.

[4] W.B. Yeats, *Explorations: Selected by Mrs. W.B. Yeats* (New York: Macmillan, 1962), 319.

[5] Stephen MacKenna, "Synge," *Irish Statesman*, 3 November, 1928, 171.

[6] J.M. Synge, *The Collected Letters of John Millington Synge*. Vol. 1, *1871-1907*, ed. Ann Saddlemyer (Oxford: Clarendon, 1983), 81-82. J.M. Synge to F.J. Fay, 10 April, 1904. Emphasis added.

[7] *Collected Letters*. Vol. 1: 178. J.M. Synge to Molly Allgood, 19 July, 1906. This is the first reference to Synge's alias as a tramp.

[8] J.M. Synge, *Collected Works*. Vol. 2, *Prose*, ed. Alan Price (London: Oxford University Press, 1966), 196.

[9] *Collected Works*. Vol. 3, *Plays*, Book 1, ed Ann Saddlemyer (London: Oxford University Press, 1968), 149.

[10] *TCD MS*: 4417, f.18v. Synge writes this on 25 April, 1896.

[11] *TCD SSMS*: 6220, f.15. Kathleen Synge to Robert Anthony Synge, 16 April, 1888. Emphasis in original.

[12] Ibid.

[13] W.J. McCormack, *Fool of the Family: A Life of J.M. Synge* (London: Weidenfeld and Nicolson, 2000), 77.

[14] See, Synge, *Collected* Letters. Vol. 1: xix.

[15] Synge claimed that when he 'was about fourteen [he] obtained a book of Darwin's' (Synge, *Collected Works*. Vol. 2: 10). This is a retrospective analysis. Synge's diary for 30 September 1895, reads 'Began the Origin of Species' (*TCD MS*: 4416, f.129v).

[16] Synge, *Collected Works*. Vol. 2: 11.

[17] Ibid.

[18] Ibid.,1, 56.

[19] McCormack, *Fool of the Family*, 383.

[20] Synge, *Collected Letters*. Vol. 1: 94. J.M. Synge to Lady Gregory, 31 September, 1904.

[21] Frank Fay, quoted in Synge, *Collected Works*. Vol. 3: 215.

[22] Ibid., 216.

23 W.B. Yeats, *Essays and Introductions* (London: Macmillan, 1961), 319.

24 Ibid, 319-20.

25 *TCD MS*: 4383, f.11v.

26 After *The Playboy* disturbances Synge drafted (but never published) *A Letter to the Gaelic League by a Hedge Schoolmaster* where he stated: 'I believe in Ireland. I believe the nation that made a place in history by seventeen centuries of manhood, a nation that has begotten Grattan and Emmet and Parnell will not be brought to complete insanity in these last days by what is senile and slobbering in the doctrine of the Gaelic League.' See, Synge, *Collected* Works. Vol. 2: 399.

27 Eric Weitz, *The Power of Laughter: Comedy and Contemporary Irish Theatre* (Dublin: Carysfort Press, 2004), 5.

28 Lady Gregory, *NYPL MS, Foster-Murphy Collection*: TS Carbon (312), Box 5, f.4.

29 Synge, *Collected Works*. Vol. 2: 398.

30 The primary source that informs *The Well's* dramaturgy is a story that was told to Synge on Aran by Old Mourteen (Máirtín Ó Conghaile). Old Mourteen took Synge to the church of the *Ceathair Aluinn* (The Four Beautiful Persons) where the dramatist was shown a holy well that was said to cure blindness and epilepsy. As the two men sat looking at the well, another islander (nameless to the archive) approached Synge and told him of the well's miraculous effect on a blind child from County Sligo whose mother dreamt of the well. Both mother and son arrived on *Inis Mór* by curragh, whereupon she 'walked up to this well, and she kneeled down and began saying her prayers. Then she put her hand out for the water, and put it on his eyes, and the moment it touched him he called out: "O mother, look at the pretty flowers!"' See, Synge, *Collected Works*. Vol. 2: 57.

31 See, L. Petit de Julleville, *Histoire du Theâtre en France: La Comédie et les Mœurs en France au Moyen Age* (Paris: Librairie Léopold Cerf, 1886), 100-103.

32 Synge first began studying with de Julleville on Monday 29 April, 1895. His diary simply states: 'cours de Julleville' (*TCD MS*: 4416, f 54v).

33 Synge's diary for 3 October, 1903 records thus: 'Petit de Julleville[,] *Theatre en France* [sic]' (*TCD MS*: 4422, f.21v). For Synge's detailed notes on Andrieu de la Vigne's *Moralité de l'aveugle et du boiteux*, see, *TCD MS*: 4393 36r-34r.

34 Synge, *Collected Works*. Vol. 3: 265. My translation from Synge's notes: 'The morality tale of André de la Vigne opens at the moment when the saint is about to expire. His body is left exposed at the bottom of the theatre, and it was quickly carried away to church in a solemn procession. Two beggars are in the scene, one of them is

blind, and only walks around groping, the other is limping, and lies down in the middle of the street. But don't have too much sympathy for them. These are two lazy souls, two drunks; be that as it may they moan in a plaintive voice; the blind one saying: Alms to the poor beggars / Who cannot live a single day without a drop of spirits. / and the paralytic: /Be good to the lame / Who cannot move for the drink.'

35 J.N. Hillgarth, *Christianity and Paganism, 350-750: The Conversion of Western Europe* (Philadelphia: University of Pennsylvania Press, 1986), 118.

36 Synge, *Collected Works*. Vol. 3: 69.

37 Ibid.

38 Ibid., 262. Synge's letter to Max Meyerfeld points out that the space and place of the play is 'Bállinatone, Grianan'. See, *NLI MS*: 778, f.6v, J.M. Synge to Max Meyerfeld, 12 August, 1905.

39 Michael P. Carroll, "Rethinking Popular Catholicism in Pre-Famine Ireland," *Journal for the Scientific Study of Religion* 34, no. 3 (1995): 354.

40 *Collected Works*. Vol. 2: 57.

41 Ibid., Vol. 3: 79.

42 Ibid., Vol. 2: 75.

43 Ibid. Vol. 3: 85.

44 See Emmet Larkin, 'The Devotional Revolution in Ireland: 1850-75.' *American Historical Review* 77, no. 3 (1972): 625-52.

45 *Collected Works*. Vol. 3: 83.

46 Ibid. 81.

47 Ibid. 80.

48 Ibid. Vol. 4, *Plays*, Book 2, ed. Ann Saddlemyer (Gerrards Cross: Colin Smythe, 1982), 107.

49 Synge, *Collected Works*. Vol. 4: 99.

50 Ibid. 83.

51 Ibid. 107.

52 Ibid. Vol. 3: 83.

53 Dáithí Ó hÓgáin, *The Hero in Irish Folk History* (Dublin: Macmillan, 1985), 46.

54 Synge, *Collected Works*. Vol. 3: 85.

55 Ibid. 101.

56 Ibid. Vol. 2: 34.

57 Ibid. Vol. 3: xxii.

58 Ibid. Vol. 2: 398.

59 Ibid.

60 *TCD MS:* 4405, f.10v.

61 Ibid.

62 Synge, *Collected Works*. Vol. 3: 117.

63 *TCD MS:* 4405, f.10v.

[64] *NLI MS*: 13,617, ff.7r-7v. J.M. Synge to W.G. Fay, February 1905. Synge does not stipulate the date on which he wrote the letter, apart from 'Thursday night'. Certainly, during this month Synge was in Dublin. See, Synge, *Collected* Letters. Vol. 1: xxiv. Emphasis in original.

[65] Synge, *Collected Works*. Vol. 2: 239.

[66] Ibid. Vol. 3: xxii.

[67] Ibid. xxiv.

[68] Ibid.

[69] Ibid.

[70] Joseph Holloway, *NLI MS*: 1803, 11 January, 1905, f.23.

[71] Holloway, *NLI MS*: 1803, 11 January, 1905, f.23.

[72] Ibid.

[73] W.G. Fay and Catherine Carswell, *The Fays of the Abbey Theatre: An Autobiographical Record* (London: Rich and Cowan, 1935), 168.

[74] Synge writes this on 3 March, 1896. See, *TCD MS*: 4417, f.11r.

[75] Synge writes this on 25 April, 1896. See, *TCD MS*: 4417, f.18v.

[76] Synge, *Collected* Letters. Vol. 1: 94. J.M. Synge to Lady Gregory, 31 September, 1904.

[77] Synge, *Collected Works*. Vol. 3: 80.

[78] *TCD MS*: 4393, f.5r.

[79] James Joyce, *Ulyssees* (London: Penguin, 2000), 256.

[80] Mrs. K. Synge, quoted in *J.M. Synge: 1871-1909*, ed. David H. Greene and Edward M. Stephens (New York: Macmillan, 1959), 180.

[81] Fay concluded that: '[t]he great majority, thinking of religion and themselves, abominated the play on both counts. It had bad press and we lost money and audience over it'. See, Fay and Carswell, *The Fays of the Abbey Theatre*, 169. Similarly, George Roberts remembered that '[t]he play was not at all popular on its first performance. At that time we were not accustomed to very large audiences, but there was an exceptionally small audience for the first performance of "The Well of the Saints." The second and third performances were even worse. I remember counting the people in the house on one of these nights and there were less than 20 present'. See, George Roberts, "Memoirs of George Roberts," *The Irish Times*, 2 August, 1955, 5.

[82] Synge, *Collected* Letters. Vol. 1: 286. J.M. Synge to the Editor of *The Irish Times*, 30 January, 1907.

11 | The Glass Ceiling and the Gag: Fifth Wave Feminism & Ireland's National Theatre,   2010-2014

Meidhbh McHugh

> I walked into a glass door; I didn't see it, but it was there.
> There is something in the water: but she's coming up for air.
>
> What is feminism? Simply the belief that women should be as free as men, however nuts, dim, deluded, badly dressed, fat, receding, lazy and smug they might be. Are you a feminist? Hahaha. Of course you are.
> -Caitlin Moran, *How to be a Woman*.

Hahaha. Of course you are a feminist. What could you possibly object to, asks the popular figurehead of contemporary feminism, Caitlin Moran: equal pay, the right to vote, Madonna... jeans? It's absurd, senseless. It's incongruous *not* to be a feminist; inequality is no longer the butt of a joke, it *is* the joke. Imagine being owned by your husband, or forced to quit your job upon getting married. Haha. Good one! (Aside: I have had one part-time job in which the marriage bar seemed a good idea, but quitting without the stress of a wedding was an easier option all round).

In recent years feminism has been a headlining narrative across popular culture, debate, discussion, TV, film, print, social and online media. Writers like Caitlin Moran, films such as *Bridesmaids*, HBO TV series *Girls* and comedians such as Tina Fey and Amy Poehler working in Hollywood have all contributed to an emergent culture of highly visible women seeking not only equal opportunities, but an end to the idea that feminism is man-hating, humourless, strident or sour. Instead, these women are creating their own work, raising their voices, occupying public space, and most importantly, consciously campaigning for better conditions for women, while retaining and *harnessing* their sense of humour. Moran and her counterparts are significant for putting 'feminism' and 'hahaha' in the same sentence in mainstream, public consciousness and for making the alternative (I'm not a feminist) seem, well, a joke. If it's a fifth tide of feminism that has come into being in the past three years, as I shall call it, it's categorized by one thing: it's funny. It's marked out by a sharp sense of humour: an innate, generational understanding of irony, as well as serious intent.

Across the Atlantic, Lena Dunham has also been hailed as a feminist icon for her observational comedy and brutally honest examination of female friends in her HBO series, *Girls*. In particular, her portrayal of the body has broken new ground in a world where twerking pop stars assimilate patriarchal porn culture and embrace it as 'empowerment', or size-zero actresses self-mutilate their bodies to conform to patriarchal institutions such as Hollywood. Dunham's originality in showing us her real-life, 'imperfect' (meaning, by our mass-media normative standards) naked, womanly body onscreen, repeatedly, is not a subtle subliminal message; it's a full-on, in-yer-face political and feminist statement. In doing so she has interrupted and altered the script of the female body on American television. She is politically aware too: 'I have to write people who feel honest but also push our cultural ball forward'.[1] Caitlin Moran says the same. In a discussion on feminism published on *Salon*, she says, 'You start with the cultural change, so it's acceptable for people to talk about these things'.[2] The conversation is changing and becoming louder. A funny woman is no longer a punch line: it's a prime-time desirability. 'I have never made any observation of what I apprehend to be true humour in women,'[3] said the Irish-educated playwright William Congreve in 1695, but fast-forward to 2014 and Dunham, Moran and Co are laughing all the way to the bank.

And yet Congreve's comment cannot be assigned to ancient ideology; it is indicative of years of cultural conditioning that sought to control or repress women's humour and laughter, and continues. As recently as 2007 Christopher Hitchens wrote a column in *Vanity Fair* in which he argued that women are less funny than men because they make babies: 'a higher calling that is no laughing matter'.[4] Surely it is, conversely, a higher calling that requires an innate and survivalist sense of humour. Regardless, with its relationship to the fool figure, comedy was historically seen as on the edge of madness, and female madness, like sexuality, was deemed more dangerous, less containable.[5] Even the Bible warns of the threat of women's humour. Frances Gray notes that, ' Christian writers of the time don't suggest you can't have a laugh with women, rather that you can and that is evidence of their guile'.[6] This threat (the fear of which connects humour and power) was managed with a centuries-long campaign to present women as less funny; receivers of humour rather than creators. Thus passive not powerful, objects not subjects; we know the dichotomies. The feminist movement, too, has long been associated with and accused of sterile humourlessness. As Regina Barecca writes, 'feminist criticism has generally avoided the discussion of comedy perhaps in order to be accepted by conservative critics who found feminist theory comic in and of itself'.[7] But feminism has always had a 'witty sense of theatre'[8] as Frances Gray points out in her study *Women and Laughter,* in that bra-burning itself was a clever parody of male destruction. If inherent examples of humour or irony were not widely detected in earlier waves of feminism or feminist theory, or feminists themselves did not willingly utilize comedy for the cause, it cannot be ignored in feminism's most recent incarnation in popular culture, which has foregrounded gender equality with brilliant, often biting wit. Significantly, this secures the comic high ground: *hahaha, of course you are.*

Live comedy and theatre are also riding fifth-wave feminism. In what is arguably comedy's most organic sphere, stand-up, there are tangible stirrings of a sea change regarding the perception, and acknowledgement, of women and humour. Bridget Christie won the Edinburgh Comedy Award in 2013, although she is only the third woman to win in its 33-year history. 'I'm not sure if it's a zeitgeist-y thing,' she said, 'but this award does feel like it's part of something bigger,' in an article in the UK *Independent*, which said 'in ridiculing everyday sexism, her highly entertaining hour-long show couldn't be more timely'.[9]

Christie's avowedly feminist show, entitled *A Bic For Her* (which refers to a pastel-coloured biro marketed at women), used humour and a wry tone to send up the absurdity of such gendered demarcations, with satirical concerns that the Brontë's would not have written their great works without such a femininely pleasing pen. Again there seems to be a consistent commitment to the subtly subversive comic tone in articulating feminist ideas. This strategy of humour is a conscious one; it makes argument difficult. No one wants to be accused of not getting the joke, indicted for a deficient sense of humour. The inanity of sexism and misogyny; the absurdity of gender inequality, and the oppressive effect of patriarchy on both women *and* men, is now a cause for laughter, and by looking and laughing we might shake the foundations on which its culture stands. Women are seizing comic power and it is as vital as any other instrument of social change. American essayist Agnes Repellier wrote, 'Humour distorts nothing and only false gods are laughed off their earthly pedestals'.[10]

***

Much like calorie-counting, it's dull being a gender-counting obsessive, as well as disheartening (much like calorie counting), but women are underrepresented in all aspects of public life in Ireland. Due in part to a Catholic past we have a historically repressive culture towards women and sexuality; women are not in full control of their fertility and they are still constitutionally tied to the home as mothers and wives. Although not unique to Ireland, the ever-present pornography industry, and its influence on marketing and media, is also oppressive to real women as sexual objectification is now systematic and endemic. Emerging technologies increase the images we consume on a daily basis creating a regressive culture of objectification. This is damaging to both men and women. Feminism isn't popular solely for its jokes. We need it more than ever. The figures in Irish theatre history aren't cheering either.

***

THE ABBEY THEATRE

With a theatre culture particularly associated with ideas of national identity, and a historically entwined relationship between theatre and politics, the statistics of playwrights-possessing-XX-chromosomes working at Ireland's national theatre, the Abbey Theatre, has been worryingly low. In my lifetime, only two women dramatists have had premieres on the Abbey Theatre's main stage: Marina Carr, arguably the only Irish female playwright to near canonical status, and Elaine Murphy with *Shush* in 2013. Attempts to address this imbalance are being made. In 2010/2011 the theatre premiered four new plays by Irish women at the Peacock Theatre, the Abbey's smaller space, two of which I include, significant for their comedic value, in addition to Murphy's *Shush*. They are *B for Baby* by Carmel Winters (2010) and *No Romance* by Nancy Harris (2011). In this context, it's easy to see why Brenda Donohue wrote on Marina Carr, 'the very act of working as a professional female playwright in Ireland today can be considered a meaningful feminist act'.[11] In addition to getting their plays produced on a national platform, thereby occupying space in national cultural discourse and joining a dialogue on national identity, I see these chosen writers' uses of humour, in particular, as central to the feminist impulse of their work. These playwrights, significantly, put comedy centre stage with their own, default female perspective, and this can be interpreted as an act of power. To tell a joke is a sign of confidence, to do so in public is leadership.

Of course the issue of whether humour/laughter can forge social change is complex, as the political implications of any humour transaction include who is producing the humour, who is receiving it and at whose expense the joke is being made. At the Abbey Theatre between 2010 and 2013, however, Winters, Harris and Murphy made jokes and incited laughter amongst a relatively mainstream audience from a woman's perspective, sometimes (though far from exclusively) at the expense of male behaviours, which necessarily alters the conventional configuration. Hélène Cixous told us to write the body and to destroy the hierarchy with the laugh.[12] Laughter in the spectating body politic has the kinetic potential at least, to incite a questioning of ideas of gender and power, by laughing at, with or about them. The hierarchy is destabilised, contextually as well as by content, if not entirely dethroned.

Shush, for example, could be accused of leaving gender conventions untroubled, and while that may be a valid argument, the fact of having a play on the Abbey's main stage, with its depiction of a certain Dublin milieu and an individuated expression of middle-aged female experience, can be seen as a feminist act. This is not to say that the terms 'woman-centred', 'women's writing' and 'feminism' should necessarily be interchangeable, but in addition to the production context discussed above, years of 'Irish plays' (deemed to have national significance) propagated stereotypes of – and proffered identities upon – Irish women, with their female characters continually cast as either suffering mothers or chaste maidens.

A deviation from such typing and a new voice centre-stage can be seen as feminist *by* its woman-centric focus, regardless that the characters' desires and actions focus heavily on men. Purveyors of the contemporary theatre context may think such gender and nation debates tired and trite, yet if only two female writers have premiered main-stage plays at the national theatre in twenty-five years, the scope of the argument refers further back in the historical timeline than it would otherwise. That *Shush* is a conversation-based play and not built as a conventional comedy doesn't detract from the fact that Elaine Murphy is the producer, not receiver, of the humour. Likewise, the humour capital of the play is too easily undervalued or dismissed as an afterthought in review. Frances Gray writes, 'Where women are visibly making people laugh, they deny the existence of a conscious creative process'.[13] This may be too harsh an indictment of critical responses to *Shush,* but it is not a totally unfair question whether comedy itself is not an adequate measure of achievement for a play on a national stage. Who decides what's funny? I attended the opening night and distinctly noted the high volume of laughter in the auditorium, a personal observation extending to all three plays.

THE PLAYS

Deconstructing humour defies an entirely objective study; 'funny' is a highly subjective (although often politicized) concept, but there are similar strategies of humour, evident to me, running through all three plays. These strategies account for much of the comedy produced by the plays and in the playing, and are evidence of fifth-wave (my definition: funny) feminism in operation in contemporary Irish theatre. Much of the humour, to my mind, comes firstly from the exposed gap between fantasy and reality; the playwrights variously highlight the absurdity of human constructs and behaviour and invite us to laugh at our own folly in what is not, in fact, 'innate' or 'natural', but a social construction. Secondly, they draw attention to the construct of language itself, deriving humour from punning and mischievously foregrounding language's slippery surface. Thirdly, all three playwrights have an innate sense of how to utilize the comic potential of incongruous elements, connections and juxtapositions, which can simultaneously surprise, shock and delight while de-familiarizing 'normative' sexist patterns. This strategy seems to me feminist in its very understanding of inconsistency and illogic, which is what the feminist movement comes up against time and again. *I have never made any observation of what I apprehend to be true humour in women.* It is particularly 'fifth-wave-feminist' to use irony, or wry humour, to expose illogic as it relates to gender ideas or indeed more generally to expose our ability as humans to think or behave illogically. Congreve's maxim, it follows, reads as a joke.

In calling attention to the often-absurd nature of human mores, the plays signal the possibility of change and do so by foregrounding other possibilities made apparent through comedy. It is, we know, difficult to decipher if or when comedy is temporary relief or an instrument of real social change, but it *can* suggest alternative realities. Gray quotes Søren Kierkegaard's contention that, 'humour *tends in the direction of* social change and the comic apprehension evokes the contradiction or makes it manifest by having in mind the way out, which is why contradiction is painless. The tragic apprehension sees the contradiction and despairs a way out.'[14] Feminist movements, in their quest for social change, must likewise expose the contradiction, highlighting the social construct and its alternative, having in mind a way out.

The first part of the triptych structure in *No Romance* comically exposes the gap between the imaginary and real, the flight of fancy and the fact, not only for the character in question, Laura, but by association, the same gap in wider culture. Laura is making an erotic photo book for her partner and has come to the home/studio of Gail for the job. She's immediately recognisable as a comic character, arriving as a nervous bundle of energy with a bag of gaudy costumes envisioned as 'looks' for the shoot. The costumes symbolize characters; roles she will assume in her quest to be feminine, sexy and desirable in the final images. Not necessarily herself, but another woman: an imaginary one. As she produces feather boas and wands, we see her imagination has been shaped by popular images of femininity as well as iconic women from history, pop culture and mythology. Guinevere, Queen Medb, Madonna and Cleopatra offer models of strong, fierce womanhood but they soon fizzle out into types more akin to fancy-dress suggestions; a jazz singer, a French maid, a princess, a fairy. The lines blur further when images of the Moulin Rouge are layered with less romantic ones of sex workers in Amsterdam's Red Light District, begging us to consider the inferences beneath surface enshrinements.

The humour in the scene comes from the ridiculousness of Laura trying to 'unleash (her) inner ... whatever. Diva', according to these received images. Harris wittily debunks images of canonical femininity in favour of the real person in front of us, Laura, who eventually takes the pictures naked. We are given access to how the character's imagination operates; her mind pictures herself lounging 'sexily' on a piano, 'sort of swinging my legs over the keys and throwing my head back', and we are invited to laugh in shared recognition. To fantasize is human, regardless of gender, and the limitlessness of the imagination is a source of much mirth.

Conversely, how our imaginations get caught in cliché also offers laughs. Significantly though, this signals the constructed nature of these images, how we view ourselves through the prism of culture and even cliché and type, and the ultimate impossibility of living up to outmoded, gendered mythology. The image can only ever be one dimension of the real person and it is often a false one; a commodification of male-orientated fantasy. By throwing into comic relief the absurdity of received images, particularly as they relate to gender, Harris seeks to strengthen our cynicism of the images we are bombarded with in our hyper-image-based society, particularly as women or of women. Theatre, by its nature, both imitates and imagines, it looks back and forward through the live performance. The image can be subject to a process of change, as something new is imagined. Harris does this by *laughing* at artificial images in our culture, by pitting them against the live body in front of us. This is the latent feminism, or use of humour with the potential for social change, which highlights the absurd gap between fantasy and reality and challenges us to distinguish between them.

B for Baby also operates on this level. Much of the humour in *B for Baby* is derived from the *learned* behaviour of the character B, who has a learning disability and lives in a care home. His appropriation of the world we deem 'natural' makes it seem unnatural – much like normalized perceptions of reality can appear altered, artificial or absurd when viewed from the perspective of an outsider or a child. The play begins with B performing the role of a hairdresser, cutting an imaginary person's hair. It's later understood that he is acting out a memory or a series of memories; snippets of conversation he evidently acquired or recalls pepper his dialogue, the past experience is layered over his present re-enactment:

> **B.** Dip your chin for me ...lovely. Now stay still, good man, we don't want to scalp you, sure we don't? Indeed'n we do not. Look at you and your lovely silky hair ... (*To Dee*) Doesn't he have lovely silky hair?

The well-worn sketch of the talkative hairdresser, done in this way by B, evokes the learned behaviour we all adopt and assume, our unconscious parroting and mimicry. The performance of identity, as it relates to gender amongst other things, is therefore also obliquely called into question.

Carmel Winters goes further to make language itself seem suspect, unnatural, the constructed nature of language apparent as slippages and manipulations begin in the opening minutes. Language is shown to be a tool for manipulation, a system of power, not necessarily a natural bedfellow with fact or truth. Dee pretends to B that 'volume' is a 'dirty, filthy word':

> **Dee.** It's the word for a woman's you-know-what.
> **B.** Her boobydoobydoos?

Dee. Her what?
B. Her boobydoobydoos?
Dee. Worse than boobyboobydoos
B. BoobyDOObydoos
Dee. Whatever. 'Volume' is worse. Lower. Down there. Before-the-butt-hole. Bogsville. The place you're called after.

If 'vagina', the V word inferred, has become an unpleasant and unused word in cultural discourse, a point popular-feminist Caitlin Moran takes up in her book *How to be a Woman*, why couldn't 'volume' also be given such smutty significance? Of course the absurdity of a 'hairdressing word' as B rightly defends it, as the name for a woman's genitalia offers great comedy, particularly as Dee's commitment to the joke/manipulation results in B getting an erection, much to his embarrassment:

> **Dee.** You started it. Going around putting 'volume' into people's hair. How would you like it if I put my volume in your hair?

Winters' dark humour is subversive in its treatment of language. The title of the play alludes to this too; *B is for Baby*. Naming something brings it into existence; it is an action. Similarly if there is shame attached to a signifier (a name), it extends to the signified. In the case of the word 'vagina', that impacts half the human race. Harris also picks up on this in *No Romance* with a sequence on a sex-blog called, 'The Story of C', the online font of inspiration for Laura's cast of calendar characters. Does 'C' stand for 'clitoris' (deemed vulgar) or 'cunt' (deemed vicious)? In the context of the scene it eventually comes to connote Laura's cancer, the real vicious C in existence and one outside our control, unlike women's relationship to, and language surrounding, their bodies. If language is how we define reality, and gender constructs are built with words and images formulated through language, then Winters shows us the unreliability and even betrayal of linguistic paradigms and engineers ways to expose them to comic ridicule. Again the humour has a feminist bias in its subtle but subversive attack on a culture of patriarchy, which underpins even language as we know and use it.

The third most obvious way these writers make their audience laugh is in their knowing use of incongruity. The use of surprising, incongruous elements and our reaction to them can point out the illogic of our logic, the surreal quality of our reality and, allowing for an adjustment, point the way to change. For example in *No Romance*, particularly in the second and third parts of the triptych structure, much of the comedy comes from incongruous elements. The second scene in the play erupts into high black farce when a middle-aged man, Joe, is confronted by his wife Carmel, over his suspect internet-activity. Comically, the action occurs over his mother's dead body in the funeral parlour. The imminent arrival of the family relations adds a dramatic ticking clock and increases the comic pace. Incongruity happens in witty, one-line absurdities such as the idea of a 'state psychologist', a mistake with reverberating humour, or it is situational such as the extraordinary inappropriateness of Carmel holding up a pair of women's stockings which Joe has ordered online, from a girl called Abbi (with a 'heart over the i'), in what should be his last moments alone with his mother's corpse.

The third part of *No Romance* also derives its comedy from the incongruous (in society) idea of the sexual older woman. This works in a similar manner to Marina Carr's *The Mai*, in which much humour is found in the older woman character, Grandma Fraochlan's, outspoken desire, but it has roots further back in Irish theatre history, in the likes of J.M. Synge's Widow Quinn in *The Playboy of the Western World*. In Harris' play the comedic tone of the scene comes from the (still) somehow surprising way the older woman, Peg (the name calling to mind the famous, but not for her love life, Peg Sawyers) acknowledges sex and desire as part of her life, albeit an inner life at this stage. We learn that she writes the sex-blog from Part One, tying the three scenes together. Her knowingness on sexual matters exemplifies Harris' wry tone:

> **Peg.** No matter how enlightened a man might appear, no one is immune to chlamydia.

Lines such as this, a reasonable assessment of the non-discriminatory nature of venereal disease, can provoke laughter not only at what is being expressed, but also by whom and in what context. Our strained expectation of the scene (an old woman with her grandson) is overturned and we may laugh at the incongruity.

Shush makes comic use of the same idea. Marie, in her sixties, tells her daughter Clare, in her thirties, to 'close your ears' before divulging marital advice:

> **Marie.** I know it's exhausting with small kids, Ursula, but it's important to keep these things alive. Bernard and I still take the Micra down to Dollymount Strand the odd night.

The mental picture of two adults, by domestic necessity, going to the beach like teenagers to consummate their passions within the confines of a small car invites laughter, but an element of surprise at the older woman's vocal desires and discussion may also account for the laughs. Why we still find it incongruous that an older woman should be sexual, however, points out an inconsistency in our culture. Would an older sexual man seem as surprising on stage? Granted it could still be funny, as bawdiness is an entry to humour of its own, but it would arguably have a lesser strain of incongruity. Putting these voices on a national stage, a range of women's voices, is a start in normalizing a range of women's voices. Ideally, we might laugh at an onstage woman's coarse humour because she is coarse and not because she is female.

Similarly, it is in its context rather than content, that Murphy's *Shush* is most apparently feminist. The bawdiness and frank conversation of the middle-aged, female characters, at an age where women now feel culturally invisible, finding a voice on the Abbey platform feels new. Professor of Sociology and anti-pornography activist, Dr Gail Dines, has an excellent speech online on the rampant, destructive effects of the pornography industry, available on YouTube, which outlines how women in today's society are categorised as either 'fuckable' or 'invisible'.[15] The women of *Shush* refuse to be invisible by occupying the Abbey stage. The play may remain within the domestic sphere and the theatre's marketing department did the critical reception no favours with its add-on beauty offers to boost ticket sales, but the darker thread of the play is a depressed, suburban, middle-aged woman who feels past her sell-by date in more ways than one. Death hangs over the play. *The Irish Times* may have dismissed it as a 'chat in two acts',[16] but by starting a cultural conversation on an often-unseen milieu, and again using comedy to do so, Elaine Murphy has opened the door for someone else to push the cultural ball further, to turn the chat into an argument. It may be a play of small moments, but when Murphy's character Irene passes wind on the national theatre stage at the end of the play, she strikes another small blow at the trope of mother/girl; as she de-ladyizes and de-thrones the ideal woman, contorting the image of the classic Colleen so long at home on the Abbey boards, with some well-timed gas.

Although I have previously posed the question whether laughter alone is sufficient for national theatre success, another question might concern itself with whether these writers *had* to be funny? Is comedy now the only way that certain female expression, particularly if it is woman-centred and concerned with everyday life, will get produced,

accepted or received? That may require another study, and regardless
whether necessary or voluntary, humour is a conscious strategy, aligned
with contemporary popular feminism, to seize comedic power for a
serious purpose. Ultimately these playwrights want to do more than
make people laugh. Emily Toth refers to the 'humane humour rule' in
an article 'Female Wits'. She notes that women rarely use the typical
scapegoat figures in their humour, such as blonde jokes or mother-in-
law quips. 'Rather,' she asserts, 'women humourists attack – or subvert
– the deliberate *choices* people make: hypocrisies, affectations,
mindless following of social expectations.'[17] As Regina Barecca puts it,
'women's comedy takes as its material the powerful rather than the
pitiful'[18].

While a blanket term of women's humour is certainly problematic, it
is interesting to note a recent essay by Susanne Colleary on the Irish
comedian Maeve Higgins. In it she quotes Higgins' critique of the very
concept of male/female humour, with a sketch about men and period
jokes, but Colleary also notes Higgins' response to male stand-up
comedy, which is telling of certain, possibly gender-specific approaches:

> I think, just say something about yourself, it doesn't have to be
> too deep or anything, just say what you think about something,
> not just like some corny...like my girlfriend said this to me[19].

Women humourists it seems, and it is true of the three plays under
discussion, often return to the emotional heart of the scene/play,
behind the humour. Laura, from *No Romance*, may be a comic
character but she's also a real and complex woman, who far from being
a 'pathetic' girlfriend trying to please a man with risqué photos, is
dealing with serious issues about the expiration of her body, sex and
death. Peg from the same play, has a comic sexual knowingness but has
also lived through a marriage to a gay man, a sacrifice made, tragically,
to conform to society's norms. We can infer that he denied his
homosexuality and/or both disregarded divorce. If the character is
eighty in 2011, both divorce and homosexuality were illegal most of her
married life. In *B for Baby*, the laughs come thick and fast, but by
curtain close we wonder if we've laughed our way through a serious
crime, as Mrs C manipulates and exploits her position of power in the
care home to fulfil her own deep desire to be a mother. After *Shush* we
might ask how the woman suicidal at the beginning of the play will fare,
living alone in enforced retirement, abandoned by her husband and her
son, around whom she had formed her life and identity. None of these
plays are built as easy comedies, but they do use humour to highlight

the poignancy that is at the heart of their drama and through comedy's reverberations offer the possibility of change. Look, they might say, look at the laughable incongruity of this contradiction; there is a way out.

I have said that by virtue of projecting their voices from 'national' stages, these writers can be construed as feminist. Another definition of feminist theatre, by Lizbeth Goodman, is theatre that 'works in some way to present positive images of women or to raise the status of women in the theatre'.[20] Again the definition concerns *both* the context of the play's production and/or the content of the play-world itself. By this definition, we could also categorize *No Romance, B for Baby* and *Shush* as feminist theatre. All three, by occupying a comic platform, by creating rather than receiving humour, raise the status of women in the theatre. Their characters too are, for the most part, self-realizing women, offering nuanced, complex roles to female actors in Ireland. Although connections can be made to the currents of (funny) feminism evident in popular TV, film, online media, and stand-up comedy, culture cannot be compartmentalised; what these playwrights are doing is not necessarily part of a movement but an honest examining, re-examining, dissecting, resisting, challenging, sometimes accepting socially-constructed notions of women's identity today. But what's central is they themselves are doing it. Writing the female, writing the body. They are situated as the subject in the theatre machine, not the object, and they are laughing. Humour is not a by-product but the key to the feminist spirit of these plays.

One recent study, *Inside Jokes: Using Humor to Reverse-Engineer the Mind (MIT Press),* by Hurley, Dennett and Adams, explains why we possess the faculty for humour at all, in evolutionary terms. The theory is this: we need to be able to contradict and correct our assumptions to better understand the world around us and we wouldn't do that if it was a tedious process, hence evolution made it pleasurable, much like it made the process of reproduction (however unfunny Christopher Hitchens finds it).[21] It is this power of comedy, to contradict and at best correct our assumptions, which makes it an ally to any feminism movement, or quest for social change, and it is happening in Irish theatre too. Sometimes the playwrights succeed, sometimes they won't, but what matters are the opportunities to take that chance. As Peg says at the end of *No Romance:*

I never said it was a triumph. Freedom is supposed to be a right.

***

Those who don't find rape jokes funny, or jokes that systematically undermine women are often accused of lacking a sense of humour. But who's definition of humour is that, and is it really the best on offer? Finally the parameters of comedy have expanded to include a new generation of funny women who have better gags than ones about vicious attacks or dumb blondes. Finally women playwrights are being produced at the national theatre who are writing back to entrenched tropes of stage Irish womanhood with honesty and hilarity. Fifth-wave feminists today are witty and sexy; able to both laugh at men and like men and laugh at themselves and like themselves; if men are threatened then they are victims, too. It is a culture of patriarchy that is the enemy, it's never been men, and it's that culture that should feel nervous of women's laughter. Nervous at the looking down years of oppression, objectification and unopposed power, pointing and howling, saying I will laugh you off your earthly pedestal. We might keep our bras from the fire this time, because we paid for them and some of them are quite nice, but we will laugh until the glass in that proverbial ceiling cracks. Until the roof of what Moran calls 'patriarchal bullshit', i.e., anything women are dealing with which men aren't, comes tumbling in. Hahaha. Haha. Ha. Or can't you take a joke?

WORKS CITED

Barreca, Regina. They used to call me Snow White...but I drifted: Women's Strategic use of Humour. New York: Penguin Books, 1991.

Cixous, Helene. The Laugh of the Medusa 1975. in *The Portable Cixous*, Edited by Marta Segarra. New York: Columbia University Press, 2010.

Gray, Frances. *Women and Laughter*. Basingstoke: Macmillan, 1994.

Fitzpatrick, Lisa. *Performing Feminisms in Contemporary Ireland*. Dublin: Carysfort Press, 2013.

Harris, Nancy. *No Romance*. London: Nick Hern Books, 2011.

Moran, Caitlin. *How to be a Woman*. United Kingdom: Random House Group, 2011.

Murphy, Elaine. *Shush*. London: Nick Hern Books, 2013.

Weitz, Eric. *The Cambridge Introduction to Comedy*. Cambridge: Cambridge University Press, 2009.

Winters, Carmel. *B for Baby*. London: Methuen Drama, 2010.

The Psychologist, vol 26 no 4, April 2013.

---

[1] Andrew Goldman, 'Even Lena Dunham's Dog Is Getting Frisky With Her,' New York Times, June 8, 2012, accessed March 12, 2014

http://www.nytimes.com/2012/06/10/magazine/even-lena-dunhams-dog-is-getting-frisky-with-her.html?_r=0

2 Lorraine Berry, 'Caitlin Moran: Women have Won Nothing,' October 16, 2012 , accessed March 12, 2014
http://www.salon.com/2012/10/16/caitlin_moran_and_bitch/

3 Congreve, quoted in Frances Gray, *Women and Laughter* (Basingstoke: Macmillan, 1994) p.3.

4 Christopher Hitchens, 'Why Women Aren't Funny', Vanity Fair, January 2007, accessed March 12, 2014,
http://www.vanityfair.com/culture/features/2007/01/hitchens2007 01

5 Frances Gray, *Women and Laughter* (Basingstoke: Macmillan, 1994, p.118.

6 Frances Gray. *Women and Laughter* (Basingstoke: Macmillan, 1994) p.6.

7 Ibid., p.118.

8 Ibid., p.12.

9 Veronica Lee, 'Foster's Comedy Award winner Bridget Christie: 'I was standing in a bookshop when I realised that this was a show I just had to do'', The Independent, 25 August, 2013, accessed 12 March 2014 http://www.independent.co.uk/news/people/profiles/fosters-comedy-award-winner-bridget-christie-i-was-standing-in-a-bookshop-when-i-realised-that-thiswas-a-show-i-just-had-to-do-8784433.html

10 Agnes Repllier quoted in Regina Barecca, *They used to call me Snow White...but I drifted: Women's Strategic use of Humour* (New York: Penguin Books, 1991).

11 Brenda Donohue, 'Marina Carr – Writing as Feminist Act' in *Performing Feminisms in Contemporary Ireland*, Ed. Lisa Fitzpatrick, (Dublin: Carysfort Press, 2013) P.39.

12 Helene Cixous, 'The Laugh of the Medusa 1975' in *The Portable Cixous*, Ed. Marta Segarra (New York: Columbia University Press, 2010)

13 Frances Gray. *Women and Laughter* (Basingstoke: Macmillan, 1994) p.8.

14 Søren Kierkegaard, cited by Frances Gray. *Women and Laughter* (Basingstoke: Macmillan, 1994) p.32.

15 https://www.youtube.com/watch?feature=player_embedded&v=-Z5iANEfQUU

16 Peter Crawley, 'A sister act that's somewhere between a sitcom and a kitchen sink', *The Irish Times*, June 13, 2013.

17 Emily Toth quoted in Regina Barreca, *They used to call me Snow White...but I drifted: Women's Strategic use of Humour* (New York: Penguin Books, 1991) p.13.

18 Ibid.

[19] Maeve Higgins quoted in Susan Colleary, 'Eating Tiny Cakes in the Dark: Maeve Higgins and the Politics of Self-Deprecation in *Performing Feminisms in Contemporary Ireland*, Ed. Lisa Fitzpatrick (Dublin: Carysfort Press, 2013) p.23.

[20] Lizbeth Goodman, qtd. Elaine Aston, *An Introduction to Feminism and Theatre* (London: Routledge, 1995)p.64.

[21] Qtd. Christian Jarrett, '*How many psychologists does it take to explain a joke?'*
in The Psychologist, vol 26 no 4, April 2013

12 | The Savage Eye Sees Far: 'Militant Irony' and the Jacobean Corrective in Contemporary Irish Satire

Susanne Colleary

INTRODUCTION

> It's beginning to snow again. The flakes, silver and dark, are
> falling obliquely against the lamplight. It's probably snowing all
> over the island – on the central plain, on the treeless hills,
> falling softly on the graveyards, on the crosses and headstones,
> upon all the living...and the dead.[1]

It falls to the eponymous star of *Father Ted* (Dermot Morgan) to make
this speech, a version of the last lines of James Joyce's short story '*The
Dead.*' He speaks, in part, as a requiem for Father Jack (Frank Kelly)
who 'dies' in the last episode of the first series. The situation-comedy
series, *Father Ted*, centred on the lives of three priests living on the
fictional Craggy Island off the west coast of Ireland. The show was
produced for (British television channel) Channel Four and broadcast
through the 1990s to both national and international audiences. As
Claire Connolly notes, this scene is both:

> sombre and funny ... reinforced visually by scenes that are
> strongly reminiscent of ... the closing scene of John Huston's
> film version of *The Dead* (1987): snow, Celtic crosses, a
> cemetery, all filmed in mournful monochrome.[2]

At the end of the monologue, Father Jack sits up in the coffin and
tells Father Ted to, 'Shut the Feck Up', which quickly deflates any
poeticism. However, Connolly makes note of the show's drawing on
Joyce as inspiration in a 1990s situation comedy; a show that was also
heavily influenced by the modern traditions of televisual comedy
including *Seinfeld* and *Fawlty Towers*. For Connolly, the twinning of

Joyce with this 'sombre and funny' moment in *Father Ted* also symbolises a requiem for Ireland's past. This is what the spirit of *The Dead* speaks to, 'an attempt to convey a moment of change in Irish culture: the old images passing, fresh representations being put in their place'.[3] Twenty-odd years ago *Father Ted* was attempting to express moments of transition in Irish culture as the past loosened something of its grip. Those moments are mirrored in certain respects to contemporary reconfigurations of Irish cultural, social and political life, heightened perhaps by the catalyst of the construction boom and the Celtic Tiger years.[4] How that tiger has reshaped the surfaces of Irish society, its mores and cultural practices, along with the depth of those transformations remain very much in play. Share and Corcoran argue as much when they state that:

> Post-industrial Ireland is layered over a bedrock of enduring social patterns of behaviour, of ideology and of social inequalities of power and influence. The illusion of the 'new Ireland' continues to reveal the contours of these older patterns.[5]

It is within these series of transitional cultural and economic backdrops that programmes such as the satirical sketch show, *The Savage Eye*, were forged.[6]

The programme has mapped and road-tested the tensions within a changing society during and in the aftermath of the economic boom. As a means to look at how the satire in the show is working, I would like to connect *The Savage Eye* to Northrop Frye's formulation of 'militant irony,' along with Peter Berger's treatment of Frye's paradigm. Secondly I would like to combine 'militant irony' as satire to the qualities inherent in Jacobean city comedy's notion of the corrective moral. Twinning these concepts and bringing them alongside the work of *The Savage Eye* allows me to examine the show with particular focus. I wish to look at how the show uses satire to expose cultural anxiety around ethnicity, identity and prejudice in contemporary Irish life.

'AS YOU KNOW I WAS A BLACK WOMAN FOR MANY MANY YEARS.'[7]

In Irish theatre discourse, notions of Irish identity and ethnicity have, in the past, figured heavily and been actively refigured through the lens of contemporary criticism. Writing in 2007, Lisa Fitzpatrick associated traditional and contemporary notions of Irish identity with conceptions of a globalized, affluent society. She described the re-imagination of

Ireland and Irish identity in the age of the Celtic Tiger within a range of expression in recent theatrical performance. On one level, those expressions can be linked to the 'globalisation of the economy and the country's embrace of European integration...[which] represents the shift from a homeland of mammies and tweed and potatoes and bogs to a curiously featureless, sterilized, suburban nowhere'.[8] She goes on to suggest that in the age of the tiger's roar, the Irish emigrant abroad finally lost the stigma and disenfranchisement so familiar to previous generations.

At the time of Fitzpatrick's writing, the Celtic Tiger migrant abroad constituted personal choice and affluence, with the one-time experience of the Irish emigrant being 'displaced in the media onto the body of the Other: the new Irish, economic migrants and refugees'.[9] Eric Weitz also takes up the subject of the immigrant experience as theatrical performance in his discussion of the Dublin-based theatre company, Arambe Productions. Weitz looks at the works of Nigerian-born Irish theatre practitioner Bisi Adigun, and explores recent experimentation with theatrical humour dynamics in Adigun's staging of both African and Irish texts for a contemporary Irish audience.[10] Adigun directed Jimmy Murphy's *The Kings of the Kilburn High Road* in 2006. According to Weitz, Adigun staged *Kings* in order to point up ideas on the experience of immigration for him and his fellow Africans, whilst being very aware of Ireland's own past (and present) relationship with mass emigration, performed for a multicultural audience in Ireland. Weitz states:

> Ireland's recent immigrant populations have begun a process of 'learning' the host culture they have entered, while, of course, remaining irrevocably tethered to their own. Meanwhile, the collective Irish consciousness harbours a memory or two about the travails of emigration.[11]

Sadly the travails of emigration are more than memory for many now. Since 2008, Ireland has been plunged into the depths of a double-dip recession, with forced and mass re-location of its people occurring in numbers that rival or outstrip the dark days of the 1950s and the 1980s. Leah Hyslop, writing for the *Telegraph*, discusses the recent emigration figures for Ireland to April 2012. She states, 'statistics from the Irish Central Statistics Office show that 87,100 people left the Emerald Isle in the financial year [to April 2012], almost 2% of the entire population'. According to Hyslop, these are the highest figures since new records began in 1987. Of that number fifty-three percent were Irish citizens.[12] That said, Adigun re-figures plays such as *Kings* and Ghanaian playwright, Ama Ata Aidoo's *Dilemma of a Ghost* in 2007, which continue to speak to the condition of both the Irish emigrant abroad and the African experience of immigration[13].

Fitzpatrick looks to the 'body of the Other,' to ground her discussion of the 'new' Irish. Weitz examines the emigrant/immigrant experience through close examination of the humour transaction in performance of African and Irish texts for a multicultural audience.

Clearly then, theatre practice and scholarship are invested in these discourses and so too is current televisual culture; most notably *The Savage Eye* has taken to the subject of the immigrant experience in Ireland with vigour. The brainchild of David McSavage (David Andrews Jr), *The Savage Eye* is written by McSavage and collaborators/-performers John Colleary, Patrick McDonnell and Dermot McMorrow, all of whom have backgrounds in stand-up performance as well as film and television work. The satirical programme has been nominated three times for best entertainment programme and twice for best director for the Irish Film and Television Awards. It takes the format of an anthropological documentary by way of vox pop and sketches, which McSavage describes as 'sketchumentary'.

Structurally and thematically broad, *The Savage Eye* has trained its satirical sights on every topic under the pre- and post-Celtic Tiger sun, and each week the show examines various topics including health, religion, alcohol and racism. At times surreal and absurd, the show has been described as 'exposing every toe-curling aspect of Irish life'.[14] Asked about the graphic nature of the show, McSavage responded:

> In the present time when the church, the banks and Government are all collapsing I feel I have free rein to do what I want. I find if a sketch makes a good point and is attacking the right targets, people don't complain. They only write in if it's not funny.[15]

Sketches involving ideas of emigration, ethnicity and identity recur through all of *The Savage Eye* works. However, Series Two, Episode Five is wholly dedicated to the subject as the show's title 'Racism' makes clear. One sketch involves the daughter of Irish middle-class parents dating an African man. She brings her boyfriend home to dinner and they all sit down to share a meal together. As the tension mounts, the father, despite his best efforts, betrays himself. He is, at best apprehensive that his daughter is having a relationship with a black man. The direct approach is taken in another scene, as viewers

are presented with images of black men, with the word *Fear*
emblazoned across the centre of the screen. And seamed throughout all
of these interrogations, is the President for Life (PFL), who was a 'black
woman for many, many years' and whose Irish Citizenship classes will
soon become the central focus of this discussion. However before truly
turning toward the PFL, I want to take a closer look at ideas of 'militant
irony' as satire sketched earlier. In addition I want to examine how
'militant irony' may work alongside the qualities of Jacobean city
comedy as a useful means through which to capture the characteristics
of the show's satiric eye.

MILITANT IRONY AND THE JACOBEAN CORRECTIVE

Peter Berger borrows from the work of Northrop Frye in his discussion
of satire. In Berger's view, Frye's definition of 'militant irony' as satire
comes very close to his own formulation, namely:

> in satire, the aggressive intent becomes the central motif of
> comic expression. All elements of the comic are then, as it
> were, welded together into the shaping of a weapon. Most often
> the attack is directed against institutions and their
> representatives, notably political or religious ones. It may also
> be directed against entire social groups and their cultures, say
> against the bourgeoisie and its mores ... its emotional tone is
> typically malicious, even if the motive for the attack is this or
> that high principle.[16]

Berger continues, suggesting that while irony can be quite subtle,
satire cannot be overly gentle lest it lose its 'attitude of attack,' its
militant qualities.[17] So both Frye's 'militant irony' and Berger's 'shaping
of a weapon' may be understood as comic expression created in the
inherent tensions between an attitude of attack and ironic intent, both
of which are heavily mediated by its social contexts. Berger goes on to
list what Frye advocates as essential elements for satire, 'fantasy (often
grotesque); a standpoint based on moral norms; and an object of
attack'. However Berger disagrees with Frye's point that the satirist and
the audience must be agreed on the object of attack. Rather Berger
states that:

> To be sure, there must be a commonality of social context
> between satirist and audience...But it is not necessary that the
> audience agree with the satirist to begin with. Satire can also be
> educational: it may be a *result* of the satirist's labours that the
> audience comes to understand the undesirability of what is
> attacked.[18]

Lastly, Berger agrees with Frye when he states that satire, because of its dependence on social context is particularly 'time bound.' At its best, satire points to an horizon beyond the current historical context, giving a sense of freedom beyond the present cause(s) of suppression.[19]

Just as there are a range of critical theories to underpin ideas of satire, so too, Jacobean city comedy can also be described from various critical standpoints. Broadly, 'city' comedy was in vogue from 1605-1630. Its writers, including Jonson and Middleton produced plays about London life, which differed from older romantic representations of the city.[20] The scholarship is comprehensive and well beyond the scope of these pages. For my purposes the work of Susan Wells is useful here. Wells argues that scholarly representations of Jacobean city comedy can be read as falling into two main camps; that of the sociological criticism of L.C. Knight's and the generic criticism of Brian Gibbons. Gibbons states that city comedy:

> worked a limited range of materials – satire, jest book, the
> Roman comedy – into a rather stylised sub genre in which
> trickery and swindling are celebrated, while the greed that
> motivates them is exposed.[21]

Thus Wells argues that city comedy in this reading can be understood as 'corrective moral comedy, liberally salted...with moral ambiguity.'[22] On the other hand, Knight has described city comedy as 'a response to the changing nature of British society, citing the rise of the middle class and the commercial growth of London as its determining influence'.[23]

Wells goes on to argue for a cross-fertilisation of these oppositions by twinning ideas of then nascent capitalism and conceptions of the Bakhtin marketplace to best illuminate city comedy as illustrating contradictions within contemporaneous hegemonic ideologies in the city of London. Connecting city comedy and seventeenth-century London life to contemporary Dublin and Ireland is possible by looking at the historical contexts of both cultures. Both emerge from unprecedented commercial growth and capitalist ethos. And both utilize the weaponry of satire as response, in order to expose the inequalities and hypocrisies generated by each society's boom time.

Also, there are crossing points here between Frye and Berger's concepts of satire and city comedy. Both look to an object of attack as targets for comedy. Both seek to denounce that which they are attacking through celebratory or ironic tactics (or both), and both are seamed through to varying degrees with moral subtleties and ambiguity.

Further, both have an educational or corrective quality, that is, by exposing that which is denounced however ambiguously, such satire is able to take on the quality of corrective moral comedy as Wells suggests. Implicit in the comic form of satire as corrective or educational here, then, is that sense of liberation beyond the present moment that Berger speaks of. I would argue that satire can act simultaneously as agent for militant, ironic, ambiguous and corrective comic expression. So, if satire's horizon can accommodate these differing but related concepts, can and does the *The Savage Eye* shape its own satiric weaponry in anything like the same way? To highlight and argue the point, there follows a sketch, which makes attack on issues of ethnicity and identity in contemporary Ireland. The sketch takes aim at racial prejudice in Irish society, employing the device of a Dublin taxi man stereotype as the vehicle for attack.

The scenario centres on one of the main stock characters of *The Savage Eye*, that is, the President for Life (PFL), played by McSavage. The character would seem to be loosely based on Mary Robinson, Ireland's first female president from 1990-1997, and later the United Nations High Commissioner for Human Rights, 1997-2002. The PFL can be understood as an often absurd and always-incisive pseudo representation of the figure of 'Mother Ireland,' so deeply embedded in the Irish psyche.

Throughout the series, the PFL conducts Irish Citizenship classes in order to interrogate predominant values and customs in Irish culture. In this scenario, the PFL is attempting to resolve the taxi wars of Dublin. The scene opens with the PFL sitting in a reception room in Áras an Uachtaráin, the official residence of the President of Ireland, and seated either side of the PFL are Declan, a Dublin taxi driver, and Jikambe, an African-born taxi driver. The PFL speaks directly to camera. She welcomes all who are watching to her Irish Citizenship classes and states that she will now bring about an end to the taxi wars of Dublin. She addresses Declan, the Dublin taxi driver, asking him why he has a problem with Jikambe, who is just trying to create a good and safe life for himself and his family in Ireland. Jikambe nods and looks concernedly toward Declan. Declan, who has a deep Dublin accent, replies, 'I'm not racist (pointing at Jikambe) but the majority of the colours look the same, so it's easy for them to share licences right?' Declan then crosses his arms across his chest defensively, and says, 'There's no room for black taxi drivers in Irish taxi ranks'. PFL berates Declan in motherly tones of disappointment, she feels that Declan is 'misguided' and reminds him, despite his protests, of the Irish Diaspora in the United Kingdom, the United States and Australia. All the while, Jikambe nods agreement.

PFL now turns her full attention to Jikambe. She tells him that she is going to take him on a journey into Declan's mind. The camera zooms in on Declan's ear. The PFL and Jikambe are now in Declan's halls of memory. They move through a hazy corridor toward the camera, stopping at certain doors along the way. At the first door the PFL looks knowingly at Jikambe and says, 'Childhood'. Esoteric music, overlaid with childhood sounds can be heard in the background. The door opens on a memory of home, with a young Declan sitting in front of the fire. His parents are seated on the sofa where his father is reading the newspaper. During the scene, the camera pans back and forth between Declan and his parents. Declan's father begins rattling the paper aggressively and starts to speak, 'Blacks! Chinese, Russian bastards!' His mother responds with equal vitriol, 'Dirty black bastards! The dirtier the dirt, the blacker the black bastards'. The camera then pans back to the sympathetic face of PFL regarding Jikambe.

They move to the next door, which reads 'Education'. Here the door opens on a schoolroom. The teacher is writing in Irish on the board and asks a question of Murphy (Declan). Declan is asleep at his desk. The teacher becomes irate when he sees Declan, he shouts at Declan to wake up and he begins to beat him with a strap. The other children are clearly frightened as the teacher continues to beat Declan violently, shouting, 'I'll teach ya, I'll teach ya!' The teacher does not stop and the PFL looks sorrowfully at Jikambe as they withdraw from the room.

They move to the final door, 'Experience in London'. This scene takes place in the kitchen of a London hotel or restaurant. Declan is a young adult and is working as a kitchen porter. He is washing dishes at a sink. A waiter enters carrying dirty dishes. He puts the dishes in the sink and speaks to Declan. Throughout Declan wears an expression of acceptance and a submission of sorts, he certainly makes no attempt to reply. The waiter greets Declan as, 'Paddy', and sarcastically calls him 'mate'. He then makes a vicious attack on Declan for being Irish: 'You fucking Paddy wanker. Look at you, you fucking filthy inbred terrorist bog wog, coming over here and taking our fucking jobs!' The camera zooms out; the PFL and Jikambe are back in the reception room, sitting as they were at the beginning of the sketch. The PFL is holding Jikambe's hand. Jikambe now speaks to Declan who is wearing a very worried expression. Jikambe says, 'Oh my God, I'm so sorry'. He gets up and approaches Declan, his hand outstretched. Declan takes his hand, replying, 'I'm sorry too'. They are crying when they embrace each other as movie climax music peaks in the background. Behind both men the PFL has her arms outstretched as if in a sign of faith. Both men sit back down again and hold the PFL's hands. She looks directly to the camera and says to all who are watching, 'Welcome to Ireland'.[24]

Initially, Declan's subjectivity would seem to come under some attack. However, as the story unfolds, the audience are given insight into Declan's character, and sympathy with some understanding is earned. The sketch clearly takes up an aggressive stance against those in Declan's past who projected their racist attitudes onto the young boy. The aggressive edge sharpens when attacking acts of violence are carried out against Declan, as deep betrayal by those charged with the care and educaton of the young in the name of church and state.

Finally, the sketch paints a disturbing picture of Declan's own abuse as an emigrant in London. The object of attack could be understood as being the racist waiter here, whose vitriolic assault on Declan is centred on the idea that the Irish are taking jobs away from the British. However the fact that Declan, who now, as an adult has at least some agency to reply, yet remains silent, is the biggest indictment of all. The parental invective at work in the first part of the sketch is aggressive but not heavily scored with irony. However, the teacher's promising to 'teach' Declan as he beats the young boy speaks to stronger ironic impulse. The teacher does not need books to school Declan, but educates him to internalize feelings of powerlessness, and to accept the use of violence against him as typical and permitted behaviour. Throughout the waiter's tirade, Declan does not speak. Through his silence, there is an outright, if unspoken, denounciation of those who have had an active hand and part in shaping his life.

The harshest irony is that 'London Declan' has learned his lessons very well. He has learned from his childhood experiences and has come to accept and internalize both physical and racial abuse as normative behaviour. The beginning of the sketch clearly signals that Declan is caught in a pattern of repeating that which he has learned, as the PFL repoaches him for his racist stance. Through the Irish Citizenship classes, the PFL hopes to enlighten and guide her wayward people toward a more tolerant and inclusive understanding of Irish society.

There is an element of mischief and trickery at work here, which carries an ironic sonic boom. Initially that irony would seem to be embedded in the PFL's almost naive idealism as she reconciles Declan and Jikambe, so symbolising the end of the taxi wars of Dublin. However, the PFL's understated sense of joy as she makes harmonious that which was previously in conflict works to expose the deep fissures beneath. Her reconciliation of multicultural relations in Ireland is deliberately juxtaposed against the blight of intolerance, stereotyping and cultural unease that underpin those relationships.

I spoke earlier of Jacobean comedy that celebrates trickery and swindling while exposing the greed that motivates them. The PFL's compassionate reconciliation of past and present abuses toward accord exposes the complex nature of a newly minted multicultural society and of prejudicial attitudes that crest the waves of a diverse populace. The corrective moral, however ambiguous, is alive here, and chimes well with that educational quality that Berger speaks of, where the satirist seeks to make an audience understand the 'undesirability of what is being attacked'.[25] Although firmly anchored in the present, the sketch can play an audience into acknowledging and recognising the fissures beneath the surface of Irish society. That exposure allows the discussion to take a lungful of air in the open, adding voice to current discussion on how best to seal some of those ruptures.

I began this article by suggesting that Father Ted's use of Joyce's words signalled moments of transition in Irish culture twenty or so years ago. *The Savage Eye* is, in a way, something of a chronicler of such moments now. The programme looks backward in acknowledgement to its comic forebears and the iconic *Hall's Pictorial Weekly*, for one, resonates here. Grounded as it is in the present moment, the show does interrogate Ireland's past while casting a weathered eye toward a future horizon.

City comedy, as Wells suggests, illuminated and contested hegemonic and political ideologies in the nascent capitalism of the emerging city of London. In light of a late capitalist, post-industrial society, and facing the hardships of a double-dip recession, *The Savage Eye* has attempted to capture the most recent seismic shifts in Irish life. The PFL as pseudo 'Mother Ireland' is one of the most powerful characters that the show has created in order to signal those transitions in Irish culture.

Another is the show's use of the ubiquitous political press conference. Throughout all the series, the show's satirical blade sharpens and crystallises on Irish political ineptitude and ineffectuality. The political podium in the world of *The Savage Eye* is forever populated by the eternal ministers; the Minister for the Awareness of Problems, the Minister for the use of Three Similar Words, the Minister for using Breathlessness to Convey Sincerity and the Minister for Laughing Inappropriately are in attendance. Their inane responses to cultural anxiety around ideas of ethnicity and difference in Irish life reenforce that ineptitude. The Minister for using Breathlessness to Convey Sincerity has this to say:

> I think it's wrong to assume that the Irish people are in denial about racial issues. Even in the old Irish language, we have a word for black people. Na Daoine Gorma, it means the blue people.[26]

The current blight of mass-emigration is dealt with in an equally absurd way. The Minister for the use of Three Similar Words has this to say:

> Emigration is a wonderful strand of the Irish experience, and ah ... we have created a high exodus from this country ... ah ... creating an enormous Diaspora, ensuring a very very healthy tourism industry ... ah of the future (applause from the other ministers).[27]

Perhaps the most poignant mapping of transition and forced change in Ireland is portrayed in a long scene at the end of the second series, where Ireland (McSavage dressed in an Ireland costume) is saying goodbye to the exodus of its people as 'Ireland's economic tide goes out'.[28] Forlorn, he eventually walks away with the local priest (who gives him a comforting squeeze of the buttocks). We are confronted immediately by the political press conference. The eternal ministers are present. They are dressed in conventional suits topped by a red 'Ming the Merciless'-type collar and devilishly painted eyes. The Minister for Using Three Similar Words speaks:

> Well, we've carried on like there was no tomorrow,
> And it turns out we were right to do so.
> Ah..we were correct to do so.
> It was appropriate for us to do so.
> I don't think the Irish people like looking forward.
> (Close up on McSavage)
> I think it's an Irish thing to do,
> I think that Irish people certainly want a bit of mystery in their lives,
> And this government provided that.
> (Black out)

This scene aired in early 2011. In interview for the episode, Bob Geldof made clear his feelings, stating that the actions of Irish politicians during the Tiger years were a 'betrayal of a generation and any idea of a chance in this country, and that's a great act of economic violence'.[29]

A *Savage Eye* vision employs the scope of a militant and ironic attitude in order to satirize and map a deeply troubled present and an uncertain future for the people of Ireland. Claire Connolly suggested that Joyce's *The Dead* wished to express moments of change, 'the old images passing, fresh representations being put in their place'. *The Savage Eye* attempts to capture those moments of change also, in this instance through the interrogation of ethnicity, identity and prejudice in contemporary Irish life. However, believe it or not, some of the 'old images' prove very difficult to oust. The spirit of the eternal ministers ghosts the proceedings. They may have changed the colour of their shirts for the moment. They may be decked in the sackcloth and ashes of newly humbled and responsible public representatives. They may too be worrying their beads and praying under the tooth, wishing for the return of the glory days.

WORKS CITED

Benson, Mary, and O'Flaherty, Eoin, 'Landscapes of Recession in Contemporary Ireland' in *Ireland Of The Illusions: A Sociological Chronicle*, 2007-2008, Vol. 7, ed. Mary Corcoran and Perry Share (Dublin: IPA, 2010), pp. 79-100

Berger, L. Peter, *Redeeming Laughter: The Comic Dimension of Human Experience* (Berlin and New York: De Gruyter, 1997)

Connolly, Claire, 'Ireland in Theory', in *Theorising Ireland: Readers in Cultural Criticism*, ed. Claire Connolly (Hampshire: Palgrave Macmillan, 2003), pp. 1-13

Corcoran, P, Mary, and Share, Perry, 'From Enchantment to Disillusion', in *Ireland Of The Illusions: A Sociological Chronicle*, 2007-2008, Vol. 7, ed. Mary Corcoran and Perry Share, (Dublin: IPA, 2010), pp. 1-19

Fitzpatrick, Lisa, 'Nation and Myth in the Age of the Celtic Tiger: Muide Eire? in *Echoes Down the Corridor: Irish Theatre – Past, Present, and Future* (Dublin: Carysfort Press, 2007) pp. 169-179.

'Future', Series Two, Episode Six, *The Savage Eye*, (Dublin: Blinder Films Ltd, 2011)

Higgins, Maeve, Unpublished Interview with the Author, 25 March 2010.

Hyslop, Leah, 'Emigration from Ireland soars', *Telegraph*, 5 October 2012, <http:// www.telegraph.co.uk/expat/expatnews/9584756/emigration-from-Ireland-soars.html>

Leonard, Liam 'The Galway Water Crises', in *Ireland Of The Illusions: A Sociological Chronicle*, 2007-2008, Vol. 7, ed. Mary Corcoran and Perry Share (Dublin: IPA, 2010), pp. 65-76

Linehan, Graham, and Matthews, Arthur, 'Grant Unto Him Eternal Rest', Father Ted: The Complete Scripts (London, 1999)

'Racism', Series Two, Episode Five, *The Savage Eye*, (Dublin: Blinder Films Ltd, 2011)

Stott, Andrew, *Comedy; The New Critical Idiom* (Oxon: Routledge, 2005).

Weitz, Eric, 'Who's Laughing Now: Comic Currents for a New Irish Audience', in *Crossroads: Performance Studies and Irish Culture*, ed. Sara Brady and Fintan Walsh (Hampshire: Palgrave Macmillan, 2009) pp. 225-236

Wells, Susan, 'Jacobean City Comedy and the Ideology of the City', *EHL* 48:1 (1981), pp. 37-60

---

[1] Graham Linehan and Arthur Matthews 'Grant Unto Him Eternal Rest', *Father Ted: The Complete Scripts* (London, 1999), p.90, cited in *Theorising Ireland: Readers in Cultural Criticism*, ed. Claire Connolly (Hampshire: Palgrave Macmillan, 2003): 11.

[2] Connolly, 12.

[3] Connolly, 12.

[4] For a comprehensive discussion on the physical and figurative transformation of the Irish landscape in recent years see *Ireland Of The Illusions: A Sociological Chronicle*, 2007-2008, Vol. 7, ed. Mary Corcoran and Perry Share, (Dublin: IPA, 2010).

[5] Mary P. Corcoran and Perry Share, 'From Enchantment to Disillusion', in *Ireland Of The Illusions: A Sociological Chronicle*, 5-6.

[6] RTÉ (the national Irish broadcaster) has in recent years, increasingly filled its entertainment schedules with homegrown comedy programming, large aspects of which are hosted or created by successful Irish stand-up comics. They include Jason Byrne's *The Byrne Ultimatum* (2009), Maeve Higgins's *Fancy Vittles*, (which Higgins describes as 'stand up to camera' (2009), *The Modest Adventures of David O Doherty* (2007), *Naked Camera* (2005-2007), *The Panel* (2003-) *The Republic of Telly* (2009-), *The Hardy Bucks* (2009-2011), *Irish Pictorial Weekly* 2012 -) and *The Savage Eye* (2009 -).

[7] President for Life, 'Racism', Series Two, Episode Five, *The Savage Eye*, (Dublin: Blinder Films Ltd, 2011), 9.40-10.32

[8] Lisa Fitzpatrick, 'Nation and Myth in the Age of the Celtic Tiger: Muide Eire?', in (Dublin: Carysfort Press, 2007) pp. 169-170.

[9]Fitzpatrick, pp. 169-170.

[10] For further discussion, see Eric Weitz, 'Who's Laughing Now: Comic Currents for a New Irish Audience', in *Crossroads: Performance Studies and Irish Echoes Down the Corridor: Irish Theatre – Past, Present, and Future Culture*, ed. Sara Brady and Fintan Walsh (Hampshire: Palgrave Macmillan, 2009), pp. 225-226.

[11] Weitz, pp. 225-226.

[12] Leah Hyslop, 'Emigration from Ireland soars', *Telegraph*, 5 October 2012,
<http://www.telegraph.co.uk/expat/expatnews/9584756/emigration-from-Ireland-soars.html> [Accessed 09.13.13]

[13] With the permission of the playwright Jimmy Murphy, Adigun rewrote *The Kings of the Kilburn High Road* for African characters as *The Paddies of Parnell Street*. The play, which was also directed by Adigun, was staged in August 2013 at The Teachers Club in Dublin.

[14] 'Savage comedy "pushes boat out"', *Irish Independent*, 30 November 2012,< http://www.independent.ie/savage-comedy-pushes-boat-out.html> [Accessed 9 March 2013]

[15] 'Savage comedy "pushes boat out."'

[16] Peter L. Berger, *Redeeming Laughter: The Comic Dimension of Human Experience* (Berlin and New York: De Gruyter, 1997) p. 157

[17] Berger, pp. 157-158.

[18] Berger, p. 158.

[19] Berger, p. 158.

[20] Susan Wells, 'Jacobean City Comedy and the Ideology of the City', *EHL* 48:1 (1981), pp. 37-60 p. 37.

[21] Brian Gibbons cited in Wells, p. 37.

[22] Wells, p. 37.

[23] Wells, p. 37

[24] 'Racism', Series Two, Episode Five, *The Savage Eye*, (Dublin: Blinder Films Ltd, 2011), 16.48 – 19-03.

[25] Berger, 158.

[26] Future', Series Two, Episode Six, *The Savage Eye*, (Dublin: Blinder Films Ltd, 2011), 20.06 – 20.18

[27] Future', Series Two, Episode Six, 23.05 – 23.15

[28] Future', Series Two, Episode Six, 22.30 – 22.40

[29] Bob Geldof in interview, 'Future', Series Two, Episode Six, 18.30-20.15

13 | Playwrights, Screenplays, Criminality, Gangland and the Tragicomic Imperatives in *I Went Down* and *Intermission*

Eamonn Jordan

INTRODUCTION

There is nothing new about people working across different art forms, but since the 1990s what is of significance is the sheer number of writers, who initially made their names as playwrights, and also wrote and sometimes directed very accomplished screenplays that are more often than not set in criminal and urban underworlds. Indeed the styles and approaches of these writers are as much influenced by screen writers and film directors as they are by theatrical traditions, practices and genres.[1] In this essay I will be focusing in particular on the implications of tragicomic genre impulses in Mark O'Rowe's screenplay for *Intermission* (2003),[2] which John Crowley directed, and Conor McPherson's screenplay for *I Went Down* (1997),[3] which is directed by Paddy Breathnach and was initially commissioned by Breathnach and Robert Walpole, who were looking for a particular style of movie that they felt would have broad appeal.[4]

In both of these works Dublin serves as a real, lived-in place, as a screenscape, and as sensibility or consciousness that is central to the framing or interfacing of criminality, capitalism and social marginalisation.[5] But despite all of the horrors and terrors of criminality and gangland, its bonds, rules, threats, disorganisation and violence, the distinctivenesses of these two works are found in the fact that each film seldom reaches the levels of gruesomeness found in the very many representations of the darker criminal underworlds evident in other metropolitan centres. This is due to the fact that the city of

Dublin in both films is framed in such a way as to accommodate substantially the distinctive tragicomic impulses that are fundamental to the genre mechanisms of each of these works.[6]

CAPITAL CITY/ GANGLAND CAPITAL

Dublin is not an iconic city, *per se*, as it does not have the landmark buildings of New York, Rome, Paris or London. In many ways Dublin is a relatively nondescript city, defined in many films by its mountains, its small bridges like the Ha'penny or new Beckett bridges across the river Liffey, by its proximity to the sea, by its buses, trams and trains and by a few landmark buildings and monuments, including the Spire, the two Poolbeg chimneys, IFSC and more recently its redeveloped sports stadia, the Aviva and Croke Park, and new Conference Centre. Dublin is a city equally not defined by its commodification or iconicity.

Jen Harvie notes how 'cities are ever-changing geographical, architectural, political and social structures where most people live and work, densely gathered in extremely complex social structures'.[7] Since the early 1990s, and with few exceptions, the city of Dublin is portrayed as one of density and complex social dynamics, but is seldom a city of rejuvenation, comfort, professional living, and cultural privilege.[8] Instead the domestic, working and social spaces represented are more often than not bleak, stagnant, stultifying and degenerating. The socio/economic disadvantages represented are associated predominantly with unemployment, a lack of social mobility, social repressions, structural inequalities, broader welfare benefit dependencies, and large scale social housing – comprising down-at-heel inner city apartment or flat complexes or suburban estates.

In addition, these cinematic worlds are dominated by criminal activities and the rule of gangland, making them almost, but not quite dystopian in perspective.[9] Robberies, extortion, racketeering, bribery, smuggling, dealing in illegal fire arms and drugs, prostitution, human trafficking and the torture and execution of rivals, opponents, or indeed anyone who gets in the way, are common to almost all of these works. In these cinematic criminal worlds, for those central or on the periphery of gangland, concerns about safety are an ongoing anxiety, freedom is compromised and life is clearly cheapened. Gangland's almost feudal hierarchies are based on dominance, intimidation, ruthlessness, indebtedness, misplaced loyalties, and spurious moral codes.

Individual or clusters of criminal or gangland figures generally accumulate significant wealth fostered by greed, exploitation and their own sense of entitlement. Substantially smaller dividends trickle down to their minnows and occasionally when some money is distributed to the poorer socio-economic classes these actions are sometimes framed nostalgically and unconscionably as a sort of Robin Hood-type effect. The forces of the law are ineffectual in the protection of the innocent or in apprehension of the guilty, and are almost futile in the fundamental discharging of natural or civic justice. This criminalisation of a cinematic Dublin does not make it a world elsewhere, as it mimics in so many ways the representations of other first-world underworld cultures in film generally. The Dublin of the two films discussed here does not carry the burden of such a negative stature, but nevertheless, there is the transposition of the general darkness associated with Dublin's underworld.

In a complex, almost Robert Altmanesque movie that involves multiple intertwining narratives, multi-protagonists and multi-antagonists, and multiple locations, somewhat similar to *Nashville* (1975) and *Short Cuts* (1993), *Intermission* in the first instance is sharply defined by its various Dublin locations and by the dominant Dublin vernacular spoken by the characters across different social classes.[10] Shot on hand-held cameras, *Intermission*'s Dublin includes various locations from domestic family places to work places, from a pub and adult video shop to a mature-aged adult night club, from inner-city flat complexes to mountainous locations beyond the city's boundaries.

Intermission opens with Colin Farrell's exotically named, working class Dublin character Lehiff, who initially appears to be seducing a shop assistant (Kerry Condon). Then, the shift in sensibility that accompanies the instance of his horrible violence towards her demonstrates one of the many challenges audiences face in the processing of attitudes towards charm, violence, sensation, and voyeurism. Also there are also the challenges audiences face with the traditional processes of empathising with the plight or aligning themselves with a lead actor's character, such as Farrell's.[11] Lehiff proves to be a thief, carjacker and kidnapper, and late in the film he shoots an unarmed policeman.[12] And although Farrell's character is central to the dramatic arc, the emotional trajectory of the piece has more to do with the complex relationship between Deirdre (Kelly MacDonald) and John (Cillian Murphy). Lehiff's tiger robbery plan is John's opportunity to get money, but more importantly, to extract some level of revenge on her and her new boyfriend, bank manager Sam (Michael MacElhatton), with whom Deirdre has struck up a relationship soon after breaking up with John. John's prior criminal activities include the stealing of Chef Sauce (Brown Sauce) with his friend Oscar (David Wilmot) from the nearby Fruitfield Factory.

If these characters, John, Deirdre, Oscar and Lehiff are from lower down the social ladder, they are offset by Megamart's store manager, Mr Henderson (Owen Roe), and the middle-class couple, Sam and his wife Noeleen (Deirdre O'Kane). The media classes are also prominent through the figures of television producer Ben Campion (Tomás O'Suilleabháin) and his immediate boss, Thomas Downes (Daragh Kelly), who determines what stories are aired on the magazine programme, 'Little Big City'. Further linking all of the characters and multiple narratives is Jerry Lynch (Colin Meaney),[13] the maverick street cop with fifteen years experience of policing and a penchant for Celtic mysticism.

In his guiding of Ben through the world of Dublin's high-rise flats and abject poverty, Jerry variously labels those who are socially disadvantaged, as members of Dublin's 'underbelly,' as 'piss, waste', and 'scum'. To his police colleagues Jerry is not a maverick law enforcer, but a puffed-up, self-aggrandising idiot. Jerry's narcissism, self-deceptions and contentious social awarenesses are clearly played for these views to be satirically exposed. In Lehiff, Jerry has his own natural antagonist.

Placing characters out of their depths in gangland is a common trope in McPherson's screenwriting more generally, but these figures regularly rely on cunning and industriousness to survive such encounters.[14] Set predominantly in a working-class environment, the tragicomic buddy road movie, I Went Down, also has Dublin as an unruly city, partially contaminated and determined by criminal intent. In I Went Down there is also criminal indebtedness, punishment beatings, double crossings, kidnappings, disappearances and killings, but these are represented in surprisingly different ways to most of those films set in Belfast's paramilitary/criminal underworlds.[15] Representations of social housing are confined to Bunny Kelly's (Brendan Gleeson) visits to his family home, where his wife comedically tries to hide out of sight: in this location the words 'Drugs Out' are either painted or chalked on the street.

The opening scene showing Git (Peter McDonald) in prison is not an opportunity to capture the oppression that is often shown to exist between prison inmates and rival gangs; instead its focus is on the relationship between Git and his ex-girlfriend Sabrina Bradley (Antoine Byrne), who is now dating his friend, Anto (David Wilmot), and she wants Git's approval. Their exchange takes place in a brightly lit space. In *I Went Down* there are only a few night scenes, and the darkness and shadow of some of the already mentioned internal urban locations are offset by many of the external scenes that are brightly lit by Cian de Buitléar's cinematography. *I Went Down* takes Bunny and Git away from Dublin to Gort, Co. Galway, to Cork, and back up to the capital through the southwest and midlands of Ireland.

The characters travel down back roads and narrow rural lanes as they try to stay away from the main roads.[16] The rural landscape is predominantly flat, unlike the island and mountain shots evident in many Irish films from prior decades. And when it comes to violence, the spectator frequently only gets to see the aftermath of such scenes, namely Git's blinding of one of French's lieutenants, Johnner Doyle (Michael McElhatton), or later when Git is beaten up in the pub in Cork, the spectator does not see the attack, only the outcome, a bloodied face and broken nose which Bunny tries later to re-set. When the characters later on find themselves in the forest, one could be watching a pirate movie and the digging up of hidden treasure, or witnessing a mafia-like disposal of human remains. While the forest is the burial place of three gangland figures, French (Tony Doyle), Grogan (Peter Caffrey), and Sonny Mulligan (Jonny Murphy), and despite the ruthlessness of the gangland milieu in *I Went Down*, neither the woods nor the streets are simply 'conduits of death – dumping grounds for mutilated corpses and escape routes for the killers'.[17] Instead the incidents in the forest provide an opportunity for Git and Bunny to escape gangland's hold over them.

DEDICATED FOLLOWERS OF CITATION

Intermission and *I Went Down* feature in Debbie Ging's wide-ranging and comprehensive study; she gives a full chapter to marginalised and socially excluded men in films of the 1990s and 2000s, where the 'ostensible politics of anti-conformism' of the new working-class 'anti-hero' are 'not always easy to decode'.[18] Ging's analysis brings together British underclass films as theorised by Claire Monk (2000) and Steve Chibnall (2001) – who proposed the notion of 'gangster-light' – and Jeffrey Sconce's term 'smart film' (2002), which includes work shaped by irony, fatalism, black humour and relativism,[19] but it is also 'characterised by disaffection, nihilism and anomie. In particular of interest is the "fucked by fate" attitudes of the smart films' protagonists and their sense of alienation within contemporary consumer culture.'[20]

The fact that both works use mediatisation, intertextuality and citation implies that they are particularly self-conscious about their own genre positioning and alert to cinematic practices elsewhere. For instance, *Intermission* as already mentioned owes a debt to films like Altman's *Nashville* and *Short Cuts*, but also Paul Thomas Anderson's *Magnolia* (1999).[21] *I Went Down* is very much inspired by comedy capers/road movies such as Martin Brest's *Midnight Run* (1988),[22] and of course Ridley Scott's *Thelma and Louise* (1991).[23] In different ways, both films absorb the influence of Hollywood's generic formulations, and not only re-apply many of them in an Irish context, but also add to them in particular ways. One relies on the competencies of the audiences to accommodate genre flux, and the utilisation of genre-within-genre, art-within-art, or media-within-media form is particularly notable in *Intermission*. As Dervila Layden notes, 'Genres are always about narrative form and thus by their nature are intertextual as they interact with the evolving generic archetype(s)'.[24]

What the film world in general proves is that genres evolve and categories are not only unstable and there to be broken but they also offer promiscuous springboards into alternative forms by way of overall genre comprehension. And without seeing indigenous film as simply countering and subverting Hollywood norms, it is important to keep in mind Christine Gledhill's comments that, 'if postmodern practices dissolve the discrete identities of genres, globalization and multinational co-production threaten the existence of the distinctly national. Thus genre theorists confront the apparent breakdown of traditional genre categories as generic features float off into the global stratosphere, ever more promiscuously crossing both generic and national boundaries'.[25]

The genres proffered in the two works discussed here are not simply parodic nor are they related to Hollywood in a parasitic way, rather their intertexual presences exist as resonators, and as curious validators of the overall ambitions and promiscuous tendencies of the pieces. It is less and less the case that genre regulations are a means by which to disparage evolving forms. The combinations of both genre reassurance and experimentation have invoked complicated responses to *I Went Down* in particular. For instance, Barry Monahan prefers to make reference to the 'generic' deficiencies of the protagonists:

> Not only do Bunny and Git become ridiculous in their ineffectiveness at achieving modes of performance that specific

generic narrative structures require of them, but comedy is also provided by their reflection and commentary on this. The inability of the small time gangsters to fill the mainstream roles that both narrative and mise-en-scéne have drawn for them is paralleled with a breakdown in communication and a failure of linguistic logic.[26]

I can only partially agree with Monahan here. I do think that they fill the 'mainstream roles' determined for them, and the malfunctioning of logic is tragicomic in intent rather than implicit failures. They are as Monahan concludes anything but the gangsters of 'Hollywood's classical era', but are the dislodged tragic clowns of Beckett or O'Casey in many respects. And Lance Pettitt argues something slightly different, concluding that its world 'takes reference from other cinematic representations and is true to this medium rather than reality.' He adds that *I Went Down* 'is unconcerned with the sociologically-driven naturalism'.[27] While I do agree that the film is true to the 'medium rather than reality', in many respects it still maintains a firm enough foothold in a particular reality as I have been arguing.

In terms of *Intermission* Ging argues, 'It is the multiplicity of masculinities, coupled with the film's use of irony, which renders it highly polysemic'.[28] Ging continues, although there is 'sufficient violence, action and celebration of hardcore working-class masculinities to qualify *Intermission* as a youth-orientated tale of male (mis)adventure such as in *Trainspotting* or *Twin Town*, 'it is also a much more self-conscious exploration of the paradoxes and inconsistencies that underpin contemporary performances of masculinity'.[29]

The fixations on gangsters and criminality in both works are not determined only by sensationalism and by a need to shock, for to my mind they have far greater purpose. So it is here where I turn my attention to the relationship between criminality and the brutality and oppressions of the everyday of the underworld and how a tragicomic disposition both heightens awarenesses and also softens the impact and implications of violence.

GANGSTERS RAPPED

Diane Negra cites Lee Grieveson, Esther Sonnet and Peter Stanfield's comments that 'gangster films are not simply narratives for telling the stories of ahistorical, unidimensional criminal figures or gangs but sites of instability of wider cultural resonance'.[30] Further, Lance Petitt notes of *Veronica Guerin* that, the level of consumption and pleasure in clothes, motorbikes, inflicting sadistic violence, sex and gambling is an index of the gangster's contempt for the 'workday' capitalism under which the rest of society obediently works, but its excess merely embodies *in extremis* the underlying principles of consumerism and 'cut throat' competition that drives the wider economy.[31]

Taking both quotes together, in different ways each film discussed here forces us to think differently about cultural 'instability', and about wider social/political relationships between consumerism, '"workday" capitalism', workday criminality, to coin a term, and various forms of violence.

Slavoj Žižek identifies 'subjective violence' as being the more visible forms of violence 'performed by a clearly identifiable agent', which is measured against a norm of non-violence; thus it is seen as a 'perturbation of the "normal" peaceful state of things'.[32] In many instances, gangland violence is seen as a shattering of norms on the one hand, but, on the other, that its violence is isolated to certain areas and in the main self-contained and not mainstream. Equally, this subjective violence is deemed random and pathological in many instances. So it tends to be ruthless psychopathic figures that populate and dominate gangland in representations of American organised crime as in mafia films generally, in television series like *The Wire* (2002-8), in the French crime series *Spiral* (*Engrenages*) (2005-), or in sectarian/paramilitary/criminal scenes in the gangland Belfast that Martin McCloone talks about.[33]

But for Žižek one also needs to take a step backward from such subjective violence and 'to identify a violence that sustains our very efforts to fight violence and to promote tolerance'.[34] He sees this 'objective' violence as 'precisely the violence inherent in the "normal" state of things. Furthermore, Žižek regards objective violence as a systematic and fundamental oppression designed to maintain the mechanisms and inequalities of liberal capitalism. For him, objective violence then is 'often the catastrophic consequences of the smooth functioning of our economic and political systems', thus 'something like the notorious "dark matter" of physics, the counterpart to the all too visible subjective violence.'[35]

Seen in this light, the criminal/gangland cultures in each of these two films also potentially reminds the spectator how they contrast with the many Hollywood films where social hardships in disadvantaged neighbourhoods are deemed as a fundamental consequence of a ruthless, exploitative and proximate gangland culture only, but not as a condition of broader socially ranked, inequitable relationships. In both of these films and in different ways the subjective, visible violence that is nominally the forte of gangland is considered not in isolation, but in relation to this broader systemic violence that Žižek identifies. This objective violence is often made manifest with strong, if unusual, correlations between capitalism and inequality in the two works considered here. This impulse is not akin to Žižek's Marxist analysis, but more from the perspective of a socially democratic justice platform. The sense of entitlement of gangland figures like French in *I Went Down* or, indeed, Perrier (Brendan Gleeson) in O'Rowe's screenplay for Ian Fitzgibbbon's *Perrier's Bounty* (2009), maps onto a similar sense that exists within the elite of a society, some of whom have earned certain economic privileges, and others having accumulated wealth by less than honourable means. However, Git's father possesses a false sense of entitlement when he loots a rammed electrical shop, a deed which ends up with a jail sentence for his son, and this is a detail which complicates any simplistic nostalgia or idealisation of the working classes.

Furthermore, that Jerry in *Intermission* sees Ben (the eventual slayer of Lehiff) as a 'warrior soul, a kindred soul' is as fantastic as it is delusional, but it is also indicative of wider bourgeois allegiances and collusions between the forces of law and media elites. The media false narrative of Lehiff's death and Jerry's heroism is part of this complicity. The failed attempt to document the working-class, inoffensive activities of the rabbit man (Mikel Murfi), and the exploitation of the story of Deirdre's sister, Sally (Shirley Henderson) and mother, Maura's (Ger Ryan) involvement in the rescue of victims of a bus crash say much about the framing imperatives that a predominantly middle-class media wish to circulate, particularly about those lower down the social scale. Such manipulation is a different form of ideological oppression.

There is a clear divide between the relatively humane and self-judgemental characters like John and Git and the merciless, if measured, psychopathic figures like French, Jerry and Lehiff. That said, many of the working-class male characters in both of these two works display low levels of contentiousness, defy duties and responsibilities, are not motivated to work, and possess reactionary and militant qualities that easily take them outside the law and frames of legitimacy. It is not so much taking justice into one's own hands, but easily embracing criminality as a default setting. John and Oscar are good examples of this. In *Perrier's Bounty*, the film's main character,

Michael McCrea (Cillian Murphy), is described as a 'perpetual waster' by the film's grim-reaper narrator.

Perversely, by the film's end Sam in *Intermission* is now the submissive partner in his relationship with his wife, as his status as elite society member is partially subverted by his new role as Noeleen's house slave. The final assault on Mega Mart's Mr Henderson by the young boy on the bicycle is a further elaboration on this work's subversive class-based impulse, but in ways that the boy's delinquent behaviour is seen as bringing a positive retributive outcome.

Ging's conclusion to many films about working-class disenfranchised male characters is close to my own argument, that, 'indeed the extreme polarity that came to characterize Irish media representations of young working-class men in the 2000s – as lawless and dangerous in the news media, yet reified as popular cultural heroes in advertising and the entertainment media – may have ultimately served the same purpose, namely to stigmatize and essentialize underclass masculinity as social inevitability rather than as a symptom of inequality'.[36] While I agree with her on the issue of class, I do think that McPherson's or O'Rowe's work exposes the systematic inequalities of these male characters.

According to Ging global 'cinematic tropes of male disempowerment and victimhood do not necessarily signal patriarchal defeat; on the contrary they can be read as strategic attempts to reclaim agency and power through the representation of their loss',[37] or even when 'working class masculinities are excluded from most of the patriarchal dividends, they often benefit in the sense that they are used as exemplars of masculine strength, 'and authority' – pace Connell (1995).[38] However, unlike Ging, I do not see the role of working-class criminally minded males in the films discussed in this article as evidence of a form of patriarchal reclamation. In the two films, the psychopathic are killed and those without empathy are scorned, and few are in receipt of 'patriarchal dividends'. The low-waged disaffected, the slacker rebels, the nonchalant anti-authority and protest figures, the classed-based non-conscientious scapegoats are evidence of the intermingling of contradictory and rival value systems and are more about grasping the systemic contradictions and anamolies of liberal capitalism. These apply across genders – Noeleen, Sally, Deirdre and Maura in *Intermission*, and Sabrina and Teresa (Carmel Callan) in *I Went Down*. (It is French's wife who double-crosses French and Grogan, as she is not the figure traded between men, but the one who determines what is exchanged.) While both films are predominantly heterosexual and homosocial in focus, Bunny's bi-sexuality does not simply remain on the margins and Jerry's use of homosexuality as a term of abuse is upbraided.

Equally, there is no evidence of Mick and John being under police investigation for their roles in the attempted tiger kidnapping, and there is no reporting to authorities or investigative follow-through of John's bullet wound. Like John, Bunny is also wounded, but it has no lasting effects. The disappearance of French is concealed in hearsay, innuendo and urban legends and Bunny and Git face no further investigation. While the underworld is almost always ruthless and unforgiving and the victory in I Went Down of the two minnows over the gangland boss is a celebration of survival, and the conviviality of both Git and Bunny. (McDonald and Gleeson take a certain glee in the gormlessness and limited – but constructive – inventiveness of their characters.)

Git and Bunny may be out of their depths in the gangland but there is optimism in their plans to go to America, after profiting from illegality, having gained the possession of forged dollar printing plates. The final scene has them leaving in a car, wearing shades and Hawaiian shirts. America is a place known to them, not by experience, but by media and fictive representations. (Of course, there is no reference to whatever visa problems both ex-convicts might face.)

Further, the buddy structure is marked by the usual early tensions between them and the emergence of mutual respect and friendship is akin to Hollywood buddy movies more generally. (Their relationship is not marked by the usual destructive dyads that Nina Witoszek and Pat Sheeran have identified in their work on the relationship between Irish literature and the funerary traditions.[39]) Deleted exchanges between Sabrina and Git during the final editing process drive the work in the direction of male/male relationships.[40] Git does not get back with Sabrina, the film suggests she knows it is the right thing for her, but she fails to take any initiative.[41]

By the end of Intermission there is not only the comedy-inflected romantic renewal of John and Deirdre's relationship, and a budding bond between Oscar and Sally, whose 'ronnie' is an ongoing joke throughout the movie. Her unwillingness to self-groom is not only equated with a lack of femininity, but also as indicative of an unwillingness to transact with those of the opposite sex. However, this behaviour is prompted by the harrowing experiences of an abusive relationship at the hands of her ex-boyfriend. So the ending is bittersweet. Intermission places significant emphasis on 'the flutts', on heteronormative relationships, rather than on homosocial relationships. The extensive focus on mother-daughter relationships is very notable, as is the emphasis on female friendship, most notably between Noeleen and her friend, Karen (Barbara Bergin).

Rather than being 'fucked by fate', many of these upbeat outcomes suggest that these characters, male and female, have taken some semblance of their fates into their own hands, and their licence is to love and not to work, opting out, to move forward, and instinctively to reject the capitalist model, without either a criminal delinquency or another alternative in mind. Prompted by Rick Altman's work, Layden cautions in sentimentalising 'countercultural unsanctioned behaviour' because genre can function as a 'safety mechanism in the maintenance of social order.'[42]

CONCLUSION

Without de-familiarizing criminality and gangland too much and without starkly displacing the horrors of these realities by making them palatable, the violence presented in the two works discussed here is neither grimly authentic nor vacantly or self-consciously postmodern, neither self-indulgently gratuitous nor simplistically voyeuristic. *Intermission* demonstrates other forms of violence that are to be found in the workplace, in policing, and in media reporting, and it also illustrates the lack of empathy, particularly amongst the middle classes towards those lower down the social scale. *I Went Down* demonstrates the ease with which people fall into indebtedness, and the pressures crime-lord figures bring to bear on characters to do their bidding. If gangland is 'dis-organised' in *I Went Down* as its DVD sleeve suggests, the criminality of *Intermission* is more opportunistic and *ad hoc*, as it illustrates the various forms of criminality dispersed across social classes. (In McPherson's, *The Actors*, Barreller's criminal gang is not ruthless, but Perrier's in *Perrier's Bounty* is.)

These two works do not picture gangland and criminality as anomalies, as worlds apart onto which one can displace or project anxieties of civic unrest or worlds that one can look upon voyeuristically from a superior social or cultural perspective. Instead, the existence of gangland and criminal violence also clearly re-iterates the functioning of broader systemic inequalities, and how the codes and structures of gangland and the greed and aspirations of criminals mimic those of society more generally. (Lehiff fantasies about having his own 'abode'.)

Overall, the Dublin of these two works is defined by what it is not as much as by what it is. It is not a funerary space, not a 'pariah city', not a world where the violence of gangland is omnipotent. Here, it is city that is marked not by gangland's omniscience, but by the repeated ability of the characters to survive the traumas of gangland not only in the works of McPherson and O'Rowe discussed here but also in the likes of *The Actors* and *Saltwater* and *Perrier's Bounty*. If the tendency is for tragicomedy to draw the comic longing of loser/heroes into tragedy, it is fair to say that these two films turn on the failures and capitulations of tragic 'anti-heroes', clowns, layabouts, dreamers, losers, and scapegoats into comedies of ambiguous success. Dublin is a place defined by its heterotopic possibilities, a city aligned with possibility and renewal, a city that prioritises life over death; both screenwriters are determined by their theatrical roots in the Dublins of O'Casey and Beckett and in the tradition of dramatic tragicomedy, which modulates the American filmic forms with which they are most associated.

WORKS CITED

Baron-Cohen, Simon, *Zero Degrees of Empathy: A New Theory of Human Cruelty* (London: Allen Lane an imprint of Penguin Books, 2011).

Barton, Ruth, (ed.), *Screening Irish-America: Representing Irish-America in Film and Television* (Dublin and Portland: Irish Academic Press, 2009).

Crosson, Sean, 'Vanishing Point: An examination of some consequences of globalization for contemporary Irish film', p. 8. http://vmserver14.nuigalway.ie/xmlui/bitstream/handle/10379/591/Vanishing%20Point%20article.pdf?sequence=1 (Accessed 1/8/2013)

Crowley, John, (Director), Intermission (2003).

Ging, Debbie, *Men and Masculinities* (Basingstoke: Palgrave McMillan, 2013).

Gledhill, Christine, 'Genre and nation' in Brian McIlroy (ed.), *Genre and Cinema: Ireland and Transnationalism* (London and New York: Routledge, 2007), pp. 11-26.

Harvie, Jen, *Theatre & the City* (Houndmills: Palgrave Macmillan, 2009).

Judell, Brandon, 'Ireland's Son of Altman: John Crowley Takes No Shortcuts with Intermission'. http://www.indiewire.com/article/irelands_son_of_altman_john_crowley_takes_no_shortcuts_with_intermission (Accessed 21/7/2103)

King, Greg, "Peat Fiction? Greg King Talks to Irish director Paddy Breathnach about I Went Down, the quirky new crime thriller from

Ireland," The Reel Ring, December 1997
http://www.filmreviews.net.au/1997/12/i-went-down/ (Accessed
1/8/2013)

Layden, Dervila, 'Discovering and uncovering genre in Irish cinema', in
Brian McIlroy, (ed.), *Genre and Cinema: Ireland and
Transnationalism* (London and New York: Routledge, 2007), pp. 27-
44.

McDonagh, Martin, *In Bruges* (London: Faber and Faber, 2008).

McLoone, Martin, *Film, Media and Popular Culture in Ireland* (Dublin
and Portland, OR: Irish Academic Press, 2008).

McIlroy, Brian, (ed.), *Genre and Cinema: Ireland and
Transnationalism* (London and New York: Routledge, 2007).

McPherson, C., *I Went Down: The Shooting Script* (London: Nick Hern
Books, 1997).

Monahan, Barry, 'Playing Cops and Robbers: Recent Irish Cinema and
Genre Performance', in Brian McIlroy, (ed.), *Genre and Cinema:
Ireland and Transnationalism* (London and New York: Routledge,
2007), pp. 45-57.

Negra, Diane, 'Irishness, Anger and Masculinity in Recent Film and
Television, in Ruth Barton (ed.), *Screening Irish-America:
Representing Irish-America in Film and Television* (Dublin and
Portland: Irish Academic Press, 2009), pp.279-298.

Pettitt, Lance, *Screen Ireland: Film and Television Representation*
(Manchester and New York: Manchester University Press, 2000).

------, '"We're no fucking Eye-talians": The Gangster Genre and Irish
Cinema', in Ruth Barton and Harvey O'Brien, (eds.), *Keeping it Real:
Irish Film and Television* (London and New York, Wallflower,
2004), pp.25-38.

Pine, Emilie, 'This is what I need you to do to make it right': Conor
McPherson's *I Went Down* in *The Theatre of Conor McPherson:
'Right beside the Beyond',* Lilian Chambers and Eamonn Jordan
(eds) (Dublin: Carysfort Press, 2012), pp. 103-112.

Pinker, Steven, The Better Angels of Our Nature: A History of Violence
and Humanity (London: Penguin Books, 2011).

Witoszek, Nina and Pat Sheeran, *Talking to the Dead: A Study of the
Irish Funerary Traditions* (Amsterdam-Atlanta, GA: Rodopi, 1998).

Žižek, Slavoj, *Violence* (London: Profile Books, 2009).

---

[1] Apart from the writers discussed here, the list would include Gary
Mitchell, Jim O'Hanlon and Tim Loane, Stuart Carolan amongst
others. Declan Hughes' *Twenty Grand* (2000), Mark O'Rowe's *Made
in China* (2001), Stella Feehily's *Duck* (2003) and Roddy Doyle and
Bisi Adigun's re-working of *The Playboy of the Western World*
(2007), set in contemporary west Dublin, with Christy Mahon, now
the Nigerian refugee, Christopher Malomo, are examples of plays

that deal with gangland. Richard Dormer's *Drum Belly* (2013) concerns itself with an Irish gang in New York in the 1960s. In Northern Ireland, Gary Mitchell's work often dealt with the relationship between loyalist paramilitaries and criminality, post-Peace Process. See for example *As the Beast Sleeps* (2002).

2 O'Rowe's screenplay for *Perrier's Bounty* (2009), which Ian Fitzgibbon directed, has a darker if somewhat similar tragic-comic mood.

3 *I Went Down* got the Spanish Circle of Screenwriter's Award for Best Screenplay and the San Sebastian film festival award for Best Film.

4 It is not possible here to theorise the relationship between screenplay and film in the way that theatre theorists like Patrice Pavis and many others have articulated the relationship between text and performance. My focus is specifically genre related, which is informed by both the screenplay's sensibility and its realisation on the screen in terms of directorial approach, cinematography, editing and acting idiom.

5 Dublin is evoked successfully and poignantly in Martin McDonagh's *In Bruges* (2008) with the city serving as a form of lapsed moral compass and is evoked brilliantly in the moments when Ken (Brendan Gleeson) sacrifices himself whilst trying to protect Ray (Colin Farrell) from Harry (Ralph Fiennes), accompanied by 'On Raglan Road', which was written by Patrick Kavanagh in 1946. Even at such a moment of poignant self-sacrifice, there is the obstinacy of McDonagh's comic impulse, for the gun that Ken has stored in his pocket to help Ray with his self-defence falls apart on landing, after he has plunged from the bell tower.

6 The tragic-comic imperative evident in Sean O'Casey's *Dublin Trilogy*, comprising *The Shadow of a Gunman* (1923), *Juno and the Paycock* (1924) and *The Plough and the Stars* (1926) are clear influences on both McPherson's and O'Rowe's writings more generally. O'Casey's work offers exceptional templates for the melding of tragedy and comedy, where the tensions between plot, character and theatrical space are constantly generating major anomalies. Additionally, to varying degrees the self-conscious and subversive irony in the writings of the Dublin-born Samuel Beckett has influenced both writers.

7 Jen Harvie, *Theatre & the City* (Houndmills: Palgrave Macmillan, 2009), p.6.

8 Gerry Stembridge's *About Adam* (2001) and Liz Gill's *Goldfish Memory* (2003) deliver what Martin McLoone calls 'hip hedonism'. See *Film, Media and Popular Culture in Ireland* (Dublin and Portland: Irish Academic Press, 2008), p.46.

9 Examples are many including Joel Schumacher's *Veronica Guerin* (2003), and the more recent television series *Love/Hate* (2010) - written by Stuart Carolan. There is also this spate of films about the

notorious gangland figure Martin Cahill, aka The General, who was killed by the Provisional Irish Republican Army. John Boorman's *The General* (1998) has Brendan Gleeson playing Cahill, Thaddeus O'Sullivan's *Ordinary Decent Criminal* (1999) has Kevin Spacey playing Cahill, fictionalised as Michael Lynch, and in David Blair's *Vicious Circle* (1999) Ken Stott plays Cahill's role. All three films deal with Cahill in very different ways, and *Ordinary Decent Criminal* has Spacey's character survive at the end. Today's Dublin is not the Dublin of contrast with the raw working class environment of Jim Sheridan's *My Left Foot* (1989).

[10] Some of the reviews of *Intermission* point up pejoratively the nature of the accents and sometimes suggest the need for subtitles for American and international audiences.

[11] Farrell delivers an ironic rendition of the song 'I fought the law and the law won' (written by Sonny Curtis), which also sets the tone of the piece.

[12] Another criminal character in *Intermission* is the young boy on a bike, Philip (Taylor Molloy), whose red jacket is pointedly co-ordinated with Farrell's sleeveless red hoodie. The boy wreaks carnage with his ability to throw rocks casually through the windscreens of passing vehicles. Lehiff, the bus driver, Mick (Brián F. O'Byrne), and Mega Mart's manager Mr Henderson all fall foul to this particular delinquency.

[13] Colm Meaney had played the father figure in Stephen Frears' *The Snapper* (1993) and *The Van* (1996), based on novels by Roddy Doyle.

[14] *See* McPherson's *Saltwater* (2000), which he wrote and directed. It is an adaptation of his play *This Lime Tree Bower* (1993) and *The Actors* (2003).

[15] Early drafts include robberies, kidnappings, vigilantes, terrorists. See Conor McPherson, *I Went Down: The Shooting Script* (London: Nick Hern Books, 1997), pp.110-11.

[16] Lance Pettitt notes how, 'the midland of Ireland and in particular the bogland scenes provide a location that is at once identifiably Irish yet also shot to look like a US prairie.' See *Screen Ireland: Film and Television Representation* (Manchester and New York: Manchester University Press, 2000), p.276.

[17] Martin McLoone also makes reference to the Dublin of Neil Jordan's *Michael Collins* (1996), where the film's 'prevailing imagery consists of shadowy urban nightscapes – dark, misty-blue and subterranean, mirroring the underground world inhabited by Collins' secret army,' a description which is in close alignment to how he sees Belfast portrayed in most films. See *Film, Media and Popular Culture in Ireland* p.87.

[18] Debbie Ging, *Men and Masculinities* (Basingstoke: Palgrave McMillan, 2013), p.163.

19 Ibid., pp.157-9.

20 Ibid., p.159

21 In an interview John Crowley notes: 'But certainly, when I was preparing for this film, I watched *Magnolia* many times, just like I watched *Short Cuts* and *Nashville* as examples of films which juggle multiple plot lines and how you do that. How you try and ensure that the plot doesn't go off the boil'. See Brandon Judell, 'Ireland's Son of Altman: John Crowley Takes No Shortcuts with *Intermission*' http://www.indiewire.com/article/irelands_son_of_altman_john_c rowley_takes_no_shortcuts_with_intermission (Accessed 21/7/2103)

22 Sean Crosson notes that 'Right from the opening scene of *I Went Down*, the choice of both music and credits is evocative of *Pulp Fiction* [1994], while the use of intertitles also invites comparisons. Likewise, the general theme of two gangsters, Git Hynes (Peter McDonald) and Bunny Kelly (Brendan Gleeson), on a mission reminds one of the duo of Vincent Vega and Jules in *Pulp Fiction*.' See 'Vanishing Point: An examination of some consequences of globalization for contemporary Irish film', p. 8, http://vmserver14.nuigalway.ie/xmlui/bitstream/handle/10379/591 /Vanishing%20Point%20article.pdf?sequence=1 (Accessed 1/8/2013)

23 Greg King reports in his interview with Breathnach, 'The influences would be much broader in general. I would be taking contemporary cinema and seeing what's going on, and then try to find a niche in that rather than try to focus on any one film maker.' In the early stages, there were a lot of people who wanted the title changed, but Breathnach was adamant that the title, both cheeky and irreverent and rich in ambiguity, was perfectly suited to the film. 'It sounded like a genre title because it had a resonance about it, like *I Married A Witch* or *I Was A Fugitive From A Chain Gang*. Things beginning with an 'I' in the title have a kind of genre feel from the [19]30s, in particular, and I thought that wasn't a bad thing, because it immediately sends a signal that this is a genre film.' The title actually comes from Plato's *Republic*, which dealt with an epic journey into a shadowy world of illusion and danger where there's no easy way to clearly define good or bad. However, Breathnach deliberately uses the title because of its deliberate ambiguity. The phrase has references to being sent to prison, often for a crime that you didn't commit, as well as a more lurid sexual connotation. See 'Peat Fiction? Greg King Talks to Irish director Paddy Breathnach about *I Went Down*, the quirky new crime thriller from Ireland,' *The Reel Ring*, December 1997. http://www.filmreviews.net.au/1997/12/i-went-down/ (Accessed 1/8/2013)

24 Dervila Layden, 'Discovering and uncovering genre in Irish cinema', in Brian McIlroy (ed), *Genre and Cinema: Ireland and*

Transnationalism (London and New York: Routledge, 2007) pp. 27-44, p.38

[25] See Christine Gledhill, 'Genre and nation,' in McIlroy (ed), pp.11-26, p.11.

[26] Barry Monahan, 'Playing Cops and Robbers: Recent Irish Cinema and Genre Performance', in McIlroy (ed), pp. 45-57, p.50.

[27] Lance Pettitt, *Screen Ireland: Film and Television Representation*, p.276.

[28] Ging, *Men and Masculinities,* p.175.

[29] Ibid., p.176.

[30] Diane Negra, 'Irishness, Anger and Masculinity in Recent Film and Television,' in Ruth Barton (ed.), *Screening Irish-America: Representing Irish-America in Film and Television* (Dublin and Portland: Irish Academic Press, 2009), pp.279-298,p. 280, citing Lee Grieveson, Esther Sonnet and Peter Stanfield (eds.), *Mob Culture: Hidden Histories of the American Gangster Film* (New Brunswick, NJ: Rutgers University Press, 2005), p.9.

[31] Lance Pettitt, '"We're no fucking Eye-talians": The Gangster Genre and Irish Cinema', in Ruth Barton and Harvey O'Brien, (eds.), *Keeping it Real: Irish Film and Television* (London and New York, Wallflower, 2004), pp.25-38, p.32.

[32] Slavoj Žižek, *Violence* (London: Profile Books, 2009), p.1.

[33] Simon Baron-Cohen's work demonstrates someone with Anti-Social Personality Disorder can also be psychopathic or have Psychopathic Personality Disorder, also called Zero Negative (Type P): Baron-Cohen asserts that this cohort comprises fewer individuals again, less than 1 per cent of the male population and about 15 per cent of the prison population. To support his argument, Baron-Cohen uses Hervey Cleckley's research on psychopathology: Cleckley identifies the following dispositions: superficial charm, lack of anxiety or guilt, undependability and dishonesty, egocentricity, an inability to form lasting intimate relationships, a failure to learn from punishment, poverty of emotions, a lack of insight into the impact of their behaviour and a failure to plan ahead. See *Zero Degrees of Empathy: A New Theory of Human Cruelty* (London: Allen Lane an imprint of Penguin Books, 2011). p.46.

[34] Slavoj Žižek, *Violence,* (London: Profile Books, 2009), p.1.

[35] Ibid., p.2.

[36] Ging, *Men and Masculinities,* p.181.

[37] Ibid., pp.4-5.

[38] Ibid., p.163.

[39] Nina Witoszek and Pat Sheeran identify the 'quarrelous dyads' that 'are part of a community of hatred which observes a "taboo on tenderness,"' a phrase coined by Ian D. Suttie. See *Talking to the Dead: A Study of the Irish Funerary Traditions* (Amsterdam-Atlanta, GA: Rodopi, 1998),pp.157-8.

[40] See Appendix 2, 'Conor McPherson, Paddy Breathnach and Rob Walpole in Conversation' in Conor McPherson, *I Went Down: The Shooting Script*, p117.

[41] See Emilie Pine's reflections on gender in 'This is what I need you to do to make it right': Conor McPherson's *I Went Down* in *The Theatre of Conor McPherson: 'Right beside the Beyond'*, Lilian Chambers and Eamonn Jordan (eds) (Dublin: Carysfort Press, 2012), pp.103-112, p105.

[42] Dervila Layden, 'Discovering and uncovering genre in Irish cinema', p.27, referencing Rick Altman's *Film/Genre* (London: BFI, 1999), pp.152-56.

14 | Along the thin line: Dublin comedy in recent Fishamble plays

Jim Culleton

Dublin writers have a strong reputation for comic writing or for writing that captures the humour alongside the pain and anguish of life. This is true of contemporary Dublin playwrights, such as Conor McPherson, Mark O'Rowe, and Roddy Doyle, or twentieth-century writers such as Sean O'Casey, Brendan Behan and Samuel Beckett, or further back again to Richard Brinsley Sheridan, Oliver Goldsmith, or the satirist Jonathan Swift. I am going to explore how I think the comedy in some 'Dublin' plays I have directed has worked.

It is fascinating to witness how Dublin audiences respond to seeing themselves captured on stage when watching plays set in Dublin. It is also interesting to see how, on occasions, the Dublin humour has been received differently outside Ireland's capital city.

The comedy in *The Pride of Parnell Street* (2007) by Sebastian Barry, *Noah and the Tower Flower* (2007) by Sean McLoughlin and *Silent* (2011) by Pat Kinevane, all of which I directed for *Fishamble: The New Play Company*, is often perilously close to tragedy and sadness, and can comment on society in more powerful ways than strictly 'serious' drama. The master of contemporary comedy of manners, Bernard Farrell, and Elaine Murphy, a relative newcomer with wonderful comic insight, both use comedy to teach us about ourselves; we stand to learn unpleasant truths about our behaviour in Farrell's *Bookworms* (2010) and Murphy's *Shush* (2013), both of which I directed for the Abbey.

THE PRIDE OF PARNELL STREET, SEBASTIAN BARRY

In *The Pride of Parnell Street*, Sebastian Barry captured the fun, resilience, sadness and pride of living in Dublin's inner city during the 1990s, as Janet and Joe share their experiences with the audience through a series of interconnecting monologues. The sense of recognition from Dublin audiences was sometimes overwhelming, with lifelong residents of Parnell Street saying that it captured their lives, in all their joy and heartache, perfectly. Janet's line, 'why would we live in Dublin, iffen we didn't adore her?' which was delivered by Mary Murray, smiling and nodding to the audience, always seemed to bring a smile of recognition from Dublin audiences. In other places too, audiences enjoyed the feeling that they were, for one night only, honorary Dubliners, and often seemed to nod back to Janet in agreement.

The play is full of sadness and resilience, coping with the fact, as Janet says about her husband, Joe, who is dying, 'that it was only life that done him in and made a fool a him, like it does us all'. And yet, shortly before he dies, audiences would laugh as Joe (originally played by Karl Shiels, then by Aidan Kelly in the 2009 New York run and Joe Hanley in the 2011 revival) bemoans the fact that, 'a Dublin man can't hardly make a living at the robbing anymore. It's a terrible thing when a traditional trade goes to the dogs like that, yeh?'

Within this play there is lots of humour, sometimes inspired by the divide that can exist between the Northside and Southside areas of Dublin. Janet comments on her Northsider mother-in-law coming to visit her on the Southside:

> So she crosses over O'Connell Bridge like a traveller crossing into a foreign territory. She was probably surprised there was no Customs on the bridge, and that no one asked to see her passport.

When the production toured to the U.S. or in Europe, we worried that the strong Dublin accents might make it difficult for foreign audiences to understand. In New York, during the first preview, we tried slowing the rate of delivery a little to make the accents more comprehensible, but we found that this affected the rhythm of the play which is so much a part of Sebastian's writing. So we reinstated the usual pace and timing and, as the truthfulness and pathos of the play is arguably as much in the rhythm of the words as in their meaning, the audience engaged fully with the characters, even though some local references were lost (when it is explained that a 'wheelier' is a 'buggy', audiences in the U.S. would sometimes say 'oh, a stroller' for example).

In Germany, the production had a live simultaneous translator who was concerned that German words tend to be longer than English ones. He commented that, if he didn't have time to translate every word, this would be fine, once the timing of the German version hit the audience's ear with the same rhythm as the actors on stage.

NOAH AND THE TOWER FLOWER, SEAN MCLOUGHLIN

Similar to *The Pride of Parnell Street*, we found that maintaining the authentic rhythm was also crucial when Fishamble brought Sean McLoughlin's play *Noah and the Tower Flower* to New York. This was a romance set in Ballymun, with Darren Healy as Noah and Natalie played by Mary Murray. Mary worked hard in rehearsals on ensuring her accent was true to the Northside area of Ballymun and didn't veer into the Southside suburb of Ballyfermot. The nuances of this were lost on any audiences outside Dublin or sometimes, indeed, in the city. But the accents and the rhythm were the same in New York performances as in Dublin. One American patron turned to me at the end of a preview there and said, 'I didn't understand what everything meant, but I sure understood those two people love each other. I'm going home now to my *gaff*.'

There is lots of humour in this play, as the relationship develops between Noah, who has just been released from prison, and Natalie, who is a recovering heroin addict. Despite the grim situation in which the characters live, there is great fun in Noah's impersonations of Robert de Niro, or his pretence that Westlife is his favourite band, or his fake Oscar-winning speech. When Noah tells Natalie about drinking on the job while cutting grass for Dublin Corporation, Natalie scolds him by saying, 'Shouldn't of been drinkin' on the job', to which he responds, incredulously, 'It was a fuckin' Friday', which always got a great reaction.

After a violent exchange towards the end of the play, Noah leaves to buy vodka and flowers for Natalie. She has a moment to herself and says, 'Ah fuck.' The audience thinks, perhaps, that she regrets continuing the relationship with Noah, whom she fancies but who has also shown examples of violent outbursts, and that she is going to change her mind. Instead, she says, 'I forgot to tell him to get orange juice', in a beautiful last line that is comic, sad and hopeful, all at the same time, as our hearts go out to Natalie and her struggle to cope with life without drugs.

SILENT, PAT KINEVANE

In *Silent*, Pat Kinevane captures the grittiness of a homeless man living on the streets of Dublin. This is an often dark and angry one-person play, performed by the playwright, but with great humour, too, as the character of Tino copes with his homeless life and mental health issues:

> Hello and welcome to the mental health hotline. If you are obsessive-compulsive, press one, repeatedly...if you have multiple personalities, press 3, 4, 5 and 6.

In general, the casual nature with which Tino can insult or threaten someone is accepted quite readily by Dublin and Irish audiences, but is considered darker by many audiences outside Ireland. For instance, when Tino has a yoghurt drink and asks someone in the audience whether it is 'creamy or watery', the audience member responds (usually) with his or her opinion. Tino then jokes that, if the person is wrong, he will come down and beat the person up, which is delivered with a twinkle in the eye and usually greeted by laughter in Ireland, but is often viewed by other audiences as more shocking or dangerous. Perhaps we treat threatened violence too lightly in Ireland, or accept quite readily the thinness of the line between comedy and tragedy. When *Silent* was performed in New York, Ben Brantley commented in the *New York Times*, 'the principle reason Tino rivets our focus is the feeling that he needs us to exist – and, to be honest, that he might turn violent if we ignore him', reflecting the menace behind some darkly comic lines. The sinister joke about beating someone up is often changed outside Ireland to, 'I'll come down there and rob your purse'!

At another point in *Silent*, Tino remarks that 'Cork and France are joined at the hip ... mostly, the accents – identical!' He then continues to compare the two accents, showing how 'le cigarette' and 'de cigarette' are both formed in the throat. In Ireland, this comparison is always considered amusing, as Irish audiences probably enjoy being compared to the sophisticated French but, when we performed the play in Paris, the French audience was less convinced about their way of speaking being compared to Corkonians!

Much of the play's humour comes from comments on characters' prejudices and snobbishness, such as Tino describing nasty Noelette Amberson who runs a boutique, 'a kip of a shop that sold some of the ugliest clobber north of Gibraltar', or an imagined woman named 'Foxrock Fanny' who is:

> all spray tan and veneers, posin at Punchestown races with a huge fuckin ostrich feather stickin out of her botox forehead

and round her neck [she] wears the screw tops, vintage couture, photo on the back pages of Social and Personal magazine and delighted with herself that she is not now, nor ever will be, a hobo.

The humour has a dark, savage edge, as he talks about people who have contributed to his homelessness and depression. Pat and myself try to keep the tone of the play light in places so that, when the laughter dies down, the issues of the play are felt by audiences in a powerful and moving way. It is a great pleasure to sit among audiences at the production and get a sense of people engaging in a very honest way with the issues of mental health illness and homelessness.

There are some moments in particular that do unite audiences through laughter, albeit a dark, sad laugh. Tino tells the audience about Morty and Molly Mackey, two 'coffin chasers ... the folly the box gang, who love death'. At the end of the play, following a very dark section when Tino has died and is describing his funeral, he mentions that there were very few mourners but that 'Morty and Molly Mackey were there' and audiences all over the world share a laugh of release and appreciate the chance to smile.

BOOKWORMS, BERNARD FARRELL

Bernard Farrell has been creating hugely successful plays about the foibles, pretensions and frustrations of the middle classes for the past three decades. I worked with him on the Abbey's premiere production of *Bookworms*, about a book-club evening that goes disastrously wrong when men are invited to join for the first time, and tensions build between the hostess's builder husband, Larry (played by Phelim Drew), and his bank manager, Robert (played by Louis Lovett). Bernard is superb at creating an environment in which he can trap his characters in a room, so they cannot leave until the action has unfolded completely. I was so impressed by how thoroughly he had worked out which doors can open, which ones lock from outside, and where the doors lead, so that every time someone is locked out or let in, it is consistent and authentic within the world of the play.

Marion O'Dwyer played the book club hostess, Ann, and she referred in rehearsals to a classic saying that, 'if you leave a door open, the comedy escapes'. There is a lot of truth in that when it comes to a play by Bernard, such that the humour is often based on who is in the room, and cannot escape. Even in Act IV, which is a sort of coda to the play, Bernard has cleverly ensured his characters' motivations require them to stay in the room until attempted apologies have been made. In rehearsals, for instance, we wondered why Robert would not leave after being disgraced in the previous scene, but Bernard has very thoroughly worked out that Robert's wife, Jennifer (played in the original run by Karen Egan and by Donna Dent in the revival), needs to maintain her dignity by having Robert apologize to Dorothy (Deirdre Donnelly), an influential book-club member, and Robert does not dare contradict his wife at this stage of the events.

One of Bernard's great skills is to create fun and comedy from people's insecurities and fears. The fun always points up the tensions and conflicts within the drama. With the character of Larry, for instance, great fun is created in his confusion over Dorothy's many bereavements, and his futile attempts to console her. This points up Larry's embarrassment and worry about taking part in the book club. Also, Larry's attempt at literary criticism, having just completed a quick search on the internet for Sylvia Plath and Virginia Woolf, perfectly captures his unease, as he pretends he is comfortable in this literary gathering, in order to try to improve his relationship with Robert:

> ... and I want to say now that I *do* know who Sylvia Plath is ... (*almost a memorised performance*). She was married to Ted Hughes who was the Poet Laureate and her poems are world famous, poems like "Blackberrying" and "Crossing The River" and ... and ... (*stops*) ... and another one ... and her poems deal with confessional poetry about details of her own life and she committed suicide by putting her head in the oven, just as Virginia Woolf also did, except she done it by walking into a river and that was the point I was making that they both had that in common, apart from their writings and that's what makes us always think of them together.

Bernard lets the audience in on Larry and Ann's worries from the start of the play, so the audience shares their predicament, and cares for them. Even when Ann reveals to Dorothy that she may have had an inappropriate encounter with Robert, we hope that Larry does not find out and that Ann's secret will remain safe in the final scene. We know Ann is hiding her diary, which contains incriminating entries, but Larry does not know this. The comedy in this section develops as he sits on the armchair where her diary is hidden and shifts on the cushion covering the diary. She panics more and more, and I always sensed, when watching a performance, that the audience shared her fear and hoped she would get away with it! Bernard described the cushion scene as the classic sketch with the lover hiding in the wardrobe and the husband opens the door to hang up his jacket but does not see the hidden lover, even though the audience does. Bernard allows the audience to see all of Ann and Larry's attempts to cover up for embarrassing encounters, so we share their vulnerability.

Bernard often makes great comic use of his offstage characters, who sometimes act as a sort of *deus ex machina*, with secrets revealed gradually, as well as the ability to solve problems from afar. In *Bookworms*, Larry and Ann's daughter, Aisling (played by Liz Fitzgibbon), appears from Australia via Skype, while Larry's brother, Vincent (Michael Glenn Murphy), is only seen in glimpses during Act I, until he arrives in Act II to create havoc, unwittingly. Aisling makes some interrupted appearances in the first half and then takes control in the second, providing honest and insightful observations on the insecurities and deceits of the characters.

Bernard has a great ability to allow a character cut to the core of a dilemma with a pithy line that allows an audience a sense of release after the tension of the scene. Dorothy's line towards the end, 'The men didn't fit in', always brought the house down, as the audience enjoyed the succinctness with which she summed up the mayhem. Ann's next line, 'True', was often not heard in the laughter, so we decided to leave a pause instead, and Dorothy said the next line, 'Men always fight', when the laughter died down.

Bernard was very responsive to what happened in rehearsals and in performance, and made small but very effective changes, as necessary, to help the action move continually in the right direction. For instance, during rehearsals, he cut parts of the scene in which Ann and Dorothy discuss what Ann revealed during a drunken conversation at a previous book-club evening, so as not to create red herrings for the audience, but only to develop plot twists that will have a satisfying payoff later in the play. Before the revival of the production in 2012, Bernard went to the Abbey's archive department to watch the DVD of a performance from the original run in 2010, tweaking lines, adding and subtracting words to make sure the audience is not a split second ahead of or behind the action.

The comedy in this play also works because Bernard establishes the tensions, dilemmas and sense of what is at stake in the play very early on, then complications grow as the action unfolds, reach a climax and ultimately get resolved. He exploits the tensions that come from the characters' differences, creating patterns and speech rhythms that vary for each character. He has a strong sense of visual comedy too, feeling that the actor playing Jennifer should be taller than the other women, so she is visually intimidating.

We explored what happened offstage between Robert and Jennifer to change their mood between scenes, and while this helped the actors to flesh out and clarify their emotional journey through the play, Bernard was very interesting in rehearsals about the way in which characters in a comedy need to be fully rounded, three-dimensional people, but that their reactions should be immediate and directly in response to the action involved, even if this seems momentarily out of character to their behaviour in the rest of the play – in the same way that, in real life, all of us sometimes behave out-of-character in certain extreme or unusual situations, I suppose.

SHUSH, ELAINE MURPHY

Elaine Murphy's first play, *Little Gem*, took audiences by storm, as it explored the lives of three generations of Dublin women to great comic effect through a series of interconnecting monologues. Her second full-length play, *Shush*, also explores the lives of a group of Dublin women, and is written entirely in snappy, inventive and very funny dialogue.

The action centres on Breda (played in the Abbey production by Deirdre Donnelly), who is going through a crisis in her life, and the visit one evening of her friends (Barbara Brennan, Ruth Hegarty and Eva Bartley) and neighbour Ursula (Niamh Daly) who are determined to give her a birthday party, whether she likes it or not. The visit is more like a Mafia-style intervention than a social call, as Breda's friends try to work out how bad things are for her, and do their best to cheer her up. Breda is experiencing a lot of change in her life, something she had not anticipated having to cope with in her 60s. Her husband has left her, her son has emigrated, she is being forced to take early retirement, and has a number of health problems. The play opens with her contemplating suicide, sitting at a table with a bottle of vodka and pills in her hand. As in much comedy, there is a thin line between darkness and light. The opening of the play is grim, then one of the first lines of the play is Breda reading a text message she receives – 'Happy Birthday from the O2 network' – which always got a huge laugh in performance. Similarly, toward the end of the play, during a conversation about coping with grief, Breda says, ' You know, there's more chance of us dying in a plane crash than meeting someone at our age', to which Irene responds, 'That's not true because you won't even get on a plane, Breda', beautifully undercutting the poignant conversation that has just preceded it. Then Breda's son rings her and she ends the phone call by telling him, 'I love you, I'm so happy for you, son', and, after a brief interjection at the other end of the line from Colm, she protests 'I only had two vodkas', again using comedy very adeptly to undercut the sentiment and emotion.

Ultimately, it is the truthfulness and honesty with which Elaine writes about depression, grief and resilience in the face of adversity that makes the play work and provides the comedy that goes hand in hand with the serious subject matter. Clare's attempts to avoid drinking alcohol are all the more funny because she is trying to keep her pregnancy a secret; Irene being referred to as a black widow spider is funnier because she has experienced such sadness with the deaths of three husbands; Marie's quips about keeping her sex life active by taking 'the Micra down to Dollymount Strand the odd night' are amusing because we know of her marital problems in the past.

The play is full of great Dublin humour, like when Ursula (who has baked a particularly horrible birthday cake for Breda) asks how she should get revenge on her cheating husband and Breda replies, 'Poison the fucker', to which Marie suggests, 'You could bake him a cake'; or when Marie suggests it would suit Breda if her husband (who has also been unfaithful) died, and Breda replies with retorts such as, 'God forbid the bastard would do something useful', and, later, by asserting, 'If he thinks he's selling my house to fund fucking South Fork he's another thing coming.'

As in *The Pride of Parnell Street, Noah and the Tower Flower, Silent* and *Bookworms, Shush* creates comedy from snobbishness and class distinction. Ursula is considered 'very affected' by Marie and has moved in next door to Breda, in a typically working/middle-class suburb. A lot of humour ensues through tensions between Ursula and Marie, such as when Ursula reveals she has had to make cutbacks to deal with financial pressures, then Marie responds by suggesting Ursula should sell her jeep and 'get yourself a little Punto or something', at which Ursula is horrified and replies, 'I said we were broke, not destitute.'

POSTSCRIPT

As I write this essay in September 2013, Fishamble has just produced *Guaranteed!* by Colin Murphy, directed by Conall Morrison, a play about the Irish bank guarantee, and is preparing to revive the production. A play about the grim realities surrounding the decision by the Irish government to bail out the banks might not seem like a very funny experience. But audiences watching it laughed uproariously at statements which, with hindsight, we now know to have been untrue. The laughter may be tinged with pain and regret, but the need to laugh at recent events, and demand answers, when the laughter dies away, is a strong one.

Guaranteed! is based on a tiny play that Colin wrote for Fishamble's *Tiny Plays for Ireland* project in 2012/2013. A number of other tiny plays in that production demonstrated the power of comedy to create social satire. These include *The Nation's Assets* by Michelle Read, about two fictional NAMA workers having sex in the photocopying room; *The Straight Talk* by Keith Farnan, in which a man tries to withdraw his money from a bank with hilarious and devastating results; and *I Stand Here Before You* by Tom Swift, about a politician's words being 'translated' by his interpreter. Like *Guaranteed!*, the first two plays poked fun at the world of finance and economics and Tom Swift's play satirised politics, making us laugh and ask questions in equal measure. The audience reaction suggested that the effect of satire is as powerful as it was when (that other) Swift was writing three hundred years ago.

The audience's laughter at these plays, and in all the plays discussed here, never diminished the seriousness of the message or theme at the core of the play. Instead, the comedy allowed the actors and audience to share a moment of hilarity or amusement, after which the audience's sense of outrage or regret or empathy for the characters on stage was released fully.

In great plays, there is often a thin line between darkness and light, comedy and tragedy, pain and joy. In the plays explored in this essay, I think it is the way in which the playwrights navigate that line, and allow us to laugh before we are plunged into sadness, that creates something special in the dialogue between the performers and the audience. Then, although audiences can react differently due to geographical circumstances, the play will connect with audiences, wherever they are.

15 | Stand-up comedy in a multicultural setting: Between a raw nerve and a funny bone

Kunle Animashaun

Perhaps because of the guiding interest of stand-up comedy, which essentially is to make uslaugh by talking about everyday life, it can be considered as an important site for the exploration of race and race relations, especially here in twenty-first century Ireland. As social commentators, stand-up comedians play a great role in the psychological health of a society. To further explore these claims, I decided to attend some comedy shows in Dublin and document my experiences. I was curious to discern how stand-up comedy is being used to examine race and ethnic relations, including the strategies and cues used by comedians to blend cultures. With the understanding that any room of people usually has its own life and that any venue with audiences always has its own vibe, I decided to note the audience's reaction in each of two Dublin venues, especially in terms of the general comportment. My goal was to understand the crowd dynamics and reactions of each audience to any particular comedian, with the ultimate aim of developing a series of perspectives and points of references, some of which have been documented in this essay.

The first venue was the Ha'penny Bridge Inn, where a comedian known as Tiny James (real name, James J. Akpotor) performed. I went there in the company of a friend of mine who is Irish and, as it happens, white. Apart from myself, there were about six other black people in the audience. We were definitely in the minority in terms of race composition, as almost all the other people (about fifty in number) that made up the audience that night were white. One by one, each comedian came on and regaled us with their jokes. Tiny James, the only black comedian performing that night, began his performance by finding humour in his childhood experiences, some of which he claimed were not so appealing. He talked about how he used to be bullied because of his big feet back in his village in Africa, and how all those years of suffering because of his big feet had fortuitously turned around as a blessing for him on moving to Ireland. According to him:

> I tell you one thing, Irish women can't get enough of me because of the one thing I've got, my big feet. So when someone, preferably an Irish woman accosts me on the road, probably looking for directions or whatever, pronto! I whip out that God-given organ of my body, my big....big....hmmm, feet, and they always fall for it anytime.[1]

Recognizing the correlation between the big feet joke by the comedian and situating this as his moment of power in a racially challenging environment like Ireland will not be far-fetched especially if considered alongside the fact that the person that accosted him looking for directions was a woman, and significantly, an 'Irish woman'. In another vein, the elastic blanket of the joke could be stretched to suggest the anxiety that white men have about their own sexuality in relation to their assumption of the stereotypical hypersexuality of black men. As a form of throwing up one of the deepest mythologized fears and anxieties in the racist imagination, that all black men have huge penises, this stereotypical innuendo presumably diminishes the 'humanness' of the black man by just reducing him to a body part. Apparently, the joke epitomizes how some people attribute 'foreignness' to people of a particular race, especially when a culture fetishizes the Other because the Other is unfamiliar. This sexual inference might suggest that Tiny James was using this as a retaliatory humour tool in exploring power negotiations in Irish society. Here, 'the black man' is comically flaunting his superior bargaining chip, his 'organ'. With this notion, the question is whether Tiny James was himself trading on the stereotype of the 'black man with big feet being endowed with a big sexual organ'. Nonetheless, there may well be an element that in a society that the comedian experiences as sometimes unforgiving in terms of racial micro-aggressions[2] and commonplace indignities, that he, Tiny James has the 'trump card' in the sexuality department, aired within the 'safe' environment of stand-up comedy. Arguably, this could also be his way of creating an avenue for him to 'get back' in some personal way while exposing the implications for the individual of such commonplace racist stereotyping for ethnic minorities living in Ireland.[3]

Tiny James's joke therefore could be argued as his own way of putting into the public domain his dissatisfaction with the sometimes shoddy treatment of the black people in Irish society. He was not the only comedian to use the technique that night, as one of the acts before him, a female comedian based many jokes that night on the fact that she got into comedy after she broke up with her fiancé of many years and so the need to perform stand-up comedy was a way of drowning her sorrow and probably, also as a way of getting back at the former boyfriend.

The peculiarity of Tiny James's technique was glaring because of the racial dimension to it. Cultural studies scholar Stuart Hall makes an enlightening point that racial humour depends on the existence of racism in order to be effective. Having analysed the construction of identity, an act of power, based on the exclusion of the Other, he points out that humour can be used as one of the crudest indicators of 'difference' just as ancillary preconscious processes regulate the flow of information.

In another of Tiny James's routines, he talked about the time that he visited the countryside in Ireland:

> From the suspicious looks I got as I walked from the bus stop, I thought something must be strange about the way I walk. That's why these people are looking at me the way they were all looking at me. I double checked to confirm that my shoes weren't glued to the palms of my hands and I wasn't wearing earrings on the big toes of my feet. When I entered a pub in the middle of town, it seemed like the earth itself froze as everything in the pub stopped to stare at me. I went straight for the bar and said to the bar man, 'The usual, please', and it was like hearing the clicking sound of a gun being cocked while you are in the middle of an orgasm. The expression on his face said it all. He opened his mouth and I could swear that he was actually having a real orgasm. 'What usual?' I don't think he's even seen a black man in his life. The old man sitting close to the bar mustered enough courage and came up to me. 'Young man, how are ya, eh, you added a bit of colour to this place tonight', to whom I replied, 'Yes, that was the reason that I came here, to add a bit of colour'; he looked at me, looked at me again, mouth still wide open, shock and awe or something like that, was the picture on his face.

By now, Tiny had the whole room in stitches. Although impossible to ascertain with scientific precision, it is always interesting to think about what this laughter meant for the audience as a group and as individuals.4 Just as Eric Weitz implies in his appraisal of Arambe Productions' stage adaptation of the *Kings of the Kilburn High Road* in 2006, we cannot really know what any given person is laughing at: 'In most cases, humorous intent could easily be apprehended by the audience as a whole, even if the breakdown of the joking action would be less straightforward for all involved.5 The important thing was that the audience were laughing together, especially when considered alongside the Other factor, which, according to Weitz, is:

> the audience's awareness of its multicultural makeup. The mutually acknowledged presences of black and white spectators in the theatre transaction, the occasion to laugh 'together' despite the divisive nature of the joke's setup, exert a defamiliarizing effect with implications for the increasingly multiracial Irish society here and now.6

Most importantly, however, is the fact that in that moment was achieved what Richard Schechner describes as 'communitas' an intense community spirit that infers the feeling of great social equality, solidarity, and togetherness notably achieved through play. Schechner centralizes 'play'-ful moments as a process that can be used to reinforce social normativity, but also as a process that can be used to contest it. I am taking the liberty here to apply Schechner's theory and it's centrality to performance theory to include stand-up comedy shows. Stand-up comedy/play and 'performances' therefore becomes a veritable avenue for creating social order, and more importantly, exploring the problems of order, the limits to it, and the dispensability or intemperance of it.

During Tiny's performance that day, differences seemed jettisoned even as new alliances ensconced in the relaxed ambience of the environment seemed to have been achieved. As the comedian continued with his varieties of jokes, I could not help but observe the members of the audience as a whole and their individual reactions. One could almost say that skin colour did not matter in that moment, though of course it does. Nonetheless, what happened that night could be seen as a sign of a healthy comedy culture in Ireland because it means that comedians are addressing social boundaries (as opposed to ignoring them). The irony of this was that, in terms of social discussions, it becomes clear that what could not be uttered in real life without political incorrectness, the comedian has licence to make jokes of.

Stand-up comedy can enable social critique and instigate transformations in many ways. Tiny James' performance could be argued as his moment of attainment of power status as a black man in Irish society. The humour in his routine is like a rubber sword that allows him to make a point without drawing blood. With the innuendos implanted in his routines, his intention could be to hurt the audience – though not too much. Conversely, one can also claim that the joke also punctures vanity, challenges falsehoods in a seemingly ironic way. Although not all of Tiny James's jokes that night had racial innuendoes, the interesting thing is that most of his jokes made reference to at least one or two incidents that a black person living in Ireland would have had to encounter and can relate to, and added to that is the fact that in most of his routines, one can hear him repeat phrases like, 'a big black man', or, 'the big black man'. It can be argued that his reference to being a big black man was much more than a simple case of a comedian putting himself at a personal (dis)advantage. With his massive frame, he is indeed a big black man; however, his 'big black man' reference on this occasion become a way of thrusting a debate into the audience's consciousness. In later discussion, Tiny James told me that the story about him being in an Irish town in the countryside was a real experience:

> I had this friend that used to live in Dublin and who moved to a town about two and half hours from Dublin and one day, I decided to visit him. Mind you, that was in 1998, and when I got to this town, some of the experiences that I had are not even fit to be in my comedy routine. For example, at the pub, the old man that told me about adding colour to the place and my response, you should have seen his face. In fact, my mind did some talking for him, racing through a checklist of things he would rather not say, things that were probably burning up his mouth due to restraint, lest they defy political correctness in a way that would have been hundred percent immigrant profiling and of course, that's just my way of expressing what I imagined was going on in the mind of the man, maybe it's true, maybe it's not, when people laugh at the jokes, that's what makes my day. For me, stand-up comedy gives me an opportunity to articulate my outrage at the discrimination in our society.

The next comedy show that I attended was that of a young man named Fabu D (real name David Owotade), at the Maldron Hotel in Tallaght. He was the only entertainer that performed. The audience at this event comprised of people from different age groups, demographically ranging roughly from 15 to 60 years, and seemingly split equally in terms of the racial composition. Fabu D's first routine incorporated a joke that was used to portray the shoddy treatment he once got from Irish immigration officials at the Dublin airport. He urges the audience to watch vividly as he takes them through the process of his questioning by the immigration officials, a process which non-indigenous people in the audience with skin tones than white may have experienced at one time or another. Yet, throughout the enactment, almost everyone in the hall was laughing:

> The other day at the Dublin airport, there was this pretty lady. When I say pretty, I mean pretty. She is beautiful. And she was looking at me. As a guy, I felt like, she's looking at me, why not. I'm cool, handsome, good looking. Ain't I (he asked the crowd, to which some people replied him, "Yes you are"). The problem was that this lady looking at me is a Garda. So, I was feeling a little bit emm, emm, (he scratches his head) uncomfortable. Now, don't get me wrong, Ireland is a great country; you can walk freely anywhere unless...........you don't have a GNIB card.7

The interesting thing about Fabu D's brand of comedy is his use of self-deprecating humour – in this usage, humour directed toward one's own in-group. Some of his jokes tend to poke fun at the black personality, the Nigerian father who threatens his son with corporal punishment or the African mother who stares sternly at her child in order to pass a message across to her. Fabu D could be grouped amongst the categories of comedians currently engaged in self-appraisal of their communities using humour as the quintessential searchlight.

Self-directed humour has the potential to strengthen the particular community because in a way, the searchlight beam is focused on shared experiences, albeit, also scrutinizing it by gently poking at its blind spots and assumptions. In one particular routine, he started by singing and urging the audience to join him in the process. The whole room could almost be mistaken for an African Pentecostal church service with singing and dancing and praise worship. He pulled a couple of people from the audience to join him on stage, cracking one or two jokes in the process and succeeded in working everybody into a frenzy. One of the jokes goes thus:

> Coming back from church one day, a Nigerian boy said to the mother:
> **Boy.** Mom, Today, I made a decision on what I want to become when I grow up.
> **Mother.** So, tell me.
> **Boy:** I will like to become a pastor when I grow up.
> **Mother.** Awww, my boy, that's so good of you. You just make my day. I always knew in my heart that there is something

special about you.

Boy. (*curious*) How mum?

Mother. When I was pregnant with you, every Sunday when we go to Church, you kick so hard during praise worship; I knew something was special about you.

Boy. Okay, but...

Mother. Tell me, what made you decide to become a pastor when you grow up.

Boy:. Because I think it will be fun to command the respect of people, be they younger or older than me, shout at them, and sometimes even scream, all the time calling 'in the name of Jesus' while obviously, I was only taking the mickey.

Fabu D: The look on his mum's face could light a cigarette.

The comedian's usage of inwardly directed humour, however, runs the risk of dredging up racist stereotypes that may have a negative effect on his community. In one of his recent short videos, Fabu D portrayed an African man who opened the door of his car to let out his children. The total number of children that came out of the car was eighteen. The small size of the car, the manner of his holding the door of the car and the incongruity of the number of children that disembark from the car created a humorous effect. However, the comicality of the video is instantaneously called into question because it is laden with stereotypical nuances and cadences, especially because of the caption, 'If the Irish government increase the Child benefit Niggas will be like ...' With this type of video, he was not only putting members of the African community in an uncomfortable position, but also, inadvertently seeming to perpetuate the same hurtful stereotypical rhetoric one has heard from less enlightened Irish people about those 'lazy social welfare dependent black immigrants, sponging off our social welfare system'.

In some of his other short videos, he is usually accompanied by two indigenous sidekicks by the name of Anto and Damo who he himself impersonates with a Northside Dublin accent, albeit, in a slurred/drawled manner of talking. These two characters personify addicts and junkies high on drugs, seen wandering the streets of Dublin on an average day. His portrayal of these two in his comedy videos might be seen as both humorous and somehow tragic. For example, with his very good portrayal of their emaciated bodies ravaged by drug use, and the mode of dressing, and most importantly, the exploits of the two characters, his portrayal attempts to depict in a comic light, life in the disadvantaged communities, which, for some people, may be seen to stereotype and vilify a social 'underclass' of Irish society.

Take for example the 'Bring the Pain' video on YouTube by Chris Rock in which he continuously makes use of the words, 'Niggers and Blacks'. 'You can't have anything valuable in your house', he says. 'Niggers will break in and take it all! Everything white people don't like about black people, black people really don't like about black people. It's like our own personal civil war.'[8] Statements like this though seeming hilarious to the audience, tends to perpetuate negative stereotypes towards the groups of people being depicted, denying due regard to the personal circumstances of individuals and, of course, the anecdotes, historical and contemporary social conditions that contributed to the circumstances of the groups of people being depicted. In the context of intercultural and social inclusivity in Ireland, by playing on the stereotypes of the African social welfare sponger or the drug addicted Northside Dubliner, the question is, does the comedian not run the risk of trivializing racism, entrenching stereotypes and belittling the tough social issues being experienced by the underprivileged in Irish society? It might be the comedian's contention that the human soul sometimes relies on the ability of the imagination to mock the tragic. This position becomes valid especially considering the point that trauma tends to lose its bite viz-a-viz the liberating essence of a joke at the expense of one's own in-group or community. Stuart Hall pointedly observes that:

> You can no longer conduct black politics through the strategy of a simple set of reversals, putting in the place of the bad old essential white subject, the new essentially good black subject.[9]

If done the right way, humour that targets one's own group can transcend differences. This reasoning substantiates that aspect of human culture that shows the importance of amusement and humour to peculiar sensibilities and identities and the concomitant tensions around their limits. The question to bear in mind when audiences are laughing at this kind of joke is whether they are laughing at the comedian or laughing with the comedian? Just like it would have been valuable to be able to pick apart what the audience at Tiny James's show were laughing at, so also would it be interesting to know precisely what viewers of Fabu D's videos or live shows are laughing it. One of his jokes drew so much raucous laughter that a passerby might have wondered at the commotion inside the Maldron Tallaght venue. Laying the preamble for the joke, he started off by saying this story took place in a city somewhere in Nigeria. It goes thus:

One day, a policeman arrested a man urinating at a place

clearly marked DO NOT URINATE HERE, PENALTY - FIVE HUNDRED NAIRA ONLY. The man gives the policeman a one-thousand naira note. The Policeman looks at the money, looks at the man and says, 'I don't have change, now urinate again.'

This punchline, deftly delivered by Fabu D, drove most of the audience wild. While hands were flapping and people around me were collapsing in laughter, it was interesting that my Irish friend (different from the one that attended the Tiny James show with me) did not get the joke. I am aware that cultural differences can create substantial obstacles to effective appreciation of original humorous intent since jokes are composed of linguistic and cultural elements. To understand the joke, my friend must be willing to jettison the moral virtue of holding back urine until one can find a well-maintained western toilet. Not a sure bet from the particular area being depicted in the joke enactment. I pondered how to describe the act of peeing by the roadside and some people's justification of it being a good deed in the long run because, to them, by peeing on the grass, they were actually watering it and as such, sustaining life. Nonetheless, calmly, I tried to explain the scenario to this friend that, at any location where notices like, 'DO NOT URINATE HERE', or 'WE MAY NOT HAVE SIGNS HERE, BUT YOU CAN GET ARRESTED, FINED OR IMPRISONED OR BOTH FOR PEEING IN PUBLIC ON SATURDAY NIGHTS', are seen, such places are sure to attract people who have come to urinate there *because* that is the logical place they could go in the absence of infrastructures that would have been used to cater for their needs. Possessing abundant knowledge about a target society is essential for an adequate comprehension of any joke. The above joke as humorous as it seems to me is the type of humour relating to an ethnic, racial or cultural group that often focuses on the stereotype of a people or place by locating the humorous aspects in the social irregularities and anecdotal situations within that society/community.

My attempt at explaining the joke thereafter created another problem for my friend. He could not understand how a government shirking its duty could be invested with the power of control, as the policeman is the representative of the inept government that did not provide the infrastructures in the first place. At this point, all I could muster as explanation was a muffled, 'You don't understand, it's a Nigerian thing', to which he replied, 'I may or may not understand, and come to think of it, what's there to understand, or not to understand when laughter fills the room like that?' And the spontaneous laughter by both of us accentuates the geniality of the topic under discussion even as I pondered how the episode proves that there is the need for more participation of immigrant stand-up comedians in engendering conversations about subjects we are afraid to face.

At its best, stand-up comedy can be our outlet for the unspeakable to be spoken in a way that is acceptable. Through their creativity, minority comics can undermine the potency of the prejudices, though, as we have seen, you can never be sure in all cases which way the sword will slice. But these comedians have proven something, that there is the need for stand-up comedy as a venue for minorities to challenge the assumptions of mainstream society and that their brand of stand-up comedy is a welcome development in the Irish comedy scene because apart from its entertainment purpose, it also can be renewing and uniting.

WORKS CITED

Garner, Steve, *Racism in the Irish experience* (UK: Pluto Press, 2004)

Hall, Stuart. *Old and new identities: Old and New Ethnicities: Culture Globalization and World Systems* (ed.) Anthony D. King (USA: University of Minnesota, 1991) reproduced as an excerpt in *Theories of Race and racism (a reader)* edited by Las Back and John Solomons (New York: Routledge 2000)

Hall, Stuart and Paul Du Gay, *Questions of Cultural Identity* (London: Sage Publications, 1996 4/5)

Lentin, Ronit and Robbie McVeigh. *Racism and anti-racism in Ireland* (Belfast: Beyond the Pale Publications, 2002)

Lynch, Catherine. *ENAR Shadow Report 2007 Racism in Ireland*(Brussels: ENAR, 2008)

Morley, David and Kuan-Hsing (eds.), *Stuart Hall: Critical Dialogues in Cultural Studies* (London: Routledge, 2006)

Patrick, Sheila Drudy, Kathleen Lynch and Liam O'Dowd, (eds.). *Irish Society: Sociological Perspectives*, (Dublin: IPA, 1995)

Schechner, Richard, *Performance Studies: An introduction* (USA: Routledge, 2006)

Sue, Derald Wing and Christina M. Capodilupo, Gina C. Torino, Jennifer M. Bucceri, Aisha M. B. Holder, Kevin L. Nadal, and Marta Esquilin. 2007. Racial Microaggressions in Everyday Life: Implications for Clinical Practice USA: Columbia University)

Weitz, Eric. 2009. Who's Laughing Now?: Comic Currents for a New Irish Audience' in Crossroads: Performance Studies and Irish Culture, ed. Sara Brady and Fintan Walsh (UK: Palgrave)

White, Elisa Joy. *The new Irish storytelling: Media, representations and racialised identities* (Belfast: Beyond the pale publishers, 2002)

1 Taken from personally recorded transcript of Tiny James's performance at the Ha'penny Bridge, Dublin 2 on 21st March 2012.

2 I consider racial microaggressions as brief and commonplace daily verbal, behavioural, or environmental indignities, whether intentional or unintentional, that communicates hostile, derogatory, or negative racial slights and insults toward people of colour.

3 Defined by McVeigh and Lentin as "any distinction, exclusion, restriction or preference based on "race", colour, descent, as well as national or ethnic origin, which cases as inferior or excludes a collectivity using mechanisms of power" (2002:8).

4 Admittedly it is impossible to know precisely what different factions of the audience, or even any given individual, were laughing at.

5 Eric Weitz, 'Who's Laughing Now?' (2009: 231).

6 Eric Weitz, (2009: 233).

7 The GNIB card is an immigration certificate of registration issued by the Garda National Immigration Bureau to a non-EEA national upon registering as living in Ireland. The GNIB Card stamp denotes the basis on which permission to remain in the State is granted. This passage also is taken from a personally notated transcript of Fabu D's performance at the Maldron Hotel Tallaght on 29th March 2014.

8 'Bring the Pain' 1996, by Chris Rock 1996 – The utterances of Chris in this video gives weight to the claim that routines like his are sometime damaging as this same seemingly harmless jokes can be hijacked by a racist person to express his or her misgivings about others within our society. http://www.youtube.com/watch?v=b-opnoLzBR8 (From 29:28).

9 Stuart Hall 'New Ethnicities' (1989: 444).

16 | The inmates take the mic: Irish comedians on stand-up comedy

Compiled, with additional material by Justin Murphy
Original interviews conducted by Declan Rooney

Stand-up comedy in an Irish context encompasses a variety of diffuse practices ranging from the amateur to the professional. These practices are demarcated and imbued by a range of social, economic, and geographical concerns as well as individual styles. But this heterogeneity of comedic practice in Ireland and of Irish comedians abroad is difficult to represent and often under-represented.

The interviews collated here attempt to address both problems, offering much insight into this diversity of practice, the myriad contexts of such practices, and also the attitudes of comedians themselves to their work. Fragments of a larger project of interviews with comedians, they reveal a cross-sectional view of the lives of stand-up comedians at different stages in their careers. They indicate the influence of new media on stand-up comedy. Further, they delineate a contemporary performative context, and the expectations and conventions of stand-up in Ireland and for Irish comedians abroad. Perhaps more significantly, these interviews present competing conceptions of the role of the comedian in a broader cultural and political sense.

In the juxtaposition of these brief interviews the question of whether Irish comedy *should be* political or *is* political is not the only one raised. Competing views on the centrality of religion, the viability of comedy that only tours Ireland, and the extent or value of performed 'Irishness' abroad also emerge.

Such tensions speak fundamentally to the question of what makes stand-up in Ireland and the stand-up of Irish comedians abroad unique, if indeed it is at all. The interviewees as stand-ups are best placed to address this question. However, from the interviews a simple conclusion is not evident but instead productively problematized.

[PJ Gallagher. Actor, writer, stand-up comedian. *Naked Camera* and *Next Week's News*.]

Justin Murphy: What is a stand-up comedian and what is stand-up comedy in the context of your practice?

PJ Gallagher: A stand-up comedian is somebody that stands alone on stage and makes people laugh, that's really all there is to it. There's a million different ways of making that happen but ultimately we are all trying to do the same thing. It's really hard to get it right and get good at it but defining it is easy.

Stand-up isn't art or an art form, yeah it's a craft and it takes learning and practice but it's not art. A lot of the time you are just trying to keep people happy while they drink, make people's weekend a little better or take them away from the frame of mind they are normally in. Stand-up is fun and it should stay fun, it belongs to anyone that cares enough to enjoy a giggle. I used to be a courier for a few years and it's amazing how similar it is to stand-up comedy. I drive a van across the country for a few hours, deliver some jokes and drive home again. Yeah jokes are lighter to carry than parcels but the mechanics of it all are the same. Granted I never got a round of applause for delivering a letter but you know what I mean.

JM: Is there something unique about stand-up comedy in Ireland and the stand-up of Irish comedians abroad?

PJG: No not really, stand-up comedy a lot of the time is an exercise in finding out how little you have to say to the World. We all struggle in the same way to find material, to find our own style, to find out how to make routines work and how to communicate. I can gig in a Dublin club and be very different to the local guys then go to Canada and see a local guy and identify with what he's doing immediately. It's not our nationalities that define what we do on a stage; it's how we approach it individually.

JM: Is performing for an Irish audience different to performing for other audiences? How important to your practice both financially and otherwise is material that can travel?

PJG: It's different because it's easier to write jokes about the environment you are immersed in rather than one you are just observing. I can arrive in any town in Ireland and do jokes about the place because I have a previous understanding of where I am. I'm doing more travelling this year than ever before and I'm seeing it's a bit more difficult but only because I'm not in the practice of doing it. Financially, for me I make less when I travel than when I gig at home but it is nice to test yourself and do gigs abroad. Honestly, though, I only really do it because it's a free holiday.

JM: Is it difficult to make a living as a stand-up in Ireland alone?

PJG: If you're starting out it is very difficult but it wasn't always that way. There are just so many people getting into it now and so many clubs with an audience that is spread too thin. Recently the clubs are really suffering too because people aren't spending like they used to. If anything now the established acts are doing better because audiences don't take chances on nights out anymore, they go to see people they already know. The days of the casual club-goer just going to a club to see who might be there are dying and that's a shame. I feel sorry for the younger acts coming through now because they don't have the same opportunities that we did. There were only 21 or 22 full time comics in Ireland when I started; now there must be hundreds of people looking for gigs. There are great comedians out there but how can we find them anymore, and who knows who's who? I'm one of the few that was very lucky to get in early.

JM: How has the proliferation of televised stand-up and online video-sharing impacted stand-up comedy? Does this proliferation privilege certain kinds of comedy?

PJG: If it's well produced it makes some kind of sense but it's always frustrating. You watch a stand-up DVD or stand-up on TV and you see from the audience how it must have felt on the night and you know that ultimately you're missing out. Stand-up only really works properly when it's a private affair between a certain group of people in a certain room at a certain time. You really do have to be there to fully appreciate it. Now you see people in comedy clubs with their phones in the air making a shitty recording of a show and ruining the whole thing on the comedian and themselves. They look back on it later and the sound is shit, it looks shit and it's a bullshit video. Then they ask themselves why they thought it was so funny and it's because they recorded it on a shitty phone and put it on Youtube. Then that video gets shared out of context and it goes on and on, it doesn't do anyone any justice.

[ABIE PHILBIN BOWMAN. STAND-UP COMEDIAN, JOURNALIST, AND WRITER OF *JESUS: THE GUANTANAMO YEARS.*]

Declan Rooney: Religion in comedy in Ireland. Your views.

Abie Philbin Bowman: Well my views are it is a hell of a lot easier to do now than it was in Dave Allen's day. And I have only become aware of him recently, but he really was a fantastically amazing, brilliant, mould-breaking dude. For me, religion and comedy ... religion, it's the perfect subject for comedy and even though I'm an atheist it is a subject I come back to again and again, because I'm really interested in ethics. I've always been really interested in philosophy, in how we live and how we should live and what's a good life and a lot of the interesting thinkers on that are religious people. Some of my heroes are people like Mahatma Ghandhi and Martin Luther King who were very religious people. So I'm not one of these dyed-in-the-wool, 'ah, you're all fucking lunatics' atheists who thinks that I'm right and everyone else is wrong because it seems to me that's a little bit fundamentalist for my liking.

But religion is the perfect subject because it never goes out of date. Like, the reason people don't write political comedy, I think, first of all, is a lot of audiences don't follow the news, aren't really that interested, and secondly, if you write a good, really good political joke about whatever is in the news this week, you got to change it in about three months' time. I mean you can go back to it, and people do, and there's subjects that come up again and again like terrorism, you can kind of have jokes on that and you know there'll be another attack in a few months' time and you can do it about that or gay marriage, something that comes around, and happens in different places and you can link a new story to an existing bit of root material. But basically if you write political jokes, if you write a really great joke about the government and then the government gets booted out at the next election, which will probably happen, you've got to write a whole new joke about the new government. And if it's about those people then .... So it's just a lot more hard work, whereas if you write a joke about sex, that's good forever. I broke up with my girlfriend last week dud-ah-dud-ah-dah ... You can do that for the next twenty years and good luck.

DR: Do you think that you use the genre of comedy to vent, use it as a platform to, you know, let loose the anger ... that type of thing ... do you enjoy it? Do you feel it's a route to express yourself?

APB: For me it's actually not that personal. In the sense that for me, what I'm really interested in is comedy as a means; as a weapon of political protest. I wrote a Masters in comedy as a weapon in non-violent protest because I'm a nerd and what I am interested in is using comedy to communicate political dissent. The core reason I write political jokes is because that's what I find funny. I couldn't go up there onstage and do a Jason Byrne thing because I'm just not Jason Byrne. ... I haven't got the madness in me. I haven't got the spontaneity in me. ... I can't do half an hour on what's in your handbag, I just don't have it in me. I don't talk to the audience much. It's not that I don't care about them but it is not what's interesting to me and it seems to me that comedy is about what is interesting, what's going on in the world.

See, politics is this word which a lot of people hear and they imagine two guys in grey suits and they can't give a straight answer, but the truth is that politics really is the drama. It's *The Wire*, it is how we all get on as a society, how we interact with each other, who gets what, who gets fucked over, who gets deprived of stuff, who gets resources. That's what it is really about and that is fascinating to me and so I want to hear stuff about that. And the guys who really blow me away are guys like Reg D. Hunter or Steve Hughes, who can really make you think differently about the world. So that's what I want to talk about. I don't think I'm *that* interesting and I personally feel like there is an awful lot of comedians who will talk about themselves the whole time. And fair play to them. It's really funny. They do it really well. But that part of the market is really, really well represented. If you want to hear jokes about my drinking problem, my shitty relationship, and why I watch too much TV, there are a lot of really good comics out there doing stuff along those lines and I can't compete with those guys because it's not who I am. I'm in a nerdier, smaller, more, I don't know, esoteric group of people who watch the news every day and are really interested in it and who like fucking around with that. It is a much smaller audience, unfortunately, but it is the thing that makes me laugh and tickles me and that's why I write what I write.

And I'm really interested in how comedy can be used. Its strengths and weaknesses as a means of communicating ideas to a wider populace. You know, we don't have a revolution in Ireland. I don't know why we don't, I think maybe the weather, it's just not the weather for it, but I'm really interested in getting in front of a room of people and talking about the banking crisis and feeling the anger and making people feel, one, I'm not alone, two, I shouldn't be suffering with this, three, I've a better attitude to this coming out, four, who are those fuckers, who do they think they are, I'm not taking this shit. That's what I want people to come away with.

[EDDIE NAESSENS. STAND-UP COMEDIAN, ACTOR.]

Justin Murphy: What is stand-up comedy in the context of your practice?

EN: Stand-up comedy is performed humour. Question then is: what is the aim of humour? The general line with stand-up comedy, as I understand it, is scanning life and human existence for incongruence, irony, double standards, and the like, observing human behaviour, and exposing the humorous aspects. The primary purpose of stand-up comedy is to entertain – specifically to make people laugh. And while there is much talk about comedy's potential to change people's lives, or to change how we do things in life, real change doesn't happen in a stand-up comedy club, although I am not saying that comedy doesn't have a certain power to excite ideas, I generally think the power of comedy is often overstated.

The overriding criterion in stand-up comedy is to get laughs, and anything after that is secondary. It is not about soapboxing, storytelling, or playing with words, and many other things that may be associated with stand-up comedy. So, if taking off one's shoe makes an audience laugh well, then, taking off one's shoe works in terms of stand-up comedy – if, and only if, it leads to laughter.

JM: Is there something unique about stand-up comedy in Ireland and the stand-up of Irish comedians abroad?

EN: The issue of stand-up comedy in Ireland and the stand-up of Irish comedians abroad is, essentially, when an Irish comedian is in Ireland he is "at home" among people who are of his cultural background and therefore have broadly similar reference points to relate to the comedian's material. When an Irish comedian performs outside of Ireland, obviously the breaking-of-the-ice phase involves talking about the Irishness and speaking of the Irishness to a non-Irish audience.

Of course, as an Irish comedian (or comedian of any nationality) becomes internationally known, the need to break the ice and the novelty of their nationality wanes and therefore the breaking-of-the-ice part of their set is no longer so relevant. This is a crucial aspect of stand-up comedy most people overlook. The concept of being a known quantity negates the need for the 'I'm from ... ' preamble or frame of reference. The comedian is then a citizen of the world, so to speak.

JM: Is performing for an Irish audience different to performing for other audiences? How important financially and otherwise is material that can travel?

EN: Another consideration is Irish comedians are working with an audience in Ireland that generally likes storytelling with punch lines. The London circuit is a different type of circuit in terms of tastes. It is dangerous to generalize, because it depends on what clubs and even on days of the week. The Comedy Store or Jongleurs, for example, are different to playing Downstairs at The King's Head. But in general, the club audience in London and the home counties are used to a more gag-merchant style of laddish/laddette style. Coming from outside London, it takes a few gigs to adjust; it means learning the hard way, re-writing and re-working both set and topics, and adapting to a different style. However, the North of England generally, has audiences more like Irish audiences – more amenable to a conversational style.

The need to go to the UK is mostly a financial/career-development necessity. Given that Ireland has a population of 4 million, and there is very little in terms of a network of clubs to play, very few professional performers can make a living solely from stand-up comedy in Ireland. There are a top-level 15 – 20 professional performers making a living from stand-up comedy in Ireland and the ones on the level beneath that manage to make some money from stand-up comedy and supplement that with other work: voice-overs, teaching, media, writing and teaching, and good honest graft.

For those comedians who decide to travel it is a challenge to have several modified set lists depending on where they are playing outside of the republic. Talking about local Irish issues in the UK, US, Germany or Australia doesn't usually make much sense – there are of course exceptions: they might be playing to an ex-pat Irish audience. But beyond the exceptions a comedian has to get into the mindset of what an audience expects from an Irish comedian.

JM: Do you think there is a political strain in Irish stand-up? Do you consider your comedy political?

EN: Purely political comedians are rare and not very popular – that is: they attract a more niche audience. In the UK there is Mark Steel, Rory

Bremner, and Mark Thomas for example. And they have a very limited audience; however, you will find comedians who, for example, like Stewart Lee cover much more than just politics. Politics happens to be part of their set. Dylan Moran will touch on international political issues or local political issues; Barry Murphy and John Colleary likewise. But again, it is part of an overall package of jokes and observations, whereas the purely political comedy is an extremely difficult thing to do and has a very small market. We all discuss politics with our friends, but there is nothing as off-putting as a dinner or a pint with people where the conversation from beginning to end is politics.

In terms of my own comedy I would always find that issues of contemporary media, and sometimes politics if it is topical, makes its way into what I talk about, but it is from the point of view of it being topical and it having a comic content based on double standards or absurdity or laugh worthiness. My job as a comedian is not to change the world – changing the world is only ever a hobby. Performing or writing comedy is talking or writing about the world in an entertaining way.

JM: Why is religion so central to the comedy of Irish comedians?

EN: Ireland is a theocracy. The disturbing fact of the matter is few Irish people recognize this, let alone the impact and consequences. Religion is central to Irish comedians as religion is central in the lives of Iranians or any other theocracy. We Irish find it easy to ignore because we're so used to it. The Constitution of the Irish state was written by the Catholic church. For good and bad, the church is embedded within the power structures of this country. Religion and Ireland is connected with our opposition for centuries to our UK and Northern Irish neighbours, of a different religious tradition. The Irish state is still a very immature state in many ways.

Religion is part of every town; look around at the amount of churches and iconography – everywhere there is the presence of religion in our lives. Our schools still have three quarters of an hour every day given over to religion, even though there are far more serious educational requirements. We struggle in this country to get our heads around strong religious practice in other countries, we find that alien. But non-Irish people find it alien listening to the national radio station at midday broadcasting a peal of bells for one minute. For us it's background we no longer notice. The reason why religion is so central to the comedy of the Irish comedian is because religion is so central to the Irish.

[BERNARD O'SHEA. STAND-UP COMEDIAN AND PERFORMER. *NAKED CAMERA, REPUBLIC OF TELLY* AND *THE PANEL*]

Declan Rooney: Where do you see television going in relation to where you are? Do you see yourself being on television for the next couple of years or do you see yourself going off to … ?

Bernard O'Shea: Well the whole form has dramatically changed in terms of we almost make television programmes now to satisfy the hunger for a quick sixty-second hit on Youtube, do you know what I mean? And I think that's what *Republic of Telly* … why, I think, one of the reasons it was such a hit because it was very 'you don't like this?' oh wait ten seconds and there's something you might like on after it. When you look at comedy shows from the fifties and the variety shows of the fifties American television, that's what's very popular now almost. Singles came out because they were only able to fit on that amount of vinyl but really and truly all people want is the one song, the one gag, the one joke.

DR: Do you love what you do?

BO: I got into it because I found it necessary to do what I do; because I ended up with no other options. I was the usual, you know, educated but not necessarily intelligent ⋯ I was playing music so I got into it through necessity. However, I love what I do when I'm on the stage. I hate everything, not about in terms of the industry or in terms of the people, but the thoughts of getting up on the stage. Everything before it is a drag: 'Aw, fuck it, why did I agree to do this?' and the fear of getting up. And when I get up, even if it's a shit room and there's people throwing things, I love being in there – but once I'm off it, I don't really care for it.

[Aishling Bea. Actress, comedian and writer. Performer at Kilkenny Cat Laughs. Winner of *Gilded Balloon*'s 'So you think you're funny?' award.]

DECLAN ROONEY: Do you find the audiences different in Ireland more so than England?

AISHLING BEA: Well I suppose I started stand-up in England. So when I started stand-up, when I'd go out on stage, I'm foreign. And so your point of view when you are a foreigner onstage – there's always a natural fish-out-of-water – and what I find when I come home, because I don't gig loads at home, that's why Kilkenny has been so lovely, you are not talking to people about yourself. You are talking to the audience as *ourselves*, if you know what I mean. So it's our own stories. You are not explaining why things are a certain way, you're explaining why we are a certain way, so it just is a shift of your tone. Do you know what I mean? That slightly changes. And also I had a big old panic, thinking maybe the only reason I am funny in England is because of my accent, whereas here I don't have an accent, they are just the same as us.

DR: Do you think comedians are dysfunctional?

AB: I think ... well, I think the reason comedy works is because it plays on dysfunction. So that the people of the audience feel relieved and able to laugh because they don't feel that weird, so you go on. And most comedy is observational of human behaviour ... My friend Celia has a joke about eating cheese straight out of it and seeing the teeth marks on the cheese and people laugh at that not because you're going, oh you're so dysfunctional and weird. No, they're going, we all do something mad. So I suppose we are all dysfunctional in our own way but we [comedians] have some weird sadistic urge to go up onstage and make a living out of re-living our dysfunction every single night in front of a microphone.

DR: And do you go up onstage to vent or do you go up onstage to entertain?

AB: No, entertain. Definitely entertain.

DR: Because some people go, 'It is like a vocation'. It is like a glue that you can't get rid of.

AB: Yeah, well it is. I was just discussing this with another comedian called David Morgan the other day and we were just discussing the different types of comedians. I would fall into the category of probably the 'entertaining-child-dance-for-granny'. You know and there's a lot of kids who probably grow up, you know, [as] the class clown, the people who've been doing it since they were probably able to speak English. Like the ones going 'la-la-la' probably annoying, half the time you want to punch them in the head. Then there are a lot of people who go away and have really interesting ideas and you don't know they're comedians until they walk out onto stage and blow you away. And then there can be people who are really educated.

Like there are a lot of young male stand-ups at the moment who are kind of in their early twenties who are so educated about comedy because they've grown up with comedy on telly. So they've grown up with so many comedy roadshows and stuff in the last ten years being their main BBC viewing, you know, so they've learnt the rhythm of jokes. And then there are obviously people who use comedy as a way to say something because you know if you really want to say something add jokes and people will listen. So you know there are different categories. I think I fall into the 'entertain your granny' category, if I'm honest.

[KARL SPAIN. ACTOR, WRITER, COMEDIAN. KARL SPAIN WANTS A WOMAN AND KARL SPAIN WANTS TO ROCK.]

DR: If at the touch of a button you could do something in this country to bring comedy up another level what would that be?

KS: I would raise the standards in TV comedy. I think there is, in TV in general in this country, too much of an attitude of let's just get the job done. Let's just get it done.

DR: Would that not be [related to] a lack of money as well?

KS: No, you can still, you can still see something and go 'no, that's not good enough go back and do it again'. I don't think the money factor is such a big deal because the stuff is being made. ... Now I think *The Savage Eye* is excellent, but I don't think it is *that* good, but I think the problem is it's *that* good because everything else falls down around it. So, I don't mean to take from *The Savage Eye*. My point is: it can be done. Like it's the same with *Irish Pictorial Weekly*, there was [sic] four episodes. I thought the first episode was outstanding, I thought the other three episodes were pretty good. But I think because the first episode was a pilot and then they were told 'right, we want more' and they literally were panicking going, well, you know, struggling. It is like your first album is a massive hit – where's the second, third and fourth album? And you've only got six weeks to write them. And I think it's a matter of let's just get it done, rather than let's make this as good as we can.

[MICHAEL MEE. STAND-UP COMEDIAN AND WRITER.]

DECLAN ROONEY: You've done a lot of tours; tell me how gruelling, how lonely is it?

MM: Well, I found living in the UK and doing the UK circuit very solitary I have to say, and that's not technically touring in the sense of ... like touring is actually the nice bit if you can do it. You really need to have a name like the guy off the telly or whatever. I mean I did one hundred and forty-three gigs one year in the UK and like every night it always seemed to be an hour to Victoria or an hour to Waterloo and then an hour somewhere else to Dorking or Milton Keynes. It was always two hours there and two hours back. So it's like a four-hour trip on your own having to grab food and I have an allergy problem. So having to grab something on the way, you get in, you do the gig and then you turn around and you belt off home so you don't get to talk to anybody at the gigs and get some idea whether you did okay or whatever. Whereas if you're touring, I toured with Des Bishop, you know, and often we would be kind of turning around and belting off but there would be much more feedback. I mean, really, if people go to see somebody like Des ... 'I have his DVDs, I'm going to have a good time'. Whereas if I turn up in Chatham or West Byfleet or something and there's just some guy on the bill, some Irish guy comes up ... they are tough gigs, so that can be lonely.

[NEIL DELAMERE. WRITER AND COMEDIAN. THE PANEL, REPUBLIC OF TELLY AND MICHAEL MCINTYRE'S COMEDY ROADSHOW.]

DECLAN ROONEY: Loneliness. How is that for you? You've done a lot of travelling. How many gigs have you done?

NEIL DELAMERE: If you're an Irish comedian who can tour, you're in a joyous position because it's not that big a country. So there isn't a gig in Ireland that I don't come back from. It is not like the guys you meet say at the Kilkenny comedy festival, the big American guys or the big Canadian guys, like, touring, that's three weeks or four weeks or three months or four months away solidly. I mean, then it would be lonely I think. Whereas the longest I've been away really from family or friends has been kind of six or eight weeks in festivals like Edinburgh or in Melbourne. So what happens is if you do those regularly enough you'll build friends there. So loneliness isn't a big issue for me on that one. I don't travel as much as I used to, you know. And also, if you do tour in Ireland, you tour with a guy who not only can open the gig but also you get on with. So you've a support act who is your mate.

DR: What is stand-up for? What does it represent for you?

ND: What does it represent for me? It represents a dream job for me. It's for ... what is its purpose? For me is...it's great because if you have an idea, it's so fluid, you can go out there and do it tonight, do you know? Television and radio, they are obviously more collaborative and because they are more collaborative you have to jump through more hoops and you have to check things here there and everywhere. Whereas this is instant. And also, when it's done really amazingly well, and I've only ever seen it done to its zenith a handful of times – I've seen it done amazingly well often, but to its real zenith maybe four or five times. It's a remarkable connection between the audience and the performer. It's just ... if you do it really, really well it jumps the divide between the performer and the audience that only music can. Like it's much easier to move someone with music because it's ingrained in us. ... It hits internally, you know, and if you see amazing stand-up like someone connecting with a group of people maybe on the basis of the fact that he's talking about common experiences or whatever, it can kind of, it can get to that level. That's what we, I think, probably should aspire to.

Contributors

Kunle Animashaun is a writer, poet and dramatist. He is currently Director in Residence at the Tallaght Community Arts in Dublin. Kunle holds a first-class Master's degree from the School of English, Drama and Film, University College Dublin. He is the artistic director of Camino Productions. Productions by his theatre company include, *Wedlock of the Gods*, *Sizwe Bansi is Dead* amd *Things Fall Apart*. He is the author of *Pitfalls* and *Drumbeats of Oppression* (unpublished). On the international front, Kunle has delivered an address on his praxis as a theatre director at the Committee of Regions, European Union Headquarters, Brussels. He is at an advanced stage of his doctoral research in the Department of Drama, Trinity College Dublin.

Susanne Colleary (PhD) conducted her doctoral research on stand-up comedy. She is as an associate lecturer in Creative Practices with Sligo Institute of Technology and Carlow Institue of Technology. She also works as a Dissertation supervisor for the Department of Education at TCD. She has worked as an actor in both amateur and professional fields and has published articles on Irish theatre, stand-up comedy and televisual satire. Her book entitled *Performance and Identity in Irish Stand Up; The Comic 'i'* is being published by Palgrave later in the year. She is currently engaged in practise-based research, focused on historicized ideas of Irish popular culture. Her research interests include contemporary theatre and performance practice, humour studies, popular culture studies and gender and identity in performance.

Christopher Collins (PhD) teaches at the Samuel Beckett Centre at Trinity College Dublin and The Lir: The National Academy of Dramatic Art. A Trinity College Dublin Gold Medallist and recipient of the Irish

Society for Theatre Research's (ISTR) New Scholar's Award (2012), he has published widely on heritage, history, memory and forgetting, particularly in relation to J.M. Synge's *Collected Works*. With Mary P. Caulfield, he co-edited *Ireland, Memory and Performing the Historical Imagination*, which is forthcoming from Palgrave Macmillan in 2014. He is Communications Officer for IFTR/FIRT and is on the Executive Committee of ISTR. He also works professionally as a dramaturg and a director.

Jim Culleton is the Artistic Director of Fishamble: The New Play Company, for which he has directed many award-winning productions of new plays, on tour extensively in Ireland and internationally throughout the UK, US, Europe, Canada and Australia. He has also directed for the Abbey Theatre, Amharclann de hIde, The Ark, Scotland's Ensemble @ Dundee Rep, Passion Machine, Pigsback, RTÉ Radio 1, Project Arts Centre, Second Age, Draiocht, TNL Canada, TCD School of Drama, Barnstorm, Amnesty International, Guna Nua, Tinderbox, Origin (New York), 7:84 Scotland, Frontline Defenders, the Belgrade Theatre, Irish Council for Bioethics, Woodpecker Productions/The Gaiety and RTÉ lyric fm. He has edited and contributed to theatre publications, and taught for universities including NYU, Notre Dame, TCD, UCD, NUIM/GSA and the Lir. He is engaged in a number of ongoing Training, Development and Mentoring initiatives with Fishamble.

Bernard Farrell is a playwright whose first play *I Do Not Like Thee Doctor Fell opened* at the Abbey Theatre in 1979 and is still produced in many translations throughout the world. His following 20 plays were premiered at the Abbey, Gate and Red Kettle theatres in Ireland and the Laguna Playhouse in California and include *Canaries*, *The Last Apache Reunion*, *Kevin's Bed*, *Lovers At Versailles*, *Happy Birthday Dear Alice*, *Stella By Starlight*, *The Verdi Girls* and *Bookworms*. His work for television includes *Lotty Coyle Loves Buddy Holly* (RTE) and, with Graham Reid, the 18-part BBC series *Foreign Bodies*. For radio, his plays have represented Ireland at the Prix Italia and his T*he Year of Jimmy Somers* was named the BBC Play of the Year. He has won The Rooney Prize For Irish Literature, The Sunday Tribune Comedy of the Year Award and the Best Production Award in the Dublin Theatre Festival. He is a member of Aosdana, was Writer-in-Association and also served on the Board of Directors of the Abbey Theatre and, in 2014, received the John B. Keane Lifetime Achievement Award for his services to the Arts.

Eamonn Jordan (PhD) is a Senior Lecturer in Drama Studies at University College Dublin. He is the author of numerous critical essays on Irish dramatists, such as Marie Jones, Martin McDonagh, Conor McPherson, and Enda Walsh. He edited *Theatre Stuff: Critical Essays on Contemporary Irish Theatre* in 2000. He co-edited with Lilian Chambers *The Theatre of Martin McDonagh: A World of Savage Stories* (2006) and *The Theatre of Conor McPherson: 'Right beside the Beyond'* (2012). He has written three monographs *The Feast of Famine: Plays of Frank McGuinness* (1997), *Dissident Dramaturgies: Contemporary Irish Theatre* (2010) and *From Leenane to LA: The Theatre and Cinema of Martin McDonagh* (2014).

Marie Kelly (PhD) lectures in Drama and Theatre Studies at the School of Music and Theatre, University College Cork. She worked at the Abbey Theatre between 1993 and 2006, firstly as an Executive Assistant and subsequently as Casting Director. Marie has an MA in Modern Drama and Performance (2005) and a PhD in Drama Studies (2011), both from the School of English, Drama and Film at University College Dublin. Her book *The Theatre of Tom Mac Intyre: strays from the ether* was co-edited with Dr. Bernadette Sweeney (University of Missoula) and is published by Carysfort Press in 2010.

Meadhbh McHugh has a first-class B.A. in Drama Studies and English Literature from Trinity College Dublin (2011) and a M.F.A. in Playwriting (Distinction) from The Lir Academy, also at TCD (2014). She writes a weekly social column, and contributes to the arts pages, at *The Irish Times*. She has reviewed theatre for the *The Irish Times* and *Irish Theatre Magazine*, as well as blogs such as www.meg.ie. She will begin her Ph.D. in Theatre at Columbia University, New York, in Autumn 2014. As a playwright, she is working towards a public reading with Druid Theatre Company at Galway Arts Festival 2014.

Justin Murphy is a recent graduate of Film Studies and English Literature and a postgraduate student at Trinity College Dublin. In 2012 he obtained Scholarship of the university. He will begin doctoral research in the field of comedy and humour studies in the autumn.

Christopher Murray is Emeritus Professor of English, Drama and Film at University College Dublin. He is former editor of *Irish University Review* and former chair of the Irish Association for the Study of Irish Literatures (IASIL). At present, he is chair of the board of the Gaiety School of Acting. Among his publications are *Twentieth-Century Irish Drama: Mirror up to Nation* (1997), *Seán O'Casey:*

Writer at Work, A Biography (2004), and *The Theatre of Brian Friel: Tradition and Modernity* (2014), as well as editions of the plays of Lennox Robinson, George Shiels , and of *Brian Friel : Essays, Diaries, Interviews 1964-1999*. He has also edited *Samuel Beckett: 100 Years, Centenary Essays,* and *'Alive in Time': The Enduring Drama of Tom Murphy, New Essays.*

Declan Rooney has been on the fringes of the stand up comedy scene in Dublin for the past 15 years plus. During that time he has contributed and written comedy for many projects. Shows include Channel 4's *Comedy Lab* (*The Headwreckers*) and RTE's *The Savage Eye*. Most recently he has been a performer on RTE *The Republic Of Telly*, 2012 to present. On the radio side Declan has just completed a Broadcasting Authority of Ireland documentary on the ups and downs of the stand-up comedy industry with co-writer Gerard Counihan, which will be completed later this year.

Sarah Jane Scaife (PhD) is an actor and director. She is Artistic Director of Company SJ, which fuses research and performance, specializing in the work of Samuel Beckett, W.B. Yeats and other Irish writers. She has toured many of her own productions internationally and has also directed Beckett's plays in Georgia, Mongolia, India, Singapore, Malaysia, China and Greece with actors from each country. In 2009 she directed Beckett's *Act Without Words 11* for the Absolut Fringe Festival as a site-specific piece, it has since been re-presented in many festivals in Ireland, England and America. In the 2013 Fringe Festival it was presented as a companion piece for Beckett's *Rough For Theatre One*. These two pieces are part of a larger installation project entitled *Beckett in the City*. They will be presented in Tokyo June 2014 and as a European tour in 2015. Since 2009 she has been working on the translation of Marina Carr's *By the Bog of Cats...* into Mandarin in a collaborative project with various institutions in China. She will direct it for The Grand Theatre Hunan, later this year. She is Adjunct Lecturer in Trinity College Dublin and has given residencies internationally for many years.

Rhona Trench (PhD) is Programme Chair and Lecturer in Performing Arts at the Institute of Technology, Sligo. She is Vice President of the Irish Society for Theatre Research. She has contributed to a number of collections on Irish theatre and practice. Her book, *Bloody, Living: The Loss of Selfhood in the Plays of Marina Carr* (Lang: 2010) is the first full length study on Carr. She is editor of *Staging Thought: Essays on*

Irish Theatre, Scholarship and Practice (Peter Lang: 2012) and her book on Blue Raincoat Theatre Company will be published this Summer by Carysfort Press.

Ian R. Walsh (PhD) is a Lecturer in Drama at the School of English, Drama and Film, University College Dublin. In 2012 his monograph *Experimental Irish Theatre, After W.B Yeats* was published by Palgrave Macmillan and he is currently co-editing *The Theatre of Enda Walsh* for Carysfort Press. Ian has been a Theatre Reviewer for *Irish Theatre Magazine* and RTE Radio 1 and also worked as a Director of Theatre and Opera.

John Waters, best known as a newspaper columnist and author, was born in Co Roscommon, where he grew up in the town of Castlerea. His first book, *Jiving at the Crossroads* (1991), about the cultural underbelly of Irish politics, was a massive bestseller. His other publications include *Race of Angels* (1994) a study of the roots of U2's music in Irish history and culture. His most recent book is *Was It For This? Why Ireland Lost the Plot* (2012). His award-winning plays include *Long Black Coat* (1994) and *Easter Dues* (1997). He is also a songwriter and secret musician. He has a daughter, Róisín, and lives in Dublin and Sligo.

Eric Weitz (PhD) is Head of Drama at Trinity College Dublin, teaching courses in Acting and Comedy, among others. He is author of *The Cambridge Introduction to Comedy* (Cambridge), editor of *The Power of Laughter: Comedy and Contemporary Irish Theatre* (Carysfort), and has contributed articles and essays to a number of collections and journals, including *Performance Research*, the *Irish University Review* and the *Oxford Encyclopedia of Theatre and Performance* as well as the *Encyclopedia of Humor Studies* (SAGE). His work in progress, *Theatre & Laughter* (Palgrave) will be published next year. He is a longstanding member of both the International Society for Humour Studies and the Irish Society for Theatre Research. He serves on the boards of two socially engaged theatre companies: Smashing Times Theatre Company, based in Dublin (for which he also serves as Chair) and Collective Encounters, based in Liverpool, England.